CONVERSATIONS WITH LOTMAN:
CULTURAL SEMIOTICS IN LANGUAGE,
LITERATURE, AND COGNITION

EDNA ANDREWS

Conversations with Lotman: Cultural Semiotics in Language, Literature, and Cognition

UNIVERSITY OF TORONTO PRESS
Toronto Buffalo London

© University of Toronto Press Incorporated 2003
Toronto Buffalo London
Printed in Canada

ISBN 0-8020-3686-4 (cloth)

Printed on acid-free paper

Toronto Studies in Semiotics and Communication
Editors: Marcel Danesi, Umberto Eco, Paul Perron, Peter Schulz

---

National Library of Canada Cataloguing in Publication

Andrews, Edna, 1958–
  Conversations with Lotman : cultural semiotics in language,
literature and cognition / Edna Andrews.

  (Toronto studies in semiotics and communication)
  Includes bibliographical references and index.
  ISBN 0-8020-3686-4

  1. Lotman, IU. M. (IUrii Mikhailovich), 1922–1993   2. Semiotics.
3. Communication.   4. Semiotics and literature.   5. Culture – Semiotic
models   6. Russian literature – History and criticism.   I. Title.
II. Series.

GN357.A53 2003   302.2   C2002-903939-8

University of Toronto Press acknowledges the financial assistance to
its publishing program of the Canada Council for the Arts and the
Ontario Arts Council.

This book has been published with the help of a grant from the Humanities
and Social Sciences Federation of Canada, using funds provided by the
Social Sciences and Humanities Research Council of Canada.

University of Toronto Press acknowledges the financial support for
its publishing activities of the Government of Canada through the
Book Publishing Industry Development Program (BPIDP).

To Tom Sebeok

Contents

Acknowledgments xi
Introduction xiii

PART ONE: LOTMAN'S CULTURAL SEMIOTIC THEORY

1 Lotman's Contributions to the Semiotics of Culture 3
    Lotman's Cultural and Intellectual Environment 5
      The Early Years 5
      The Tartu-Moscow Collaboration 7
      Lotman's Mature Years 9
    Fundamental Principles of the Tartu-Moscow School 10

2 The Structure of Cultural Semiotic Systems 13
    Language or Languages? Minimum Requirements for
        Dynamic Cultural Space 17
      Language versus Code 17
      Communication Acts 17
    The Creation of Cultural Texts 18
      Lotman's Communication Model 18
      Jakobson's Communication Model 18
      Sebeok's Communication Model 20
    Binary or Triadic Signs 21

3 Introduction to the Semiosphere 26
    Entropy and Communication 26
    Autocommunication 28

Semiotic Space   31
Continuity and Discontinuity   35
Collective Memory   40

4 Characteristics and Origins of the Semiosphere   42
Characteristics of the Semiosphere   42
  Boundaries   46
  Tension and Explosion   48
  The Illusion of Continuity   53
Origins of the Semiosphere   55
Energy and Entropy in Semiotic Space   58
Uexküll's Semiotic Model   60
The Functioning Semiosphere   65
  Proper Names   65
  Metatexts   66
  Memory   68

PART TWO: THE CONSTRUCTION OF SEMIOTIC SPACE
              IN VERBAL TEXTS

5 Lotman, Bulgakov, and Zamyatin   73
Lotman on Bulgakov's *Master and Margarita*   74
  The Oppositions of Home   74
The Artistic Text   77
Artistic Spaces and Textual Dynamics   80
  Space and the Road   81
  Types of Infinity   82
  Florensky and Imaginary Space   84
  Bulgakov's Journey in Time and Space   86

6 Bulgakov and Zamyatin   93
Intertextuality and Revolution   93
Zamyatin and Bulgakov   94
Textual Links between *Master* and 'Drakon'   97
Atemporal Reflections   107
Construction and Intention in the Artistic Text   108

7 Extending Lotmanian Theory   112
Zamyatin and Heresy   113
The Synthetic Texts in *We*   114

Numerical Texts   115
Mathematical Texts   118
The Taylor Series   123
Decoding of Multiple Texts   125

PART THREE: SEMIOTIC THEORY AS A COGNITIVE SCIENCE

8 Visual and Auditory Signs in Human Language: Perception and Imagery   133
Visual Categories in Semantic Structures   135
The Functioning of the Visual Cortex   137
Language Development and the Absence of Vision   140
The Relationship between Visual and Auditory Signs   142
Brain, Language, and Culture: The Construction of Meaning   144

9 The Language of Memory in the Memory of Language   147
Encoding and Decoding: Learning and Retrieval   148
Semantic Memory and Priming   153
Source Memory   154
Collective Memory   155
Interpretants and Memory   157

Notes   161
References   179
Index   193

Acknowledgments

The efforts of many people are necessary to bring to publication any serious scholarly work. In the case of this work, I am deeply indebted to many people for their encouragement, criticisms, suggestions, and technical support: Lidija Mixailovna Lotman, Viktorija Mixailovna Lotman, Kira Anatoljevna Rogova, Maria Carlson, Elena Alekseevna Maksimova, Irina Gennadjevna Guliakova, Maura High, Michael Newcity, Rebecca Hayes, and the staff of the University of Toronto Press.

Special thanks to Peter Lang Publishers (1997, *The Peirce Seminar Papers III*, 11–28) and Berghahn Books (1999, *The Peirce Seminar Papers IV*, 623–37) for permission to use arguments that have appeared in previously published articles, but with substantial modifications.

I wish to express by deepest gratitude to Thomas Sebeok for his enthusiasm and support for this project from its inception to its emergence into print.

Introduction

As we move into the twenty-first century, there has been an explosion of interest in the study of human culture. As more scholars in the humanities and social sciences shift their research agendas to incorporate questions that were once defined mainly within the domains of anthropology and sociology, there has been a burgeoning of new theoretical approaches and modelling systems that attempt to identify and explain the central aspects of cultural phenomena. One field that has been especially concerned with defining and explaining cultural paradigms has been *anthroposemiotics*, one of the most visible trends in European, Canadian, and American semiotics of the past thirty years. One of the central figures in this field is Jurij Mixailovič Lotman (1922–93). As co-founder of the Tartu-Moscow School of Semiotics, Lotman produced – either as the sole author or as co-author – an *oeuvre* that encompassed a broad range of semiotic issues, an *oeuvre* that included not only profound and innovative literary analyses (primarily of Russian literature texts), but also a series of important, ground-breaking works explicating the construction of semiotic models and principles in the areas of human language, speech acts, and textual analysis; typological descriptions of cultural space; mechanisms of the system-based level of cross-cultural interactions; and, ultimately, an approach to the study of collective and individual memory as a semiotic phenomenon.

Because of the breadth of his writings, scholars have long clashed over how to classify Lotman's works and their theoretical basis. Some have classified him as a structuralist (in the European rather than the American sense),[1] while others have described him as a literary historian or even literary theorist. Lotman himself, according to his older sister Lidija Mixailovna Lotman, was quite comfortable being called a historian of culture. Boris Gasparov (1985: 13–16) uses the terms 'postformalism' and 'poststructuralism' to describe the scholarship of Lotman and the Tartu-Moscow School, while acknowledging the presence of semiotic principles in their work. My preference is to call Lotman a semiotician – a term that I believe comes closer to capturing the essence his writings over forty years. One of my goals in the following discussions is to present what I believe is Lotman's central *semiotic* contribution – his work on the *semiosphere*, which is his most developed contribution in defining the 'semiotics of culture' and the 'semiotics of space.'

To provide an adequate descriptive and critical analysis of Lotman's contribution to cultural semiotics and the semiosphere, I have identified the following parameters upon which to build and focus my work: (1) to present in a logically consistent fashion the main principles of Lotman's cultural semiotic theory, including his definitions of culture (and how they are modified in his later works) and his doctrine of signs, the importance of the semiosphere for Lotman's approach to the study of culture, and the importance of information and different types of knowledge in his models of communication; (2) to demonstrate how Lotman's semiotic constructs may or may not be compatible with both structuralist and non-structuralist semiotic theories, especially as seen in the works of C.S. Peirce, T. Sebeok, J. von Uexküll, R. Thom, and R.O. Jakobson;[2] (3) to apply and extend Lotmanian principles on the construction of textual space to Russian literary texts as test cases; and (4) to extend the basic principles of Lotman's semiotic in a unique way to the study of human language, particularly in defining specific types of *sign–complex* interactions that model human perception and memory, in order to articulate and substantiate the importance of semiotic theory to contemporary cognitive science.

As always happens with important thinkers whose publishing careers are long, one finds significant changes, modifications, and evolution in Lotman's approaches through time. It is important to recognize that the works for which Lotman is best known in the West are not necessarily the most indicative of his mature thought. Soviet censorship coupled with very limited translation of Lotman's works into English are two of the reasons why the 'Western Lotman' is only a shadow of the actual 'Russian Lotman.' A specific example of 'Western' Lotman is the claim that his definition of the smallest structural unit of cultural space – the *sign* – is purely binary.[3] The perception by many American scholars that all of Lotman's works on semiotic modelling systems in the 1960s and 1970s are defined by multiple sets of binary signs has raised important questions regarding the viability of a Lotmanian semiotic theory – a theory that many Canadian, American, and European scholars would reject in favour of a fundamentally triadic Peircean sign (where Peircean semiotic sign theory is by definition not a part of the structuralist semiotic movement [Eco 1990: vii–xiii]). It is certainly true that defining Lotman as a binarist is a dated practice that unfairly marginalizes his work in contemporary Western semiotic discourse. Although I do not think that Lotman ever completely abandoned all his notions of binarism, I intend to demonstrate that his later works shift their focus to a more complex set of semiotic principles that do not depend directly on a binary sign. This change in perspective results in a truly unique contribution to the field of semiotics.

Because of the disjunction between the Western and Russian views of Lotman, in the earliest chapters of this book I will concentrate on updating and contextualizing Lotman for Western theorists. However, I begin in chapter 2 to move away from an exclusive focus on Lotman's contributions, toward a broader perspective of semiotic principles – a perspective that encompasses the works of Peirce, Jakobson, and Sebeok. From there, I will move into new areas of semiotic analysis that are extensions and modifications of a Lotmanian approach, branching out into more general semiotic questions. In the final chapter, which extends the analysis to contemporary cognitive science, I will present a unique approach to analyzing human language and memory from a perspective that integrates the latest discoveries in cognitive science (including neuroscience, linguistics, psychology, imagery, and imaging technologies) with semiotic theory.[4]

When defining the scope of one's work, it is sometimes useful to state what it is *not* intended to demonstrate. The reader will not find an attempt to construct a cult of personality around Lotman or to use him to deconstruct other theorists of his day, either in the Soviet Union or abroad: Lotman and his work constitute but one portion of the larger fabric of our analysis and exploration of complex questions encompassing dynamic modelling of human language, cross-cultural inquiry, and the relationship between cultural systems and other symbolic systems with which they intersect – especially human languages and the construction of individual and collective cultural memory. Some readers who have read only Lotman's better-known works of the 1960s and 1970s may be uncomfortable with this book's emphasis on the dynamic development of his particular semiotic approach at the expense of his more static structuralist approach to singularly literary texts. This is not to say that I exclude his earlier structuralist analyses, but not all aspects of Lotman's earlier modelling distinctions (e.g., primary versus secondary modelling systems) are significant in his mature work on semiotic cultural systems.

Conversations with Lotman has several types of readers in mind. Most readers will be semioticians interested in theoretical modelling and in applications of theory to local problems in cultural space. Other readers will be linguists and cognitive scientists interested in the study of *meaning* and how it is generated through language and other kinds of culture texts, or Slavists interested in the history of ideas, or historians of culture. Because this work is written in English, I have made a concerted effort to include many of Lotman's later works on general semiotic systems that have yet to be translated from Russian. Unless otherwise noted, translations from Russian sources are mine. I have included the original Russian texts in the more important quotes to provide direct access to the original for Slavists as well as for readers with a working knowledge of Russian.

A Note on the Spelling of Russian Names

As is always the case when different writing systems are used, there are numerous conventions for the realization of Russian names into English. Of the three systems currently in use, I have chosen the transcription system used by scholars of Slavic languages and linguistics. This system is used consistently throughout the book, including notes and references. However, in those cases where a particular Russian family name is well-known in the English-speaking world, I use the conventional, popular spelling of the name in the narrative itself (e.g., Vygotsky, Florensky, Bakhtin, Mikhail, Tolstoy, Chekhov, Vernadsky, Zamyatin). The only exception to the list above is the spelling of Gogol', where I will keep the diacritic. In those cases where there are two or more spellings of a name, all will be noted in the index.

PART ONE

Lotman's Cultural Semiotic Theory

CHAPTER ONE

Lotman's Contributions to the Semiotics of Culture

Lotman's most important contributions to the construction of a robust theory of the semiotics of culture are his definitions of *culture* and *culture text*. In a series of works written over a span of thirty years, he attempted to build a theory of culture culminating in the semiosphere defined as the fundamental space-context that is a prerequisite for the existence and functioning of culture and culture texts. Before discussing and contextualizing Lotman's semiosphere (developed in chapters 3 and 4), I will introduce some of Lotman's key working definitions of culture and show how he modified them in his later works. The notion of culture text will also be important in Lotman's definition of culture as one of the 'more abstract models of how reality is viewed within a particular culture' (1992b: I. 389).

Lotman provides one of his earliest discussions of culture from a semiotic perspective in his article 'O semiotičeskom mexanizme kul'tury' (About the Semiotic Mechanism of Culture), written with Boris A. Uspenskij in 1971 (reprinted Lotman 1993: III. 326–44).[1] Lotman and Uspenskij begin their discussion by outlining what the universals of cultural organization would be. First and foremost, each culture defines a model of itself based on phenomena related to that specific culture. Several principles follow from this statement, including the following: (1) each culture will have marks (or signs) [признаки]; (2) no single culture is all-encompassing – rather, it is a bounded space that abuts non-cultural space; (3) cultures are always sign systems (as opposed to non-cultures, which are not); (4) cultures replace one another over time; (5) culture and natural language are indivisible; (6) culture is non-hereditary collective memory; (7) culture is only 'acknowledged post factum'; (8) culture is first and foremost a social phenomenon (социальное явление) and, while individual culture is real, it is nonetheless a secondary phenomenon when viewed in the historical context of societal culture; (9) each culture creates its own model of its length of existence and con-tinuity; (10) culture generates structure in order to construct its social basis; and (11) every culture is based on a 'presumption of structure' by its participants (Lotman 1993: III.326–30).

None of these principles is fully contradicted by any of Lotman's later work on cultural space and the semiosphere. However, 'About the Semiotic Mechanism of Culture' contains an additional pattern of binary opposition that dominates the further elucidation of these categories. Examples include the binary oppositions defining form-based and content-based cultures (e.g., correct-incorrect, true-false, cosmos-chaos, culture-nature, ordered-unordered) (1993: III. 334, 338). Actually, this rigid schematization of dyads is not an essential part of Lotman's developed work. I would argue that although Lotman does not forsake binary oppositions in his later work, he does present them in a relativized manner that is more akin to phenomena distributed on a continuum as opposed to absolute poles of opposition (cf. Lotman 1994b: 331–81; 1992a: 17–27; 1990: 144, to cite only a few).[2] I would note that one of the models that facilitated Lotman's definition of categories as discrete points on a continuum (or series of continua) was Jakobson's speech act model, which demonstrates the importance of defining cultural and linguistic categories as *relatively autonomous entities* (that shift in conjunction with participant perspective) rather than absolute, privative categories.

In attempting to define the metalanguage that will adequately describe the phenomenon of culture, Lotman turns to specific types of texts that will lead to an invariant, sign-based 'text-construct' that will allow for the realization of a given culture in all its potential variations. It is this invariant, sign-based text construct that defines a 'culture text.' Culture texts may involve a variety of symbolic systems, including verbal language (oral or written), visual arts, rituals, and codes of law, to name only a few. Culture texts tend to fall into two subgroups – those which 'characterize the structure of the world' and how it is constructed, including its status as a metalanguage that assigns values to cultural categories, and those which 'characterize the place, position and activity of a person in his surrounding world' (Lotman 1992b: I. 389–90).

In chapters 3, 4, and 5 I show that by the 1990s, Lotman had significantly rethought the fundamental principles of defining culture. His rethinking seems to have been a result of his re-evaluation of what was initially a belief in the adequacy of a static, Saussurean approach and of his movement toward a more complex, deeply semiotic approach defined not at the individual sign/symbol level but rather at the level of conglomerate, *dynamic* sign-complexes.

Lotman's Cultural and Intellectual Environment

Certain episodes in Lotman's life stand out for what they tell us about his contribution to the founding of one of the most formidable international semiotic movements of the modern period – the Tartu-Moscow School. These episodes do not constitute a full biographical profile, but they do indicate Lotman's historical, geographic, ideological, and intellectual milieux. The factual information for this essay has been collected from a range of printed sources and personal interviews. In particular, I have synthesized presentations of Lotman's biography from a series of Russian-language sources, including Lotman's own autobiographical notes and interviews (published as 'Ne-memuary' [Non-memoirs] in Lotman 1995: 5–53 and Jegorov 1999a: 271–354); biographical information written by his colleagues in Tartu and Moscow, including Jegorov's excellent book on Lotman's life and works (1999a) and essays by Černov (1997: 5–12), Jegorov (1995: 5–9, 1997: 5–8) and M.L. Gasparov (1996); and personal interviews with Lotman's sisters, Lidija Mixailovna Lotman and Viktorija Mixailovna Lotman. (For English-language references, I recommend Stephen Rudy's article on semiotics in the USSR [1986], Ann Shukman's important work [1977, 1988] and Lucid's translated anthology of Soviet semiotics [1977].)

The Early Years

Jurij Mixailovič Lotman was born in Petrograd (Leningrad / Saint Petersburg) on 28 February 1922, the youngest of four children. His father was a lawyer and his mother a doctor. Lotman recalls a childhood that was full of love and laughter even though there was little money (1999: 323–4). He graduated from a ten-year school with highest honours, which won him acceptance to Leningrad State University without entrance examinations in 1939. The young Lotman at first could not decide whether to study biology and entomology or philology. By the beginning of his senior year in high school, however, he had chosen philology (Lotman 1999: 326).

After completing his first year of university, Lotman was drafted into the military. He spent the next six years on the front lines, fighting the

Germans in what the Russians refer to as 'the Great Patriotic War.' Lotman finished his service as a sergeant and returned to university in 1946. A large part of Lotman's memoirs is devoted to the war years (1995: 9–34).

In 1950, Lotman graduated from Leningrad State University with honours. After a great deal of searching and a pile of rejections, he found a teaching job in Tartu, Estonia. Even though Lotman, as a Jew, was not accepted into graduate school, he defended his candidate's degree (generally seen as the equivalent of an American PhD) in 1952.

At Leningrad State University, Lotman studied with many important thinkers of the day, including Vladimir Propp, Boris Tomashevskij, Boris Eixenbaum, Viktor Zhirmunskij, Jurij Tynjanov, Grigorij Gukovskij, Mark Azadovskij, and Nikolaj Mordovchenko (Černov 1997: 6; Lotman 1999: 305–7, 328–30). He was still a university student when the Stalinist anti-Semitic purges began, which culminated in Gukovskij's death and further persecution against Eixenbaum and Zhirmunskij (Lotman 1999: 306). This was not Lotman's first encounter with political persecution, nor would it be his last. It is no exaggeration to say that until the last three years of his life, his career was dominated by problems related to his Jewish heritage and to suspicion of his intellectual agenda.

One example of persecution was his failure to find employment after graduating from university. At that time in the Soviet Union, a party-based commission determined the employment of each university graduate at the end of his or her academic career. Many of Lotman's friends were sent to work in the Far East and Siberia – not enviable positions. His own fate was stranger than this: the commission decided not to assign him any employment. He was told that he would have 'free determination' – that is, he would have to find his own position. The price he paid for this 'freedom' was the loss of his important and very positive letter of recommendation from his military commander (1999: 307).[3]

While looking for employment, Lotman continued to write his candidate's dissertation. Ironically, Lotman realized only later that it was his ethnicity (Lotman uses the word 'nationality') that was preventing him from getting hired (1999: 308). Eventually, Lotman found employment at the Teachers Institute in Tartu, were he began to teach in the fall of 1950 (1999: 312). Although sentenced to internal exile in Estonia, he was able to take advantage of the vibrant intellectual climate in Tartu and ultimately form what would be one of the most profound intellectual groups of the Soviet era. Estonia, a Baltic state that had a more liberal tradition than the Russian Federation and that was generally hostile to Soviet rule, was distant enough from the eagle eye of the Soviet 'centre' to enjoy more intellectual freedom.

While teaching at the Tartu Teachers Institute, Lotman began doing some part-time lecturing at Tartu University. In 1952 he was extended a job offer by Tartu University – specifically, he was offered the position held by Val'mar Adams, who had just been arrested in an anti-Semitic campaign. Lotman declined the offer (Jegorov 1999a: 60). Shortly after that, however, he was offered another position at Tartu University, and this one he accepted. In 1954 he received the title of docent; in 1963, two years after defending his second doctoral dissertation at Leningrad State University, he received the title of professor. From 1960 until 1977 he chaired the Department of Russian Literature at Tartu University. In 1977 he was removed as chair for political reasons and transferred to the Department of Literary Theory in the Division of Estonian Philology. Even so, he continued to teach in the Russian Literature department at Tartu University (Jegorov 1995: 6–9).

By the time Lotman began his academic career in Tartu in the early 1950s, the university's journal series *Uchenye zapiski* (*Scholarly Notes* – henceforth UZ), was all but defunct. However, with the help of the First Congress of Slavicists in 1958 in Moscow – a landmark event for the international community of Slavists – Lotman and his Tartu colleagues were able to initiate a new series titled *Works on Russian and Slavic Philology*, and to publish Lotman's own monograph on Andrej Kajsarov. Later, Lotman, Zara Grigorjevna Mints (his wife), and Boris Jegorov were able to start yet another series devoted specifically to semiotics (Lotman 1999: 320). The first *Sign Systems Studies* (*Trudy po znakovym sistemam*) was published as number 160 of *Uchenyje zapiski Tartuskogo gosudarstvennogo universiteta* (*Scholarly Notes of Tartu State University* – henceforth UZTGU) in 1964. By 1992 the twenty-fifth volume of *Sign Systems Studies*, titled *Semiotics and History* (*Semiotika i istorija*), had appeared as number 939 of UZTGU.

The Tartu-Moscow Collaboration

The word 'semiotics' was quite controversial in the Soviet Union of the late 1950s and early 1960s. Many Moscow scholars were highly critical and suspicious of the Tartu group and its agenda. However, after the Moscow Symposium of 1962, Lotman became acquainted with its organizers (including Vladimir Toporov, Vjacheslav Ivanov, Boris Uspenskij, and Andrej Zaliznjak), and an important intellectual movement was able to take root. Lotman offered his Moscow colleagues an intellectual safe haven: they were able to use Tartu University for conferences and lectures, and the important Tartu series *Uchenye zapiski* for disseminating their work. Thus began a rich collaboration that became known as the Tartu-Moscow School of Semiotics (Jegorov 1999a: 101–3). From the very beginning, there were philosophical differences in the approaches of the two semiotic-structuralist groups: the Moscow group had a clear linguistic (and mathematical linguistic) orientation, whereas Lotman's orientation was historical and committed to a scientific approach to the study of literary and cultural texts. Jegorov pointed out that he and the Lotmans (the most senior members of the Tartu School) had all been educated in Leningrad in literary theory, and noted the intellectual ties between Leningrad and Moscow in the development of the Tartu-Moscow School (1999a: 120). (It is interesting that the Russian name of the school usually places Tartu first in the title, whereas the general English formulation puts Moscow first.)[4]

The first Tartu 'Summer School' (19–29 August 1964), a product of Lotman's efforts to develop a school of semiotics, rivalled the Moscow Symposium of 1962 as a milestone in the development of the school and its research agenda. Lotman specifically selected the word 'school' (and not 'symposium' or 'conference') in order to emphasize a freer format for problem solving and to broaden the discussions arising from the presentations (Jegorov 1999a: 119). He was able to produce the program and abstracts of the event before the first summer school began. Topics included the following: general theoretical questions of semiotic and science; the differentiation of literary versus linguistic methodological approaches; literary, sociological, historical, and cultural modelling systems; the modelling of folklore texts; stylistics; and the specifics of poetry. Participants from Moscow included Aleksandr Zholkovskij, Jurij Shcheglov, Boris Uspenskij, Aleksandr Pjatigorskij, Jurij Levin and Isaak Rezvin (Jegorov 1999a: 99, 120–1). The second summer school is remembered most for Roman Jakobson's visit, his presentation on Aleksandr Radishchev, and his public reminiscences with Petr Bogatyrev about the prerevolutionary Moscow Linguistics Circle (Jegorov 1999a: 118–19, 131–2).[5]

By 1970, Lotman had hosted four summer schools in Tartu. Well aware of their controversial position in Soviet academe and the stridency of censorship, Lotman and his colleagues carried out each summer program and each semiotic publication in their series as if it were the last (Lotman 1999: 322). In fact, the 1970 summer school turned out to be the last of the series, after Rector F. Klement was notified by Communist Party officials that he had to put a stop to these provocative demonstrations of free will (Jegorov 1999a: 132). Klement had always been very protective of Lotman and his department. After he retired in 1971, the level of censorship and persecution increased dramatically for Lotman and his colleagues in Tartu (1999: 154). It was only in the winter of 1974 that Lotman was permitted to host a 'symposium' as the final official Tartu-based event of the Tartu-Moscow school of the Soviet era.[6]

After 1974, as a result of increased censorship, the emigration of many key members (including Dmitrij Segal, Aleksandr Pjatigorskij, Boris Ogibenin, and Boris Gasparov), and travel restrictions on the rest, the Tartu-Moscow school was significantly inhibited in its formal work. However, through the various scholarly series and individual publication efforts of the school's core members both at home and abroad, the intellectual agenda remained strong.

Lotman's Mature Years

By the time he died in 1993, Lotman had published more than eight hundred works – including a dozen monographs – in more than fifty international scholarly journals and translated into nineteen languages (Černov 1997: 12; Lotman 1999: 351). Between 1958 and 1980 he lectured in Moscow more than ninety times – roughly four times a year (Jegorov 1999a: 156–8). As noted earlier, the early 1970s were the height of the persecution of Lotman and his close friends and colleagues.[7] This persecution continued into the early 1980s. Because of intensified censorship, the *Sign Systems Studies* series did not appear in print in 1984 (number 645) or in 1989. However, combined volumes were published in 1987 and 1990.

By 1986, Lotman was being allowed to travel abroad. One of his first international presentations was at the University of Bergen in Norway. In 1992 the University of Keele in the United Kingdom hosted a conference dedicated to Lotman's seventieth birthday. Two of the most important institutional relationships established by Lotman with foreign universities were with the Department of Slavonic and Baltic Languages and Literatures at the University of Helsinki and with the Institute of Slavic and Baltic Languages at Stockholm University. In Helsinki, seven volumes of articles have been published in the series *Studia Russica Helsingiensia et Tartuensia*. In Stockholm, two joint conferences between Stockholm and Tartu resulted in an important volume titled *Classicism and Modernism* (1994) (Jegorov 1999a: 218). Unfortunately, because of a series of strokes complicated by cancer, Lotman was unable to fully enjoy his long-desired freedom to travel abroad. Jurij Lotman passed away on 28 October 1993 at the age of seventy-one.

Lotman's legacy in the fields of semiotics, Russian literature, and Russian cultural studies is perhaps the richest of his generation. His intellectual contribution is all the more powerful when one considers the degree of censorship he faced for almost all his academic career.

Fundamental Principles of the Tartu-Moscow School

In 1973 the Tartu-Moscow School published a document outlining the fundamental theoretical principles on which the school was based. Authored by Lotman, V.V. Ivanov, A.M. Pjatigorskij, V.N. Toporov, and B.A. Uspenskij, *Theses on the Semiotic Study of Cultures* (henceforth *Theses*) specifically presents the structural principles necessary for conducting a semiotic analysis of culture. Although *Theses* focuses on Slavic texts, the principles of metadescription described are applicable to any culture. The opening statement of *Theses* highlights the essential distinction between on the one hand, how culture may perceive itself, and on the other hand, how a scientific metasystem may describe culture (Ivanov et al. [1973] 1998: 9, 33):

> In the study of culture the initial premise is that all human activity concerned with the processing, exchange, and storage of information possesses a certain unity. Individual sign systems, though they presuppose immanently organized structures, function only in unity, supported by one another. None of the sign systems possesses a mechanism which would enable it to function culturally in isolation ... In investigations of a semiotic-typological nature the concept of culture is perceived as fundamental. In doing so we should distinguish between the conception of culture from its own point of view and from the point of view of a scientific metasystem which describes it. According to the first position, culture will have the appearance of a certain delimited space which is opposed to the phenomena of human history, experience, or activity lying outside it. Thus the concept of culture is inseparably linked with the opposition of its 'non-culture.'

This juxtaposition immediately forces the reader to acknowledge the important notion of *boundary* and the inherent contrastive aspect of extracultural (non-semiotic) space to cultural space.

The central themes of *Theses* are as follows: the inalienable dynamics of semiotic space; the relationship between information and entropy; the defining properties of semiotic boundaries; the definition of *culture text*; the relationship between *text* and *sign*; the importance of discrete versus continuous modelling systems; the obligatory presence of *tension* between discrete and continuous semiotic-cultural phenomena; the relationship between *text* and *addresser* and *addressee*; the role of cultural memory; the difference between potential texts and non-texts; the broad range of semiotic text types, which include the central role of natural human language; and the inevitability of the polycultural, multilingual nature of any semiotic cultural space.

The culture text, which is the structure through which a culture acquires information about itself and the surrounding context, is defined as a set of functional principles: (1) the text is a functioning semiotic unity; (2) the text is the carrier of any and all integrated messages (including human language, visual, verbal, and representational art forms, rituals, etc.); and (3) not all usages of human language are automatically defined as texts (Ivanov et al. [1973] 1998: 3.0–3.1).[8] *Theses* also defines three distinct levels of text that are incorporated into any culture such that they involve a *hierarchy of sign systems* composed of *texts*, a *mechanism that will generate texts*, and *an overall summation of texts and their corresponding functions*. All semiotic systems function in context as *relative*, not absolute, *autonomous structures*. As a result, what is perceived as a text in one culture may not be a text in a different cultural space.

The Tartu-Moscow School's definition of *primary versus secondary modelling systems* (1962) and, later, Lotman's specific taxonomy of textual types as primary and secondary (1967) have been discussed in great detail by Sebeok (1991: 49–58) and I. Portis-Winner (1979, 1987). The distinction between the two modelling systems is, in the West, one of the better-known aspects of Lotman's work, although it may not be among the most important. I concur with Sebeok (1991: 50) that what is most significant about this opposition is the realization by the Tartu-Moscow School of the importance of the concept of *modelling* and how it dovetails with notions of Peircean iconicity and – I would add – Peirce's definitions of *diagram* and *diagrammatization* (Peirce 1931–58: 2.170, 2.227, 2.279, 8.368).

Theses is an important historical document that describes how the Tartu-Moscow semioticians constructed a new paradigm of analysis that reaches beyond traditional fields and domains. The theoretical premises of *Theses* are clearly present in Lotman's later theories on culture and tension and the semiosphere. I will argue that we can single out Lotman as the one member of the Tartu-Moscow School who provided a complete, internally consistent and comprehensive theory of cultural semiotics that extends beyond verbal textual analysis and reaches a profound level of analytical descriptive power. Perhaps Lotman's theoretical studies do not present an overarching metatheory on par with a school of literary criticism or school of linguistics; however, they do contribute to a theory of knowledge and a scientific method that not only require actual data for analysis but also posit in an original way questions of human perception and human memory.

CHAPTER TWO

The Structure of Cultural Semiotic Systems

> Мы живём в мире культуры. Более того, мы находимся в ее толще, внутри нее, и только так мы можем продолжать своё существование. Отсюда важность понятия «культура» и, одновременно, его трудность для определения.
>
> (We live in a world of culture. Moreover, we are in the thick of it, inside of it, and that is the only way we are able to continue our existence. The importance of the notion of culture, the difficulty of its definition, follows from this fact.)
>
> Ju.M. Lotman, 'Instead of a foreword'

To initiate a discussion of the relationship between language and culture, and to begin to understand culture as a fundamentally semiotic phenomenon, Lotman attempts to set out a clear and succinct working definition of *culture*. In a 1971 essay, he and his co-author Uspenskij define culture first and foremost as a bounded sign system (a relatively open system) that is made up of marks (Lotman 1993: III. 326–30). But this definition is not sufficient to distinguish the semiotic principles that define any system from the unique functional nature of culture. Semiotic systems are so ubiquitous in nature that it might seem at first blush that a semiotic definition of culture is no different from the definition of any other system. Bearing in mind that various semiotic structures may share a number of important features, Lotman sets up a hierarchy of semiotic principles specific to culture. Let us begin with these.

Cultural semiotic systems are always based on non-hereditary collective memory. Thus, on the one hand, culture is a social (collective) phenomenon that is 'acknowledged post factum'; on the other, each culture creates its own model of existence and continuity and both generates and 'presumes' structure. One of the modelling aspects of culture that *generates and presumes structure* is that culture and natural language are indivisible within a given cultural space. It follows that the fundamental *operating principle* of any culture is the *conversion (or translation) of non-information into information*. Thus, culture for Lotman is a *structure* or *mechanism* (устройство) *that requires at least two languages, produces information, and is by definition anti-entropic* (Lotman 1992b: I. 7–9). Neither of the 'two languages' can adequately and completely capture all of the essential information and principles of the internal cultural space. Furthermore, according to Lotman, it is not the case that culture and cultural systems are *solely and entirely* semiotic in nature. At the end of chapter 2 we will consider whether this statement is true, in the context of more broadly defined semiotic models and their relationship to Lotman's model.

The other part of Lotman's definition of culture concerns the need to draw a boundary between the internal space of a specific culture (or cultural system) and the external space that lies beyond it. Every culture takes it as a given that something else lies immediately outside it. Without this 'other space,' there can be no sense of cultural self (Lotman 1992a: 7–11; 1992b: I. 10). But it isn't enough simply to recognize this external space; the cultural system must also determine its *dynamic relationship* to that external space.

In specifying this dynamic relationship, I have found it useful to require more than one type of *reference* (following G.S. Brown's definition of this term), where *explicit reference* gives the 'value' of a sign in (semiotic) space and *implicit reference* specifies an objectivized (or 'outside') observer (of semiotic space) (Brown 1969: 69, 76). Once the observer's position is determined, meaning can be produced both within and between cultural spaces. The drawing of boundaries between distinct cultural spaces and observers sets up the primary tension between *continuous* and *discontinuous* phenomena. In his expanded definition of culture, Lotman defines *all* aspects of cultural space as a struggle between continuous and discontinuous categories:

> Культура как сложное целое составляется из пластов разной скорости развития, так что любой её синхронный срез обнаруживает одновременное присутствие различных её стадий. Взрывы в одних пластах могут сочетаться с постепенным развитием в других. Это, однако, не исключает взаимодействия этих пластов ... Ещё более существенно одновременное сочетание в разных сферах культуры взрывных и постепенных процессов. (1992a: 25–6)

(Culture as a complex whole consists of layers of different rates of development, such that any of its synchronic slices will unveil a simultaneous presence of different levels of development. Explosions in some layers may combine with gradual development in others. This, however, does not exclude the interaction of these layers ... Even more critical is the simultaneous combination of explosive and gradual processes in different spheres of culture.)

Note that according to Lotman, the dynamic aspects of culture must be articulated as the foundation of the semiotic system. These dynamics are inherent in Lotman's simpler definition of culture as the producer of information from non-information. Besides recognizing and codifying the dynamic essence of cultural space, Lotman also points out the source of the dynamic nature of culture – namely, the internal cross-fertilization between different structural levels creates change in a given cultural system. Thus, the more aggressive the dynamics of one level, the more these dynamics motivate change in those levels most opposed to them (1992a: 26–7).

Inherent in all this is the notion of *tension* (напряжение), which is essential to any modelling of functioning cultural space and to any exchange of information. For example, the *value* of a given information event in cultural space is determined by the amount of codified information that lies *beyond* the boundaries of intersecting spaces of established information shared by the speaker and hearer (1992a: 14–15):

> Это ставит нас лицом к лицу с неразрешимым противоречием: мы заинтересованы в общении именно с той ситуацией, которая затрудняет общение, а в пределе – делает его невозможным. Более того, чем труднее и неадекватнее перевод одной непересекающейся части пространства на язык другой, тем более ценным в информационном и социальном отношениях становится факт этого парадоксального общения.

(This puts us face to face with an irreconcilable contradiction: we are precisely more interested in engaging in the situation that makes interaction more difficult, and in the extreme makes it impossible. Moreover, the more difficult and incomparable the translation of one non-intersecting part of space with another language, the more valuable this paradoxical communication becomes in terms of information and in social terms.)

Complete disjunction of a communication event results in no information, whereas total overlap yields maximum redundancy (i.e., no new information). It is precisely in the intersecting spaces that the tension essential for information exchange is realized. Yet the most valuable production of new information goes on in the corresponding non-intersecting spaces. Any exchange and/or production of new information is manifested through *languages*. These languages can be differentiated at the level of speaker/hearer or at the level of code. As Lotman points out (1992a: 10):

> Языки эти как накладываются друг на друга, по-разному отражая одно и то же, так и располагаются в «одной плоскости», образуя в ней внутренние границы. Их взаимная непереводимостъ (или ограниченная переводимость) является источником адекватности внеязыкового объекта его отражению в мире языков.

(These languages build upon each other in order to reflect one and the same phenomenon but in different ways, just as they place themselves in one plane and thus form internal boundaries. Their mutual untranslatability [or limited translatability] is the source of the correspondence of the extralinguistic object with its reflection in the world of language.)

Here we find that although these *languages* – which may be what is generically known as human language – are *primary* when it comes to constructing cultural space and relaying information, they also serve as the basis for a secondary modelling system, fully created by the culture. For a given cultural space, this secondary system claims to resemble a *universal language* that necessarily leads to a 'single, finite truth' (Lotman 1992a: 10).[1] Examples of this trend are found in cultural models that construct the space beyond the boundary as chaotic, and in the insistence on the superiority of a particular culture's categories and hierarchies (e.g., its gender relationships, its legal system, its educational system).

All of this strengthens the notion that the semiotic *boundary* – which is inherent in any definition of culture or a cultural system – functions something like a permeable *membrane* that allows for multilateral movement within and without. In Lotman's system, the multiple and changing boundaries of semiotic space must be viewed as membrane-like structures – more precisely, as discontinuities – rather than as static, solid borders. It is only through discontinuity that the illusion of continuous perception is possible. We will return to this question in chapters 3 and 4 in our discussion of the *semiosphere*.

Now we return to Lotman's requirement that there be at least two languages to define cultural space, by considering the characteristics of a system with only one language.

Language or Languages? Minimum Requirements for Dynamic Cultural Space

In this section I define the terms *language* and *communication events*, and shows why multiple systems (as opposed to singular ones) and complex systems (as opposed to singular signs) are the minimum requirement for functioning semiocultural space. My conclusions will be broader than Lotman's original thesis.

One of the challenges we confront when placing Lotman's work in a more general semiotic context is clarifying his terms, for they are often understood in a different way by the general community. One example is how he used the terms *language* and *code*.

Language versus Code

We must first distinguish between *language* and *code* (язык и код) as Lotman used these terms. In his estimation, *code* leaves aside history (or cultural memory) and orients the listener toward notions of language as an artificial structure; in contrast, *language* is code with human history built in (1992a: 12–13). This distinction will not apply to the use of the term 'code' in the communication models presented by Jakobson and Sebeok. In those communication act models, *code* is coincident with *language*.[2]

Having noted this distinction, we next define the basic semiotic units that are always present in any speech event. To fully appreciate the importance of multiple languages as a baseline requirement, we will review some of the more important semiotic-based speech act models and evaluate how they overlap with Lotman's vision.

Communication Acts

Before we can define the dynamic operations of the semiosphere, we must first understand the construction of a semiotic *text* and the *languages* that are minimally required in order to create and interpret culturally relevant information. As a first step, I will focus on Lotman's communication model, as he offers it in his writings about the text as a 'meaning-generating mechanism' (1990: 11–19), and explore the compatibility of that model with other structural semiotic speech act models, especially those provided by Jakobson (1987) and Sebeok ([1976] 1985, 1991). My goal is to demonstrate the unavoidable and essential presence of an infinite series of potential embedded speech acts in any given instantiation.[3] It can be argued that the ultimate power of any such semiotic model of communication lies in its ability to *adequately* define the structural principles of encoding and decoding as they occur at multiple discrete and continuous levels. *Such a modelling principle will increase significantly the level of abstractness and complexity of the mechanism that converts non-information into information within cultural space.* The generation of new and transformed information is one of the fundamental sources of non-hereditary cultural memory and contributes to the indivisibility of culture and natural language.

The Creation of Cultural Texts

I now turn to the creation of cultural texts, which are the kernel of any semiotic model of culture and the prerequisite for any potential transfer of information. One way to begin such an analysis is to consider the structural and functional aspects of text construction and communication.

Lotman's Communication Model

In order to show the fundamental functions of a text, Lotman models how, at the most basic level, information is communicated through language from the perspectives of the speaker and the hearer. In his explanation, Lotman sets up the sequence shown in figure 2.1. At first glance, this model seems to describe a linear sequence of the pathway of any verbal message. But when we consider that every communication act proceeds imperfectly and requires (according to Lotman) that the most valuable new information lie outside the intersecting space between the speaker and the hearer, the diagrammatic model provided here cannot adequately explain the required semiotic mechanism. Does the Jakobsonian model improve on the situation?

Jakobson's Communication Model

In an attempt to explain adequately the multifaceted nature of human language, Jakobson models the speech event as a unity of six factors and

Figure 2.1

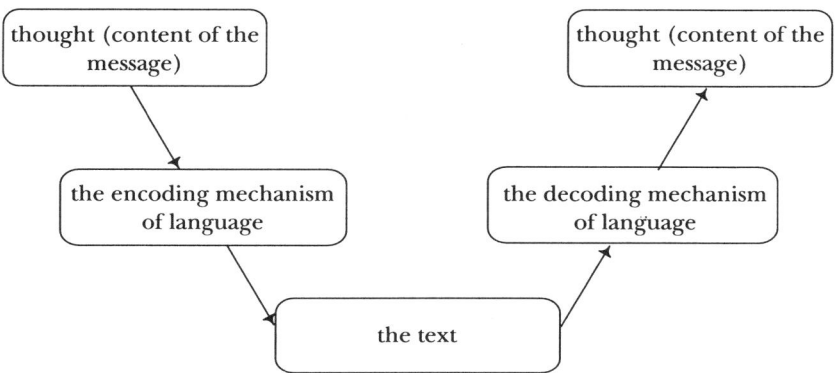

Source: adapted from Lotman 1990: 11.

functions, all of which must be present in any instantiation of language. These factors and functions are shown in figure 2.2. *Jakobson's model requires that all six factors and six functions be present in any speech act.* But clearly, speech acts are distinctly bounded and often idiosyncratic events with high levels of variability. Jakobson represents this variability by defining the model's inherent hierarchy of six factors and six functions, which are rehierarchized in every individual speech act. Figure 2.2 does not demonstrate the dynamic essence of this speech act model; however, Jakobson's accompanying narrative to this model states that these *primitives* (as given by each of the factors and functions) must be (1) present in every speech act and (2) viewed as constantly renegotiating internally their level of importance in any and all speech acts. Thus, in one instance, the dominant function may be *metalingual* (where the emphasis is *code referring to code* [e.g., 'What does "strident" mean?']), while the next speech act may have the *referential* function as its dominant function (where the *focus is on the context* [e.g., 'It's cold outside']). Furthermore, within any two speech acts where the dominant factor and/or function is the same, the subsequent hierarchy of factors and functions may be drastically different. Jakobson is careful to note that there can be no equally powerful speech act model that distinguishes fewer than these six factors and functions (1987: 66). Before returning to Lotman's original construction, I would like to consider other semiotic-based models of communication that, while including language as one potential application, purport to characterize communication for semiotic (e.g., cul-

Figure 2.2

```
                    FACTORS
                    Context
                    Message
  Addresser                            Addressee
                    Contact
                    Code
```

```
                   FUNCTIONS
                   Referential
                   Poetic
  Emotive                              Conative
                   Phatic
                   Metalingual
```

Source: adapted from Jakobson 1987: 66–71.

tural, biological, zoological) systems in general. One such model is found in Sebeok's work.

Sebeok's Communication Model

Sebeok's model of communication is similar to Jakobson's but with at least two major differences: (1) the *context* is the factor within which the entire communication act is embedded, and (2) the model includes communication that is not based in human language (Sebeok 1991: 29–30) (see figure 2.3). Sebeok makes a special point about the dynamic and adaptive nature of the process diagrammed in this figure: 'All communication systems are ... not just dynamic but adaptive; that is, they are self-regulated to suit both the external context (conditions of the environment) and the internal context (circumstances inherent within the system itself, such as the array of presuppositions and implicatures that characterize sentences)' (1991: 30).

This important observation is stated in the context of the general significance of communication, viz., only through communication do

Figure 2.3

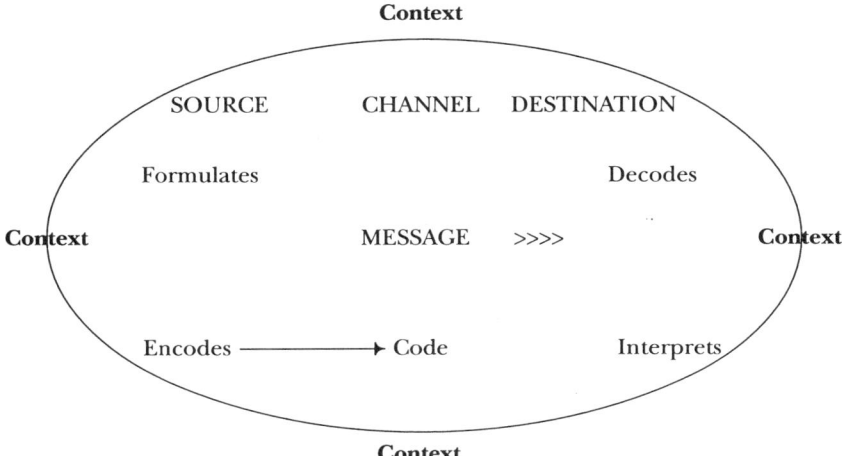

Source: adapted from Sebeok 1991: 29.

complex, living beings become part of an organizational network with potentially diminished entropic tendencies (Sebeok 1991: 22). Given the broad spectrum of definitions of the term entropy, it is essential to clarify the term's use in various semiotic venues. In Sebeok's evocation, entropy is more closely related to its fundamental definition in thermodynamics and does not coincide with how the term is used in generic information theory or social entropy theory. (For a detailed discussion of the term entropy, see the first section of chapter 3.)

Binary or Triadic Signs

In the semiotic tradition that includes the theories of Jakobson, Peirce, and Lotman, one of the most controversial issues relates to the primacy of binary or triadic sign relations. Peirce was absolutely clear that signs are irreducibly triadic in nature, consisting of a sign (or representamen), an object, and an interpretant (Peirce 1931–58: 2.227–229, 2.231–232, 5.127; Savan 1976: 3). From this basic sign structure, Peirce developed a complex set of sign categories, which in turn provided the basis for a theory of meaning, including the construction and interpretation of meaning in all semiotic systems including but not restricted to human language (ibid.: 5.175, 5.173, 5.175, 8.119, and many others). In Peirce's work the major categories of sign types result from three specific relationships: sign-sign, sign-object, and sign-interpretant.

Having said this, it is also true that Jakobson saw his work as firmly aligned with the Peircean semiotic tradition. Such an alignment with Peirce included a marked attempt on Jakobson's part to disassociate himself from Saussure – a process that began as early as the founding of the Prague School, and that is most pronounced in Jakobson's denunciation of Saussure's claim that linguistic signs are arbitrary (cf. on this point Lotman 1990: 16–17). Yet Jakobson's embrace of Peirce was not unambiguous. In particular, he focused on only one of the three triadic sign types provided by Peirce for the sign-object relationship – namely, icon, index, and symbol. Jakobson's application of Peirce's sign-object triad was central to much of his work in his American period, which began after the Second World War and did much to make Peircean semiotic theory an important trend in contemporary linguistic theory.

Nevertheless, it is unclear whether Jakobson ever completely made the leap from a basically dyadic sign (based on signifier/signified) to a fundamentally triadic one (based on sign/object/interpretant). I have discussed this problem in depth in my work on markedness theory (1990) and have argued the following points. On the one hand, Jakobson argues in his article 'A Few Remarks on Peirce, Pathfinder in the Science of Language' ([1977] 1985b) that Peirce himself believed that 'natural classification takes place by dichotomies' (Peirce 1931–58: 1.438). This statement might make more sense if combined with Savan's comment that for Peirce only mental phenomena (i.e., not physical ones) are obligatorily triadic (1976: 32). And since signs are created only in the mind, Peirce is completely consistent with his own theory and, thus, Jakobson cannot support the use of any binary sign types using this particular passage from Peirce. On the other hand, I have argued that Jakobsonian linguistic theory is in fact more triadic in nature than Jakobson himself explicitly realized. See Andrews (1990: 62–4) for an extensive review of Jakobsonian markedness theory, in which I argue that his view of markedness, coupled with his later work on speech acts and shifters, demonstrates a much more sophisticated, triadic basis for sign relations than is given in his earlier work. I believe it is accurate to say that Peircean sign theory serves as one of the most salient, fundamental logics in Jakobson's mature works in the areas of language, literature, and linguistics.

I have mentioned Jakobson before Lotman in this context since there is no question that Jakobson has had a profound impact on the theoretical works of Lotman, especially on Lotman's theoretical works concerning human language, communication acts, definitions of the different factors and functions of speech acts, and the use of mathematics in conceptualizing semiotic space and texts. And it may well be that in his construction of a semiotic-based paradigm, both explicitly and implicitly, Jakobson is more sympathetic than Lotman to the Peircean approach, and more distant from the Saussurean one. An equally complex set of issues makes it impossible to be totally certain whether Lotman should be placed in the Saussurean theoretical camp or the Peircean one. In the following discussion I will present Lotman's own statements about his semiotic approach, and try to clarify how one might negotiate the continuum of binary versus triadic sign types in Lotman's work on the semiosphere and the semiotics of culture.[4]

In the first paragraph of his seminal work on the semiosphere, Lotman notes that any contemporary re-evaluation of semiotic theory requires the acknowledgment of the two scientific traditions that have given rise to the modern state of the field, namely that of Peirce and Morris and that of Saussure and the Prague School (1992b: I. 11). Lotman concludes that each of these schools has one central common basis in a methodology that begins with the smallest element of the system, and that all other phenomena are defined and discussed vis-à-vis this basic element (1992b: I. 11). He argues that in the case of Peircean semiotics, the smallest element is the isolated sign, whereas in the Saussurean approach, the smallest element is the individual communication act. Here, Lotman aligns himself – at least initially – with the Saussurean/Prague School tradition, which begins its analyses at the level of the communication event.

Most semioticians working in the Peircean tradition, including Sebeok and myself, would argue that in this passage Lotman's description of the Peircean approach is incomplete. In fact, semiotic theory – especially Peircean semiotic theory – has reinforced the relevance of and need for further elaboration of system-based phenomena and principles, including the principles of asymmetry, markedness, and continuity. In this sense the Peircean semiotic perspective requires a revolution in technique. Such a revolution will bring into question the very object of study, as well as the instrumentation used to evaluate the object. I contend that the focal point of Peircean semiotic theory is not the sign, but rather *semiosis*, and if there has been a breakdown in the application of such an approach, it is because researchers have often avoided looking at the interface between functioning signs as they are used (Andrews 1994: 9).

Any analysis of functioning signs necessarily brings us to the larger context of the speech or communication act, which is precisely where Lotman has focused his theoretical analyses of culture texts.

Lotman moves into his presentation of the concept of the semiosphere by arguing that it is only in the context of the multifaceted aspects of variegated groups and distinct levels of functioning signs and events in multidimensional space-time (aspects of what gives rise to a definition of the semiosphere) that we can conduct any useful semiotic analysis (1992b: I. 12). Lotman's greatest concern, as expressed in his introduction to the semiosphere, is that semioticians too often attempt to describe complex objects as mere sums of primitive, simple units (12). Clearly, Lotman's statements accord directly with my claim that semiotic theory is about system-based semiosis and not about individual and unrelated signs.

Thus, Lotman disassociates himself somewhat from both Peirce and Saussure in moving toward a more developed model of semiotic space-time. Certainly, neither Peirceans nor Saussureans present a developed theory of dynamic semiotic space in quite the way that Lotman does. However, it is clear that Lotman's system is in harmony with the models presented by Sebeok, Jakobson, and von Uexküll, and also makes an important contribution to a robust semiotics of culture.

This discussion would not be complete without some note of the individual sign types that Lotman works with in the context of the semiosphere. Lotman makes repeated reference to different sign types – particular icons and symbols (1990: 17–18, 69–77, 104–11, 126, 203, 222). On the one hand, he refrains for the most part from making much of indexical signs (1990: 26); on the other, in his analyses he very often uses the Jakobsonian conceptualizations of metonymy and metaphor (as the two primary axes, paradigmatic and syntagmatic, of language, not as mere figures of speech) (1990: 39–45). Given the ambiguity in Jakobson's own applications of Peirce's sign-object triad, we find that Lotman's usage tends to be more binarized than Jakobson's. This is clearest in those instances when the *index* (of the icon/index/symbol triad) is omitted from Lotman's analyses and applications, as they often are.[5]

There is, however, one important section at the end of *Culture and Explosion* in which Lotman acknowledges and explains his perspective on triadic semiotic processes in cultural systems (1992a: 267–9):

Ранее мы говорили о бинарных и тернарных культурных системах. Протекание их через критическую линию взрыва будет различно. В троичных системах взрывные процессы редко схватывают всю толщу культуры. Как правило, здесь имеет место одновременное сочетание взрыва в одних культурных сферах и постепенного развития в других ...

(We spoke earlier about binary and ternary cultural systems. Their movement through the critical line of the explosion will be distinctive. In ternary systems explosive [discontinuous] processes *rarely* reach all layers of culture. As a rule what we have here is a simultaneous combination of explosion [discontinuity] in some cultural spheres and gradual [continuous] development in others.)

In this passage Lotman is arguing that when describing the complexities of cultural dynamics – a task that involves describing multidimensional semiotic space, different rates of change, and multiple and variegated texts – specific realizations of cultures are encountered wherein the overall space is defined by semiotic phenomena that are more triadic or more binary in nature. This may or may not be at the actual sign level itself – Lotman is not explicit on this point. However, for those semioticians working exclusively with triadic sign types, it is possible to use Lotmanian cultural theory in such a way that this passage could be interpreted as describing complex phenomena necessarily beyond the level of individual signs. Lotman is ultimately more preoccupied with the higher levels of analysis of cultural systems than with individual signs; he concentrates on establishing the system-level interactive principles and applying them to specific instantiations of cultural information, especially in the context of Russian, Slavic, and Soviet verbal and visual art forms of the eighteenth, nineteenth, and twentieth centuries.

CHAPTER THREE

Introduction to the Semiosphere

Entropy and Communication

Sebeok characterizes communication as 'that critical attribute of life which retards the disorganizing effects of the Second Law of Thermodynamics; that is, communication tends to decrease entropy locally. In the broadest way, communication can be regarded as the transmission of any influence from one part of a living system to another part, thus producing change. It is messages [i.e., information] that are being transmitted' (1991: 22).

Entropy can be defined as the physical measurement characterizing the heat of a body or cell, or of a system of bodies or cells. From a molecular perspective, entropy is the measure of probability that a particular system state will be realized. The greater the entropy, the more probable a particular system state. In all closed systems, entropy either increases or remains constant. In general, thermodynamics is concerned with system balance and with the processes that affect this balance: the first law of thermodynamics is the law of conservation of energy in conjunction with heat processes; the second law of thermodynamics sets up a direction toward which all systems move – entropy increases in all closed systems. However, the use of the term *entropy* is significantly different (almost reversed) when applied to physical and information-based phenomena.

Thus, in information theory, entropy is the 'unpredictability in the content or form of a message ... Entropy in the *content* is the equivalent of high information, and frequently requires *redundancy* to be introduced into the form for effective, easy *communication*. Entropy in the *form* is usually the result of breaking existing conventions ... Entropy correlates

Introduction to the Semiosphere 27

with *information* on the level of content, and is opposed to redundancy on both levels' (O'Sullivan et al. 1994: 106). (In information theory, where 'information' is determined by the predictability of the signal, if a form is less predictable it has high information and is called entropic; if it has low information it is called redundant. Redundancy, which characterizes at least 50 per cent of all of human language, is essential for the decoding of messages [O'Sullivan et al. 1994: 151, 259–60].)

In models of social entropy, which are open systems by definition and 'not in equilibrium' (unlike the thermodynamic models of entropy presented at the beginning of this section), an additional distinction is made between 'internal' and 'imported' entropy to account for the fact that in some systems entropy actually decreases (Bailey 1990: 71): 'Internal entropy production increases or remains constant within the system, while imported entropy can be decreased by importation of energy from the environment, thus resulting in an overall decrease in system entropy or the increase of order.' Bailey provides a nice definition that captures what all of the applications of entropy have in common (1990: 86): 'The maximum state of entropy in any system is defined as maximum disorder (randomness) or the "most probable" state of the system. Conversely, minimum entropy is always minimum disorder (maximum departure from randomness), regardless of the system in which it is applied. However, there can be great differences in how disorder is defined.'

The process of the exchange of information, including the degrees of information exchanged, is the essence of semiosis. And this exchange necessarily includes a dual process of signification and communication. As Sebeok confirms, the semiotic approach demonstrates that information production and consumption permeate the entire universe and are not restricted to human verbal systems. Examples of other systems include those used by bacteria, plants, animals, fungi, and the component parts of living organisms (cells, organelles, organs, DNA, proteins, etc.) (1991: 86). By being sensitive to the parameters of entropy and redundancy, and to the levels of information contained in semiotic events, we arrive at a more efficient and elegant model of human communication. This extension to larger segments of information exchange is critical to Lotman's characterization of the semiosphere.

In studying communication and information flow, we ultimately are focusing on both input and output, encoding and decoding. Some of the more popular models facilitate understanding this principle (see Sebeok 1991: 26–9 and 54 on his own models, and the *Umwelt* of Jakob von Uexküll). Among these models I would include a version of Thom's model of communication (Thom 1983: 278). Thom notes that it is impossible to reduce information to the content signified; rather, information is the *meaning* plus the *intentionality* which allows that meaning to continue and grow (1983: 282).

Sebeok points out the importance of maintaining the connection provided in the relationship between information and entropy. If these phenomena are viewed as mutually implicative, then they certainly belong 'on the margins of semiotics' (1991: 84). Information, defined as a measure of the number of alternative messages available, is generally applicable to a range of sign-based fields, including computer science, biology, and biochemistry. Other semioticians, such as Thom, set up a relationship between entropy and the topological complexity of a form (as opposed to making a direct correlation with information), where the greater the topological complexity of a form, the greater the entropy (1975). Thom's definition is closer to the kinds of applications found in physical applications of entropy, whereas Sebeok's definition is more restricted to information systems.

Autocommunication

As Lotman continues his analysis of the text as a meaning-generating mechanism, and of the minimum requirements for the existence of dynamic cultural space, he defines the phenomenon of *autocommunication*, where the subject is transmitting a message itself. Lotman argues that this form of communication is much more important that has previously been thought, and that autocommunication in fact only secondarily serves a mnemonic function (i.e., when the second 'I' is 'functionally equivalent to a third party' [1990: 21]). The primary role of autocommunication is a cultural one – to create new information. The new information transmitted is qualitatively restructured and necessarily involves a doubling (or even redefining) of both the *message* and the *code*; it is not redundant and is never self-contained (1990: 22).[1] In contrast, in *I–s/he communication* the *message* and *code* are *fixed* and the speaker/hearers are variable and in flux. In I–s/he communication, the amount of information conveyed remains constant. Both I–I and I–s/he communication are present in all cultures, but the degree to which they are utilized varies from culture to culture. (William Frawley provides an interesting discussion on 'false dialogue' and the importance of achieving a deeper understanding of the language for thinking, which is at once both public and private [1997: 178–233].)

One of the more salient features of autocommunication is that sign types are more indexicalized (e.g., abbreviations can be deciphered only by the text creator, complete sentences are lacking) (Lotman 1990: 26–7). Lotman even claims that rhythmical-metrical systems originate in the autocommunication system and not in the 'I-s/he' system (1990: 30). Lotman concludes his discussion with the observation that all of culture is not only 'the sum of the messages circulated by various addressers' but 'as one message transmitted by the collective "I" of humanity to itself ... a vast example of autocommunication' (1990: 33).

For the present analysis, what is important about autocommunication is the inescapable *doubling* of parts of the speech event, especially addresser, message, and code. (Lotman also discusses a doubling of the *channel.* We will return to these two modes of communication in the context of the semiosphere. For now, note that like Lotman, Sebeok uses the term *channel* whereas Jakobson uses the term *contact*, which is generally interpreted to include the notion of *channel.* As mentioned earlier, any semiotic space requires at least two languages. In the instance of autocommunication, we have a secondary level of doubling of language that involves explicitly doubling all the minimal factors of any given linguistic event.

Returning to Lotman's initial model of communication, we can now try to position his sequence within the more developed communication models provided by Jakobson and Sebeok, determine their compatibility, and define the new information that Lotman's perspective brings to the discussion. This exercise may prove quite useful in demonstrating the explanatory power of Lotman's model of text generation.

To deepen the semiotic potential of Lotman's communication model, I will try to conflate this model with the Jakobsonian model in such a way that each of Jakobson's factors will be added to the Lotmanian model as it is required within the dynamic communication process. This yields the dynamic shown in figure 3.1 (Jakobson's factors are in italics). This rendering of the two models requires that one or more factors be interacting at any given point in the sequence. According to Lotman, any singular speech act is by definition already a doublet. And if we were to extend this dynamic, multilevelled model to include more than one single utterance, we would find the relationships displayed in figure 3.2. (Note that the increase in factors is exponential.)

Sebeok's communication model sets apart *context* as both an internal and external phenomenon and thus is a major step in redefining the speech act model. I would suggest that the relationships shown in

30 Lotman's Cultural Semiotic Theory

Figure 3.1: Singular speech act

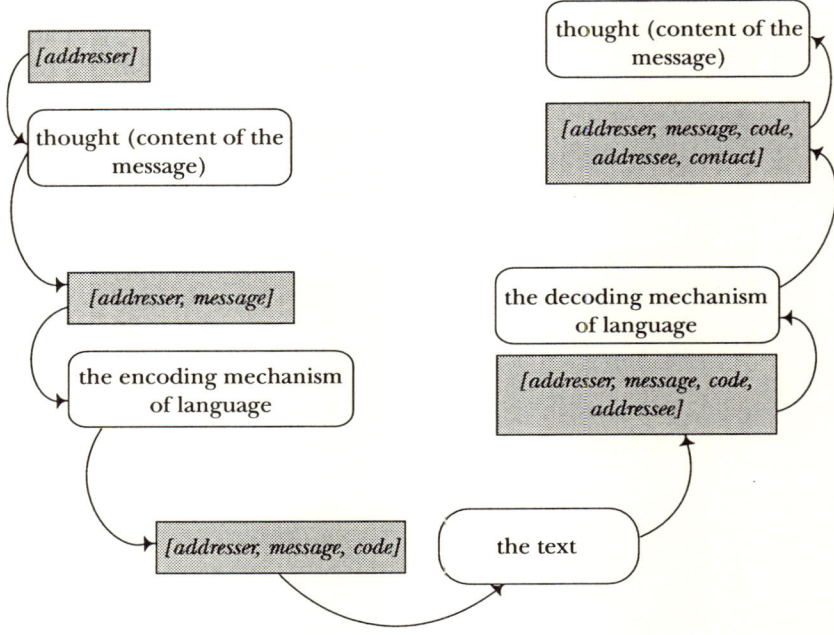

figure 3.2 would be more accurate if we were to allow context to be signalled on these two distinct levels, as shown in figure 3.3.

Clearly, there is never a *singular* speech act after the inception of the language system; rather, each speech act is obligatorily embedded in an *n*-length chain of discrete speech acts. We see that as the speech acts combine and extend into this never-ending chain at multiple, potentially infinite levels, the strings of discourse become more and more complex and, in time, begin placing strain on the participants' ability to recall previous utterances and information from the chain, and to actively produce utterances and information in the present. We can appreciate at this point Lotman's insistence on distinguishing between *code* and *language* such that *history* – or what one might call the spatio-temporal framework – is not only important but essential in defining human language. (Lotman is not unique in his preoccupation with the encoding of cultural values in language; he belongs to a rich Russian intellectual tradition devoted to this question – see in particular the works of

Figure 3.2

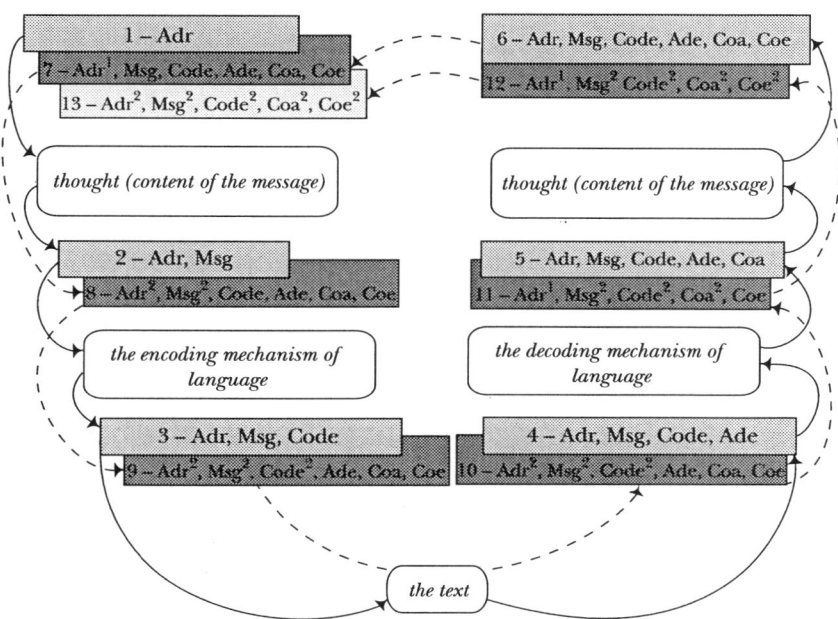

Jurij Tynjanov, Mikhail Bakhtin, Valentin Voloshinov, and Dmitrij Lixachev.) Clearly, each member of a cultural space comes into the field of culture texts and discourse acts *in the middle*. Our ability to speak and to hear is limited when it comes to negotiating the information-producing structural system – a system that both predates our participation and is a prerequisite for that participation.

Now that we have defined the fundamental principles of human communication systems, we can move forward to the larger context in which these systems are embedded. Lotman's extensive work on the *semiosphere* and the *semiotics of communication* provides some valuable insights into the structural principles of semiosis.

Semiotic Space

Lotman's begins his analysis and construction of semiotic space by noting that research based in the semiotic paradigm has proven that well-

Figure 3.3

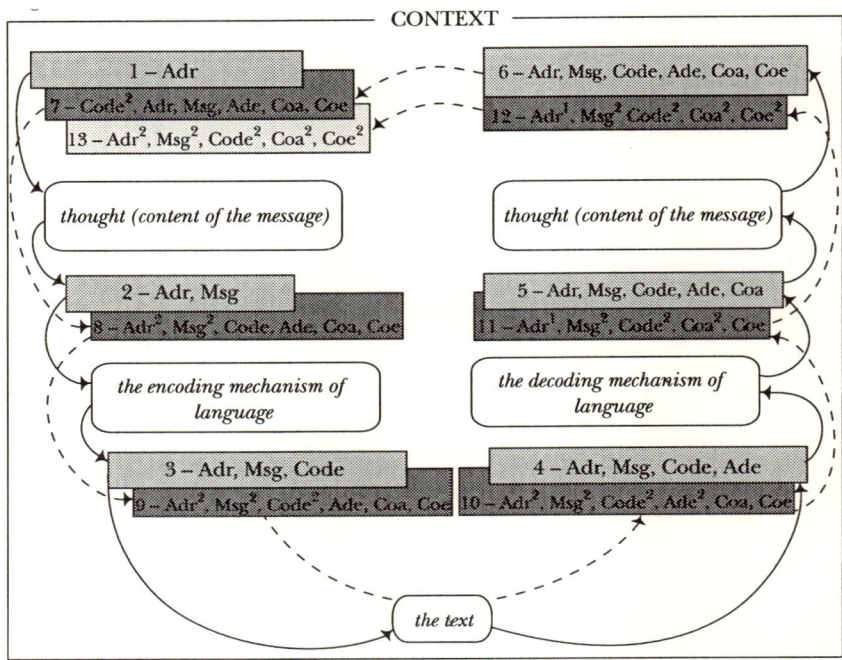

defined and functionally unambiguous systems never exist in isolation. Rather, they can only become meaningful and functional when perceived as one segment of the *continuum* of multifaceted, multilevelled, and variegated semiotic formations – that is, when they are '"immersed" in semiotic space' (1990: 123–4; 1992b: I. 12–13). Lotman deduces that this situation demonstrates that 'semiotic experience precedes the semiotic act' and, therefore we must define this fundamental ground of semiotic experience as a starting point for our structural framework (1990: 123). Lotman names this structural framework the *semiosphere* (by analogy with Vladimir Vernadsky's *biosphere*, 'the semiotic space necessary for the existence and functioning of languages, not the sum total of different languages; in a sense the semiosphere has a prior existence and is in constant interaction with languages' (1990: 123).[2] Note that in so defining the semiosphere, Lotman is making a clear shift away from the level of individual signs and their functions in cultural space toward a higher level of network semiosis and system-level phenomena.

According to Lotman, there are four fundamental concepts associated with the semiosphere:

1 *Heterogeneity* – The languages of the semiosphere run along a continuum that includes the extremes of total mutual translatability and complete mutual untranslatability (1990: 125; 1992b: I. 11–24; 1992a: 14–16).
2 *Asymmetry* – The structure of the semiosphere is asymmetrical at multiple levels, including asymmetry in terms of internal translations, centre versus periphery, and metalinguistic structures (1990: 124–7; 1992a: 25–30; 1992b: I. 16–19).
3 *Boundedness* – One of the primary mechanisms of semiotic individuation is the creation of boundaries, which define the essence of the semiotic process. Boundaries are abstractions, and are often described as series of bilingual filters or membranes that are by definition permeable and fluid, on the one hand, and as areas of accelerated semiotic processes, on the other (1990: 131–40; 1992b: I. 13–16).[3]
4 *Binarity* – The beginning point for any culture is based on the binary distinction of internal versus external space.

Lotman insists that binary oppositions in the semiosphere exist only as pluralities – that is, as mechanisms that are obligatorily included for multiplication of languages (1990: 124; 1992b: I. 13–17).

Beyond the boundaries of the semiosphere, one finds externally given, unorganized, 'non-structural' surroundings. Even if one were to imagine that there was no space beyond the semiosphere, Lotman's conception of the semiosphere nonetheless would require the construction of a *chaotic* external field (1992b: I. 15–16).

One of the remaining defining characteristics of the semiosphere and the 'highest form and final act of a semiotic system's structural organization,' is self-description, or the development of a metalanguage (Lotman 1990: 128; 1992b: I. 16–17). Once such a metalanguage is in place, the system achieves a higher level of organization; however, the presence of the metalanguage slows down dynamic development and the processing of new information. Even so, the semiosphere's metalanguage may be necessary to prevent disintegration of the semiosphere itself. (Examples of such metalanguages include legal codes, scriptural laws, and ritual texts.) This would be the case if diversity within the semiosphere were to become overly prevalent. Once again, the role of self-description in the

34 Lotman's Cultural Semiotic Theory

Figure 3.4

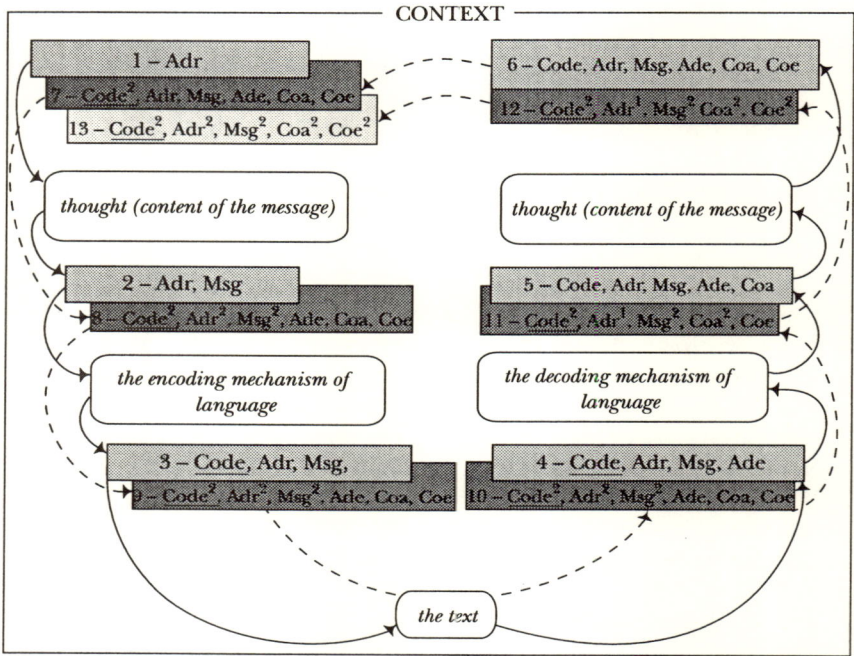

semiosphere is played out between the bounded areas of centre and periphery. The centre is defined by the metalanguage, whereas the periphery is still free of self-description and is more likely to be defined by accelerated dynamic development (Lotman 1990: 128; 1992b: I. 16–17). In the end it is the semiosphere's heterogeneity that underlies its integrity [целостность] (Lotman 1992b: I. 17).

We now return to our modified model of the communication act, and consider how this model can demonstrate the importance of a system-based metalanguage. I believe we can diagrammatically show this important feature of the semiosphere through a reordering of factors, whereby code becomes dominant at each of the levels provided as soon as it enters the system. See figure 3.4, which shows the revised dynamic. This reordering, *in which the code becomes dominant over addresser*, may seem trivial at first glance, but I would argue that it is in fact quite significant in demonstrating that the modified model is compatible with a Lotmanian analysis in general, and specifically with regard to the foundation for any communication act within the semiosphere. Furthermore, such a diagram vividly represents the important notion that the *code* is a part of *language* (where *language = code + history* [Lotman 1992a: 12–13]) and not equal to it, as well as the fact that at the inception of the semiotic act, the code's existence is directly contingent on the presence of the participant(s) and the message.

Any communication act so embedded in the semiosphere will always contain the dynamic – or in this instance, *tension* – between varying degrees of intersection of the potentially translatable linguistic acts, where the *value* of the information increases with the tension and the restrictedness of the intersecting spaces. These *spaces* represent not only the participants in the communication act, but also the information that is dynamically produced during the interaction (or linguistic exchange). In such a model the act of non-comprehension becomes just as salient as the act of comprehension (Lotman 1992a: 16). For Lotman (as is true with Peirce), all communication and all intellectual and cultural acts are *semiotic* and therefore require some form of *translation* between signs where there are *at least two* distinct sign systems involved. The most basic level of translation is guaranteed in the claim that there is no singular communication act, but *at least* a doublet at its inception.

In defining the dynamic mechanism of sign translation of the semiosphere and its contents, the next step requires that we go beyond the four properties of the system and unveil the underlying central structural invariant – the principle of continuity and discontinuity.

Continuity and Discontinuity

Continuity and its relationship to discontinuity (or discreteness) is a subject of enormous philosophical import – perhaps one of the most important aspects of any theory of knowledge. It would be impossible for Lotman to construct the principles of organization of semiotic spaces without recourse to this central distinction. Lotman is not the only semiotician to be concerned about this distinction, and to offer a full perspective on this important point, I will include other semiotic-based perspectives of this question from the works of Peirce and Thom. Furthermore, the question of discontinuity and its relationship to continuity is the basis of any viable theory of biology and human perception (see Kosslyn, Maturana, and Varela, for example). Only after addressing this important distinction can we move forward to discuss the functioning semiosphere in time and space from the perspective of both the individual and collective levels.

For Peirce, both cognition and perception, as central issues in semiotic epistemology, are continuous by definition. That is why he claims that continuity is 'the leading conception of science. The complexity of the conception of continuity is so great as to render it important wherever it occurs' (1957: 204). Continuity arises within the science universe as a direct and necessary result of the sign's triadic nature. Peirce goes on to admit that 'the idea of continuity is so indispensable ... that it is perpetually introduced even where there is no continuity in fact' (1957: 59). Continuity is a key for any system-level metatheory of perception, where perception is directly correlated with some form of perturbation (change of state or disruption). However, continuity is not the entire picture. As Thom points out, we must have a theory that has descriptive power in the context of forms and structures that are spatially and temporally bounded. Such boundaries are necessarily discontinuities in the system. Thus, in a Thomian world, discontinuity is defined as a 'change in the previous form,' and this concept plays a key role in his theory of *morphogenesis* (Thom 1975: 7).[4] For Thom, as for Lotman, the dynamics of the system can come into conflict with the need for *structural stability*. Since continuous models always become unique and reintroduce a discontinuous factor, leading back to a formal system, it is unavoidable that continuous models and/or systems have a discontinuity at some point. So it is inevitable that any semiotic space will be made up of both continuities and discontinuities that are asymmetrically defined.

Lotman represents the relationship between continuity and discontinuity in a fashion that is quite complementary to a Thomian model, in that he begins with discontinuity and only then moves on to continuity. All perception begins with 'small portions of irritation' (i.e., discontinuities), which the organism interprets as continuous and gradual (Lotman 1992a: 17). Yet both continuous and discontinuous phenomena provide the dynamic for new levels of change and evolution.

In his discussion of culture, where culture is obligatorily a complex unit (1992a: 25), Lotman points to discreteness – the mechanism for producing information segmentally – as 'the law of all dialogic systems' (1990: 144). Therefore, if culture consists of different levels moving at different speeds and at different points in development, it follows that any 'cut' (срез) will produce the immediate, simultaneous presence of variegated and qualitatively different stages (1992a: 25). In this scheme, the gradual (continuous) processes will guarantee the existence of innovation (новаторство), while the explosive (discrete) processes will guarantee succession (преемственность). These two phenomena are endlessly (and inseparably) intertwined so that a dynamic is constantly in place (Lotman 1992a: 26–7).

It is worth examining this statement more closely, since it may seem self-contradictory or unexpected that gradual changes bring innovation and explosive/discrete changes bring succession. Lotman writes (1992a: 26–7):

> Так, например, динамика процессов в сфере языка и политики, нравственности и моды демонстрирует различные скорости движения этих процессов. И хотя более быстрые процессы могут оказывать ускоряющее влияние на более медленные, а эти последние могут присваивать себе самоназвание более быстрых и ускорять этим свое развитие, динамика их не синхронна. Еще более существенно одновременное сочетание в разных сферах культуры взрывных и постепенных процессов. Вопрос этот усложняется тем, что они присваивают себе неадекватные самоназвания. Это обычно мистифицирует исследователей. Последним свойственно сводить синхронию к структурному единству, а агрессию какого-либо самоназвания истолковывать как установление структурного единства. Сначала волна самоназваний, а затем вторая волна – исследовательской терминологии – искусственно унифицируют картину процесса, сглаживая противоречия структур. Между тем, именно в этих противоречиях заложены основы механизмов динамики.
>
> И постепенные, и взрывные процессы в синхронно работающей структуре выполняют важные функции: одни обеспечивают новаторство, другие – преемственность. Пересечение разных структурных организаций становится источником динамики.

(So, for example, the dynamic of processes in the area of language and politics, morals and fashion demonstrates different rates of motion of these processes. And although more rapid processes may render an increase in speed in the slower ones, and the latter may take on the *self-naming* of more rapid processes and speed up their own development, their dynamic is not synchronized. What is more important is the simultaneous connection of different spheres of culture in explosive and gradual processes. The question becomes more complex when they take on an inadequate *self-name*. This usually mystifies the researcher. It is generally true of the latter to

38   Lotman's Cultural Semiotic Theory

conflate synchrony with a structural unity, but the aggressiveness of some *self-names* can be described as the establishment of a structural unity. Thus, at first there is the wave of *self-naming*, followed directly by the second wave of scholarly terminology that artificially unifies the representation of the process by ironing out the contradictions in the structures.

By the way, it is precisely in these contradictions that the basis of dynamic mechanisms is embedded. Both gradual and explosive processes in a synchronized working structure fulfills important functions: some guarantee novelty, others succession ... The intersection of different structural organizations becomes the source of the dynamic.)

Here we find Lotman stating clearly that all continuous phenomena guarantee discontinuities, and that all discontinuous phenomena guarantee future continuities within the cultural-semiotic system.[5] In the quoted passage he is arguing that if we could capture a paradigmatic view of multiple cultural phenomena within a specific culture at one moment in time, as in a freeze frame, we would find that each phenomenon is experiencing *at a different pace or speed* a dynamic that is either of a continuous, gradual nature or of a discrete, discontinuous one. The complication arises from the fact that these phenomena are constantly interacting; this leads to the impression that they are something other than themselves. (Lotman calls this the 'appropriation of misleading *self-definitions*' [from the neologism *самоназвание*, which literally means 'self-naming' [1992a: 26].)[6] Lotman explicitly describes this as a two-tiered process whereby the 'self-naming' occurs before the cultural metalanguage imposes its own name. The misappropriation, thus, occurs on at least two distinct levels, making the researcher's job quite complex.

At the same time, Lotman is actually focusing on something very different – the primacy of continuous and discrete dynamic forces in cultural phenomena. What is most important for Lotman is the intertwined reactivity of these two types of dynamic change, where the strength of change in one area evokes an equally powerful change in another, distinct area: the inextricable relationship between continuous and discrete (or discontinuous) phenomena, where the existence of one is dependent on the existence of the other. The more aggressive the realization of continuous processes, the stronger the reaction in the realization of discrete processes (1992a: 26). In fact, the 'crossing over' between semiotic categories of diverse structural organization is the primary source of dynamic change in any system (1992a: 27). In chapter 4 we will return to the semiotic manifestations of continuous and discrete phenomena in the form of the *explosion* (взрыв) and the resulting exploitation of the explosion.

One other piece of Lotman's argumentation – one that is relevant in concluding the present discussion – is his distinction between *actual* discontinuity and the *perception* of discontinuity. The perception of discontinuity is perhaps best described in the context of a culture's power of self-description. Even though a culture's development is cyclical in nature, the periods of self-awareness are 'usually recorded as intermissions' (as, for example, in the history of the Russian novel) (Lotman 1990: 144). The result is that the cultural *text* is viewed as a 'freeze frame, an artificially frozen moment between the past and the future' that is asymmetrical by definition (Lotman 1992a: 27 [translation mine]). The asymmetry of the relationship between past and future is defined by Lotman (1992a: 27) in the following way:

Прошедшее дается в двух его проявлениях: внутренне – непосредственная память текста, воплощенная в его внутренней структуре, ее неизбежной противоречивости, имманентной борьбе со своим внутренним синхронизмом, и внешне – как соотношение с внетекстовой памятью. Мысленно поместив себя в то «настоящее время», которое реализовано в тексте (например, в *данной* картине, в момент, когда я на нее смотрю), зритель как бы обращает свой взор в прошлое, которое сходится как конус, упирающийся вершиной в настоящее время. Обращаясь в будущее, аудитория погружается в пучок возможностей, еще не совершивших своего потенциального выбора. Неизвестность будущего позволяет приписывать значимость всему.

(The past is given in two manifestations: internal – *the direct memory of the text as embodied by its internal structure*, its unavoidable contradictions, its immanent battle with its own internal synchronism, and *external – as it correlates with extratextual memory*. Placing oneself into the present, which is realized in the text (for example, in a given painting at the moment when I am looking at it), the viewer actually fixes his gaze into the past, which converges like a cone with its end-point in the present. Looking to the future, the participant becomes inundated by a spectrum of possibilities that have not yet made their potential choice. The unknown nature of the future allows anything to be potentially meaningful. [my emphasis])

It is at this juncture that we find an important distinction between internal and external memory. In exploring its realization, we return to the core of any semiotic space – human language.

In chapters 2 and 3 I have attempted to demonstrate that fundamentally the production and exchange of information for creating, developing, and maintaining culture is embodied in communication acts. Using modelling systems developed by Lotman, Jakobson, and Sebeok, I have argued that in order to arrive at a viable theory of culture, we must develop communication act models that more precisely reflect the essence of information production and exchange. Our model is characterized by *complex, dynamic, multileveled semiotic entities defined by continuous and discrete categories in conflict* within the boundaries of a cultural *context* (where the cultural context is defined at no fewer than two distinct levels). The resulting schema in Figure 3.4 is simply a diagrammatic representation of what that process minimally entails.

Collective Memory

Any discussion of the relationship between language and memory must include both the individual and collective levels. Clearly, the speakers of a given language must assimilate a significant amount of information and behaviours in order to be recognized as full-fledged members of a particular linguistic or cultural community. This aspect of language learning depends on the mastery of a norm that is determined prior to the individual speaker's existence in the framework of a dynamic system that presupposes the participants of the speech event (including addresser and addressee), context, contact, code, and message. As I have already noted, before this communicative system can begin to operate in the Lotmanian semiotic paradigm, it must first be contextualized and immersed in semiotic space, which Lotman designates as the *semiosphere* (Lotman 1990: 124).

In the context of the semiosphere, language becomes a complex set of relations that can be called *functions* (in the mathematical, not Jakobsonian, sense), and that map distinctly heterogeneous, asymmetrical semiotic spaces (Lotman 1990: 125–6). The asymmetry of the semiosphere may be realized as centre and periphery, as the different velocities of semiotic layers, or as different temporal periods. At its highest level the semiosphere may seem to be a semiotic unity; but in fact it is a conglomerate of dynamic kernels with ever-changing internal and external spatiotemporal boundaries (Lotman 1990: 127–30). Thus, for Lotman there can be no *language* or *memory* without the guarantee of semiosis in the form of the semiosphere.

One way that cultures and languages maintain their identity is through the utilization of collective memory, which applies mechanisms for both self-preservation and propagation. Lotman identifies writing as one of the most important means of preserving information of discrete, even anomalous events (1990: 246–7). Writing as memory sets up the potential for linear (cause and effect) relationships, as well as an increase in 'the quantity of texts' and information in general (1990: 247). The other vital means of self-preservation is oral culture, where the focus is not on the generation of new texts, but on the regular, ritualistic, law-based nature of existence (1990: 246–7). Both forms of collective memory rely predominantly on language. It is important to note that writing – as opposed to oral culture – shifts the burden of *memory* from the individual to an externally given symbolic system, whereas oral culture is determined more by the accuracy of individual memory. In essence, language becomes the symbolic 'condenser' between different levels of semiosis and different segments of the time axis (Lotman 1990: 110).

If language itself necessarily exists within and beyond the individual speaker, and requires both individual and collective memory, then *texts*, as codifications of moments between past and future in an asymmetrical fashion, become meaningful in the undeterminedness of the future (Lotman 1992a: 27–8). And culture, in Lotman's definition, necessarily includes not only collective memory, which allows for the preservation and transfer of knowledge and information through time, but collective intellect, which guarantees the potential actualization of coded information in the present and the production of new information in the future (1992b: I. 200). Thus it is through the communication act, defined as a semiotic entity, that continuity and higher-level ordered (rule-based) systems such as language and culture are created from endless strings of discontinuities (Lotman 1990: 273):

> The individual human intellect does not have a monopoly in the work of thinking. Semiotic systems, both separately and together as the integrated unity of the semiosphere, both synchronically and in all the depths of historical memory, carry out intellectual operations, preserve, and work to increase the store of information. Thought is within us, but we are within thought just as language is something engendered by our minds and directly dependent on the mechanisms of the brain, and we are with language.

CHAPTER FOUR

Characteristics and Origins of the Semiosphere

In *Culture and Explosion* (1992), Lotman sets forth a mature, fully developed version of his theory of semiotic systems as they are defined by their accompanying semiotic space. The need for defining the fundamental principles of any sign system is explicated in the multiplicity of texts that serve to differentiate internal and external boundaries, different layers, and different levels of complexity within and among layers moving at many different and variable speeds. One of the key mechanisms that allows these texts to communicate with one another and to cross over the internal boundaries of cultural space is the existence of varying degrees of translation. We have already seen that there can be no communication of any sort, be it I–s/he communication or autocommunication, without translation. Translation occurs between the participants of sign events with varying degrees of intersection and success, and involves multiple natural languages and sign types (especially what Peirce would call interpretants). Furthermore, all of these semiotic acts of translation are accompanied by some degree of tension. The participants of these events, having different perspectives, will make significant changes in the potential and actual meanings that result from translation. To show more clearly how sign systems function, Lotman provides an insightful diagrammatization of the obligatory aspects of the semiotic space where, once bounded, we find distinct and multifaceted semiospheres.

Characteristics of the Semiosphere

The semiosphere is defined by Lotman as 'the semiotic space necessary for the existence and functioning of languages, not the sum total of different languages; in a sense the semiosphere has a prior existence and is in constant interaction with languages ... a generator of information' (1990: 123, 127). This space is both a precursor to and a result of ('the result and the condition for') cultural development (1990: 125). The primary characteristic of the semiosphere is its separateness (отграниченность), which is both homogenous and individual (Lotman 1992b: I. 13). Thus, the boundary (граница) becomes one of the most important 'functional' and 'structural' elements of the semiotic mechanism (Lotman 1992b: I. 14). The semiosphere, therefore, is the fundamental semiotic space that provides the context and potential for both human communication and the creation or generation of new information (1992b: I. 11–12).

We must clearly define 'boundary' in order to avoid any misunderstandings about the range of its applicability. One possible analogy is to a cell membrane, which allows for the inflow and outflow of substances. Another is to a mathematical boundary, which is a collection of points (Lotman 1992b: I. 13). Yet both these examples fail to illustrate the important quality of translatability. Nothing can penetrate the boundaries of the semiosphere (nor move from inside to outside the semiosphere) unless it is translated into one of the available languages of the internal semiotic space. Lotman's term *bilingual translation filter* provides perhaps one of the more meaningful ways of viewing semiospheric boundaries (1992b: I. 13). This being said, Lotman reiterates that the semiosphere does not represent 'the sum total of different languages' (1990: 123) – that is, the semiosphere cannot be reduced to its multiple languages. Rather, it is a complex gestalt with multileveled, highly integrated structures.

The neologism *semiosphere* coined by Lotman is based on Vladimir Vernadsky's term *biosphere* (discussed in more detail below). Specifically, Vernadsky's biosphere is the 'region of life' (область жизни) – the enclosed space where living organisms exist, change, and evolve. All semiospheres are, by definition, heterogeneous. The degree of heterogeneity will, of course, vary from space to space. The different kinds of heterogeneity are based on both the elements and the functions of each semiotic space (1990: 125). According to Lotman, the laws of the semiosphere are asymmetry and binarism (1990: 124). Because the semiosphere is in constant flux, the inherent asymmetry of all semiotic space is obligatory as a system-based principle that necessarily produces future changes as perturbations occur to the functioning system. As I have already shown, the notion of binarism and the degree of its application are central issues distinguishing different trends in semiotic theory, especially in the context of the writings of Lotman and Jakobson and their compatibility with Peircean semiotics.

The dynamics of the semiosphere lead to changes that do not really parallel biological evolution. The fundamental difference is that biological organisms may die and disappear, whereas cultural phenomena are always potentially with us and can come to life over and over again (Lotman 1990: 127). Lotman's argument actually seems to be about the difference between cultural and natural phenomena: cultural phenomena are non-hereditary and require languages. However, where cultural and natural phenomena are the same is in how they are perceived. The bottom line for Lotman is that all phenomena must be translated in order to be perceived. Thus, nothing is unsemiotic or even natural, since there is no unmitigated knowledge of the external or internal worlds. The importance of translation as part of perception, and the fundamental difference between living and non-living nature, will come up again in the context of Jakob von Uexküll's *Umwelt* theory.

The law of asymmetry of the semiosphere leads to important distinctions between the centre and periphery, multiple layers defined by their differing speeds and tensions, and variable degrees of translatability between and among these layers. Lotman's example of a randomly selected *cut* (or *section*) of the semiosphere (cpe3) vividly demonstrates the full force of dynamic change simultaneously occurring at a variety of levels (Lotman 1992a: 25–6). Figure 4.1 provides an example of what a semiospheric cut might look like. In this diagram I have selected a representation of the layering in the human brain between the cortical surface and white matter, with examples of pyramidal neurons and their axons connecting different layers of the cerebral cortex. Thus, asymmetry is the driving force behind the dynamicity of the semiotic space, which proceeds in time and space in a non-linear mode characterized by periods of continuity and explosion (Lotman 1992a: 16). We must understand the exact nature of the periods of continuity and explosion if the semiosphere is to take on the richness required of such a model (or perhaps it would be more accurate to say the superstructure or metastructure) of culture.

Lotman's definition of semiotic space and the semiosphere necessarily begins with the notion of asymmetry, which is the baseline requirement that leads directly to the constant presence of variable dynamism of the semiotic space (1992a: 16–18), movement between the individual and

Figure 4.1

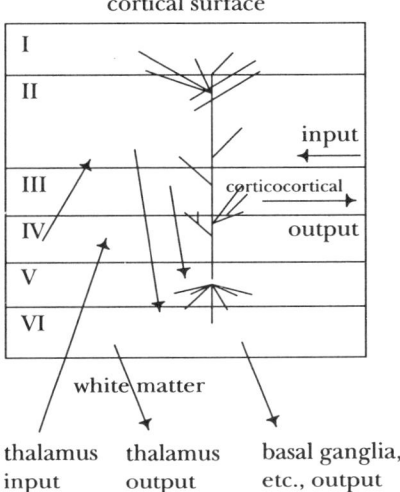

collective levels (1992a: 10–11), the different and unequal roles of speaker(s) and hearer(s) in any communication act (1992a: 14), and, perhaps most important of all, ever-present *tension* (Lotman uses two Russian terms to refer to tension – напряжение and силовое сопротивление 1992a: 14).

The question of binarism is both complex and controversial. In the first place, Lotman is careful to qualify his use of the term: 'Binarism, however, must be understood as a principle which is realized *in plurality* since every newly formed language is in its turn subdivided on a binary principle' (1990: 124; italics mine). Here, Lotman is not reducing the structure of semiotic space to dyads alone. Note also that the Peircean semiotic paradigm explicitly requires that all sign types and all forms of semiosis be triadic in nature. Although it may not be possible to reconcile these two semiotic views, I would point out once again that Lotman's view of binarism does not exclude triadic relations, and that once the semiotic space becomes sufficiently complex, the multiplication of codes in number and diversity of elements and functions is no longer reducible to binary relations.[1]

Lotman applies binarism specifically in two instances: when defining the primary subdivision of the semiosphere as centre versus periphery, and when defining the two types of dynamic change as continuous and discontinuous (1992a: 17; 1990: 127). We will focus more sharply on these two aspects of change after the discussion on boundaries.

Because the semiospheric boundary is like a membrane or filter, always penetrable (проницаема) (Lotman 1992a: 178), clearly, bilingual translation is possible from both directions (internal to external and vice versa) (Lotman 1992b: I. 13–14). The interplay across these boundaries is inexhaustible ('Это "вечное движение" не может быть исчерпано') (Lotman 1992a: 178–9). Furthermore, unlike biological evolution, cultural evolution allows for the co-existence in time and space of historical artifacts, works of art, language(s), and so on (1990: 127–8; 1992a: 178). In order for translation to occur across the semiospheric boundary, whatever is a foreign text or 'non text' to a given semiosphere must be reorganized into a text in one of the available codes of the semiosphere itself (1992b: I. 13). This kind of contact between different semiospheres is constantly occurring, and these semiotic 'currents' flow *horizontally* and *vertically* from within and without (1990: 129–30). At this point it is appropriate to consider some of the more important types of boundaries found with any semiosphere, and how these boundaries change and eventually modify the available texts and languages in a particular cultural space.

Boundaries

For Lotman, boundaries are the basic mechanism of semiotic differentiation. We have already seen that Lotman defines all boundaries as bilingual and membranelike. The most external of semiospheric boundaries differentiates the cultural 'we' from all 'others,' regardless of the nature of the space of the 'other' (be it another semiosphere or extra-semiotic space). There are many examples of how cultures construct everything external to them as chaotic, heathen, evil, and primitive (Lotman 1992b: I. 15; 1990: 131–2). The obligatory external boundary guarantees the relatively closed status of the semiosphere; this means that nothing can penetrate the boundaries of the semiosphere that is of the nature of a non-semiotic text or a non-text (1992: I. 13). These external boundaries are *relatively arbitrary*, and so is their thickness and degree of penetrability, and how they are drawn will depend on a series of cultural factors provided in the context of the semiosphere itself. Meanings are created as information is translated across these boundaries, and in no other way. Lotman pays special attention to the external boundaries of the semiosphere; whatever lies beyond those boundaries is generally characterized by a large number of diverse human cultures as uncivilized, animal-like, pagan, and chaotic – a space where all is permitted that is not permitted within the semiosphere (1990: 131–3).

Besides outermost boundaries, the semiosphere has internal boundaries. These are multiple and diverse, and are always being created and destroyed, and differentiate the internal space of the semiosphere. These internal boundaries are just as important as the external filters. The primary functions of these internal semiospheric boundaries, as a 'sum of bilingual translation filters' (1992b: I. 13), are (1) 'to limit penetration, filter and provide an adaptive reworking' of all that is external to itself as these semiotic 'features' are internalized within the given space, and (2) to speed up the semiotic processes of codifying and producing new and salient information, and to simplify the work of maintaining and ensuring the continuity of old information in new forms (1992b: I. 14–15). Note that this formulation requires that all translations occur in a series and never as monads. This fact is demonstrated clearly in the modelling of the kernel of discourse discussed in chapters 2 and 3.

One of the more important internal semiospheric boundaries is the one between periphery and centre. The central space is necessarily dominant in a given semiosphere, while constantly renegotiating itself through the translation of new information, which is initiated at the border areas and the periphery of the semiosphere. The realization of the multiple languages and texts within a given semiosphere is often not one of strict hierarchization and may be perceived to be on one and the same level. Individual texts may be contextualized within the semiosphere in languages that are inadequate for the extrapolation of meaning. In fact, the necessary codes for some of these texts may cease to exist in the given semiotic space (1992b: I. 16–17). Because of this aspect of the constant renegotiation between centre and periphery, there will always be at least some texts that are untranslatable because of the absence of the necessary codes.

Given that the semiosphere's structure includes multiple paradigmatic levels moving at different rates and changing their spatial dimensions vis-à-vis the other levels of the semiosphere, there is also the possibility that information, texts, and meaning will be created through 'vertical isomorphisms' between structural layers (1992b: I. 18). The languages and codes that facilitate translation across the boundaries of these structural semiospheric layers alternate between discrete and cyclic phenomena, demonstrating continuities and discontinuities, depending on the perspective of the observer(s) and the level of semiotic realization. Lotman notes the following (1992b: I. 18): 'Фактически можно сказать, что дискретность в семиотических системах возникает при описании циклических процессов языком дискретной структуры.' (One might actually say that discreteness in semiotic systems arises during the act of description of cyclic processes by means of the language of discrete structure.)

As new information and texts are created, so is individual and collective consciousness in cultural space. For Lotman, there is no consciousness without communication, and all communication is modelled as a dialogue in such a way that the principle of dialogue 'precedes and gives rise to language' (1992b: I. 19).[2] It is through the interaction of these two opposing forces that tension arises, a tension that ensures the dynamic, text-generating essence of cultural space. Another source of tension is found in the discontinuities that occur in all spatio-temporal perception events.

Tension and Explosion

Lotman's notion of tension and explosion is at the heart of not only the semiosphere itself but also any individual act of human communication. The 'tension' arises at multiple levels, including the asymmetrical roles of the participants of the communication act and their intersecting – but not identical – codes and memories (1992a: 12–14). As I have already discussed, in the multifaceted speech act provided in Jakobson, Sebeok, and Lotman, there is built-in tension between the factors required for a speech act to occur. If the participants of the communication event were identical and if complete overlap of encoding and decoding were achieved, then no new information would have been relayed (Lotman 1992a: 14–15). Thus, any exchange of information necessarily involves two contradictory tendencies (or tensions): the desire to increase overlap between the speaker/hearer in the context of the utterance, and the desire to increase the value of the information (1992a: 14). It is, therefore, the information that falls *beyond* the field of intersection that is of the greatest value. As Lotman eloquently points out (1992a: 15, 17):

... чем труднее и неадекватнее перевод одной непересекающейся части пространства на язык другой, тем более ценным в информационном и социальном отношениях становится факт этого парадоксального общения. Можно сказать, что перевод непереводимого оказывается носителем информации высокой ценности ... Непредсказуемость взрывных процессов отнюдь не является единственным путем к новому ... Постепенные и взрывные процессы, представляя собой антитезу, существуют только в отношении друг к другу.

(... the more difficult the translation of one non-intersection space into another language, the more valued the fact of this paradoxical interaction becomes in terms of informativeness and social relationships. One might say that the translation of the untranslatable turns out to be the carrier of highly valuable information ... The unpredictability of explosive processes is hardly the only path to innovation ... Gradual and explosive processes, being the antithesis of each other, exist only in relation to each other.)

(I hope to demonstrate in chapters 7 and 8 that this is precisely one of the reasons for the high 'value' of Evgenij Zamyatin's novel *We*: Zamyatin's text constantly requires the reader to do the almost impossible – translate from one type of text to another as a means of increasing the value of the information encoded among and between these seemingly 'nontranslatable' codes.)

The other aspect of tension is the long-term mechanism for dynamic change in cultural systems. Lotman argues that change is unavoidable. Not only that, but there are different mechanisms for dynamic shifts in the system that result in varying levels of information growth. There are two primary mechanisms for change: gradual and explosive (1992a: 17–43). The fact that these mechanisms exist for Lotman as cultural universals, and that the two are inextricably linked, coexisting and alternating, perceived as facilitating or hindering progress depending on the perceiver's point of view, makes these phenomena the cornerstone for understanding and explaining cultural evolution (1992a: 17–20).

To complete the picture, Lotman states the role of the explosion in the following way: (1) complex cultural spaces (and all cultural spaces are necessarily complex) include multiple synchronic layers moving at different speeds in such a way that at one level, explosions/discontinuities are occurring while at other, simultaneously given levels development is continuous (1992a: 25); (2) the moment of explosion is a central point for extreme information expansion for the entire system (1992a: 27–8); (3) continuity facilitates innovation (новаторство), whereas discontinuity yields succession (преемственность) (1992a: 26); (4) language interaction is always marked by tension at the intersection of the equivalent and non-corresponding linguistic acts; and (5) the moment of explosion designates the beginning of a new era (1992a: 32). Breakdowns in communication are as important as successful transmissions of information because at least two languages are required for any cultural text or space to exist (where one of the two languages may be extra-linguistically given) (1992a: 16). (An example of breakdown in communication is the mistranslation from French into Russian that resulted in the Russian idiom 'to be out of sorts' [быть не в своей тарелке – literally, 'not in my own plate'].)

Lotman takes his first conceptualization of a culture text from the Tartu-Moscow School as provided in its 1973 publication *Theses*, and develops this central notion in his work *The Structure of the Artistic Text (Структура художественного текста)* (1971: 65–74). As Lotman focuses on the sign-based nature of all texts, he continues at this point to distinguish between two basic categories of text – primary and secondary (Lotman 1971, 1975: 97–123). If we briefly consider the articulation of this particular contribution by the Tartu-Moscow School in *Theses*, we return to the following formulations: primary texts are integral, closed sign systems that are non-discrete, static, and heavily iconic and that change only through transformation of distinctive features, not individual signs; whereas secondary texts are open, sequential systems of signs that are dynamic and primarily *symbolic* (in the Peircean sense) and that change through the addition of new elements (Ivanov et al. [1973] 1998: 13–15; Irene Portis-Winner 1979: 109). Furthermore, these texts are incorporated into culture at different levels. The preliminary conclusions to which these initial principles lead require the recognition that the same *message* may not be a text in all cultures and that the character of the text depends directly on the perceiver's point of view (a type of built-in deixis).

Although these early principles of textual categorization are insightful, I believe that Lotman reaches a new, more profound level of description in his later works, when he focuses more directly on semiotic space itself, including those spaces which necessarily exist beyond the boundaries of a specific semiosphere. This broadening of perspective results in the articulation of a mandatory doubling of codes (at least two) in order for semiotic space to exist – a space where none of the existing languages is sufficient to capture it in its entirety (1992a: 7–9). From this follows the importance of cultural self-description and metalingual functioning. It is only within these systems that meanings take on form, and it is only when at least two languages exist that translation can occur between one system and another. In Lotman's model there are no ideal languages;

there is only a continuum of different kinds of language where artificial and natural are but extremes and where translation – the only mechanism for information transference – is always limited and never perfect (1992a: 8–10). Ultimately, any *text* is defined by a semiotic space. Or, in Lotman's own words (1992a: 42):

> Семиотическое пространство предстает перед нами как многослойное пересечение различных текстов, вместе складывающихся в определенный пласт, со сложными внутренними соотношениями, разной степенью переводимости и пространствами непереводимости.

> (Semiotic space stands before us as a multilayered intersection of differentiated texts brought together into a specific level, including complex internal correspondences reflecting different degrees of translatability and spaces of untranslatability.)

Thus, central to any semiotic space are the texts that define that space – there cannot be one without the other. Lotman then draws the conclusion – which is completely consistent with his model – that *culture itself* is a text, but the nature of this text is obligatorily complex, involving hierarchically defined, embedded, and intersecting layers of 'texts in texts' (1992a: 121). And these texts are never 'objects,' only 'functions' (1992a: 178–9). These functions necessarily include the 'presumption' that there are both addressee(s) and addresser(s) (as exemplified by the semiotic discourse model in chapter 2) (178–9). In the context of providing a more powerful and pervasive definition of semiotic space, Lotman presents the term *semiosfera* (semiosphere) – a concept that is as significant in modelling culture as context is in the semiotic discourse model provided in chapter 2.

Although Vernadsky extended and developed the term *biosphere*, this term was introduced by J.B. Lamarck at the beginning of the nineteenth century and used by Eduard Suess in 1875 while working in the Alps (Vernadsky 1989: 243). Teilhard de Chardin, the Jesuit priest and paleontologist, also worked with the term *biosphere*. However, de Chardin is better known for coining a related term, *noosphere*, which is the human sphere 'of conscious intervention, of conscious souls' beyond the animal world of the biosphere (1925/1968). Vernadsky also used the term *noosphere* and, ironically, only gave credit for the term to Edouourd Le Roy, who worked with de Chardin and might be considered a co-author of the notion (1989: 178). In Vernadsky's use of this term, there is a clear sense of the noosphere as an inevitable evolutionary outcome of the biosphere in geological history (1989: 150, 179–80). Here, the noosphere represents the totality of living human beings and their natural surroundings in such a way that humankind is inseparable from the noosphere itself (1989: 180).[3]

Built into Lotman's notion of explosion is the viewer or participant's perspective. For example, in the relationship between the present and the future, the present is 'a flash of a space of meaning not yet unfolded' (1992a: 28). From a textual point of view (here, 'text' is used in both its broad and narrow sense), when the reader begins to interact with the text, s/he does not know what information will become essential further on in the narrative; thus, the 'indefiniteness of the future allows one to make everything [potentially] meaningful' (1992a: 27 [brackets mine]). On the other hand, when the viewer or participant's perspective shifts from present to past, the situation changes into something that seems regular, law-based, and as if it were the only possible outcome (1992a: 29–30). As long as the semiosphere is identifiable (thus implying the existence of some observer) and dynamically interacting, there can be no final explosion (1992a: 32–4).

One other aspect of the moment of explosion is that it is differentiated into distinct segments. Lotman pays special attention to the 'moment of exhaustion of the explosion' (момент исчерпания взрыва), an important 'turning point' in the process that is realized as both the 'moment of future development' and the 'place of self-realization' (1992a: 30). What this means for the observer is that there will be a qualitative re-evaluation of the process that has just occurred. It is precisely the moment of exhaustion of explosion that provides the observer with the semiotic context for interpreting what was, in actuality, a completely random, chance event as the only possible outcome in the evolution of the particular cultural space under scrutiny.

Another important outcome of semiospheric-internal moments of explosion and high tension is the removal of boundaries of untranslatable space and the reintegration of these former discrete, non-communicating spaces into an integrated, translatable unity (1992a: 40). This process is mirrored to some extent with the external semiospheric boundaries. At the external boundary level, the semiosphere constantly negotiates and renegotiates its relationship to all external spaces, be they semiospheric or not, by expelling dormant, semiotically non-active elements to non-affiliated external spaces or by absorbing extra-semiospheric phenomena into itself (assuming that the information is perceivable as a text) (1992a: 43).

The Illusion of Continuity

Following Peirce and Sebeok, we can define semiotics only in terms of the system of dynamic signs in interaction. This brings us to semiosis itself. Semiotics, as 'doctrine' (to use Locke's term), where the primary goal is to adequately represent the dynamic sign in semiosis, will ultimately focus on the production of the *interpretant* and its affiliation with the sign-object (in Peircean terms) (1931–58: 5.473). As such, semiotics 'never reveals what the world is, but circumscribes what we can know about it ... What a semiotic model depicts is not 'reality' as such, but nature as unveiled by our method of questioning' (Sebeok 1991: 12). In other words, semiotics is a peculiarly human form of inquiry that is in its essence a theory of perception. (I use the word 'perception' as opposed to the word 'cognition' deliberately, based on the work of Hofstadter [1985: 633–4], who compares the Kurzweil scanner and its ability to recognize letters to optical character recognition by humans [also see Kosslyn 1994].

Calvin and Ojemann (1994: 109–21) distinguish at least three types of neurological perception-based activities, including recognition (a form of decoding), recollection, and the process of encoding into memory (see chapter 10 for a specific discussion of types of memory). Thus, we may want to propose a schema for talking about how memory is stored and retrieved that is, at the very least, triadic. Most certainly, memory is one of the central issues in any theory of cognition, and perhaps perception as well.

What is important to all of the above-mentioned approaches to defining the semiotic process is the interplay of discontinuous and continuous phenomena in determining the space-time *object* that may become a candidate for encoding. The perception and construction of the boundaries of the object (whether the object be a thing or a relationship), which is always dynamic and changing, are fundamental to the initializing of the encoding process. One of the central figures in developing new theoretical approaches to the analysis of dynamic systems is René Thom.

Thom's catastrophe theory is an attempt to characterize 'discontinuous phenomena by explicit equations' of dynamic systems (Thom 1983: 121). In presenting his theory, Thom proposes to bridge the gap between traditional quantitative and qualitative models, and between continuity and discontinuity. As Thom states (1983: 111): 'What is important in a model is not its accord with experiment, but, on the contrary, its "ontological range," in which it states the manner in which the phenomena take place and in which it describes their underlying mechanisms.'

Below are some of the fundamental Thomian categories that find parallels in Peirce's and Lotman's semiotic theories:

1 *Morphogenesis* – Any process that creates or destroys forms – that is, discontinuity in which change in the previous form is perceived. Morphogenesis is one of the central foci of catastrophe theory because it defines discontinuous phenomena (Thom 1975: 7–8, 1983: 14).
2 *Chreods* – Areas in a natural process that are structurally stable – 'islets of determinism separated by zones where the process is indeterminate or structurally unstable' (1983: 16). The chreod can be broken down into 'elementary catastrophes' through the introduction of dynamic models. The most stable chreods are those 'most charged with "meaning"' (1983: 17).
3 *Structural stability* – A form is said to exhibit such stability if a homeomorphic relationship can be determined between A and any A' sufficiently close to A (1983: 50). This refers to the dynamic that conflicts with the need for structural stability (1975: 19). Examples include interactive phenomena such as memory and the referents of substantives in human language (1975: 14, 1983: 50–3). Structurally stable forms (as functions) may be altered but will retain the same topological form as the initial function or form.
4 *Semantic density* – A measure of conceptual complexity implied by structural stability (1975: 327). There is at least one open set where structurally stable fields are everywhere dense (Thom 1975: 26) – the manifold M where M > 2 are not dense everywhere by definition.
5 *Catastrophe points* – Closed sets in which each point is related to at least one function that provides a point of discontinuity (1975: 18). Thom distinguishes between *ordinary* catastrophe points and *essential* catastrophe points (1975: 42–3).

For Thom, the concept of the generalized catastrophe is connected to the 'breaking of symmetry' (1975: 11). For this reason, it is hard to model. Yet the catastrophe as survival manoeuvre does not destroy one system and replace it with another; rather, it requires a given system to 'leave its normal characteristic state' (1983: 90). (This could be compared to the creation of new memory in the brain.) Thus, the system continues to exist, when it would generally be unable to do so, by exhibiting a 'jump.' The types of jumps or discontinuities that are the subject of catastrophe theory are the same as occur in linguistic change.

However, even local models developed to describe particular formal systems in catastrophe theory have few predictive powers. It is the chreod, as a structurally stable set, that gives definition to replicable properties, as shown in Peirce's final interpretant. Thus structural stability is parallel to the Peircean habit. The domains of both theories (Peirce and Thom) are *relatively autonomous* (not absolutely autonomous), and both reject the notion that forms are arbitrary. The salient defining properties of the Lotmanian semiosphere are compatible with the five structural categories offered by Thom. Thom's catastrophe theory and Lotman's semiosphere share the defining properties of discontinuities and complex, multiple spaces that are represented in a sophisticated metalanguage. This metalanguage is a sufficient and necessary condition for synthesizing and crunching information; it sets the stage for the creation of powerful modelling systems that can lead to new discoveries in the area of human knowledge and the defining properties of human perception.

Origins of the Semiosphere

As already noted, Lotman's conceptualization of the semiosphere was inspired by Vernadsky's and Teilhard de Chardin's vision of the biosphere (биосфера) and the noosphere (ноосфера) (Vernadsky 1989, 1993; Teilhard de Chardin 1968). What is typically missing from Lotman, and from other sources that point to the connection, is a detailed discussion of Vernadsky's terms and their defining parameters. In the following section I review the most salient characteristics of the biosphere and noosphere, using Vernadsky's original Russian texts. The goal is to achieve a deeper understanding of how Lotman's semiosphere borrows from these concepts and yet is very different in its essence.

To begin, let us recall Lotman's perspective of the difference between biological and cultural life:

> The evolution of culture is quite different from biological evolution, the word 'evolution' can be quite misleading.
> Biological evolution involves species dying out and natural selection. The researcher finds only living creatures contemporary with him. Something similar happens in the history of technology: when an instrument is made obsolete by technical progress it finds a resting place in a museum, as a dead exhibit. In the history of art, however, works which come down to us from remote cultural periods continue to play a part in cultural develop-

ment as living factors. A work of art may 'die' and come alive again; once thought to be out of date, it may become modern and even prophetic for what it tells of the future. What 'works' is not the most recent temporal section, but the whole packed history of cultural texts. The standard evolutionary point of view in literary history comes from the influence of evolutionary ideas in the natural sciences. (1990: 127)

In a passage directly preceding the one contrasting culture and biology, Lotman explains that it is possible to imagine the semiosphere, which is 'the result and the condition for the development of culture,' as analogous to Vernadsky's biosphere, which is 'the totality and the organic whole of living matter and ... the condition for the continuation of life' (1990: 125).[4]

In his other work on the semiosphere, Lotman quotes from Vernadsky's definition of the biosphere: 'a living element is the sum total of living organisms' (живое вещество есть совокупность живых организмов) (1992b: I. 12). Lotman then warns the reader not to interpret Vernadsky's biosphere as a reductionist model wherein the sum total of living elements yields the biosphere. In fact, Lotman argues that a living element is an 'organic whole' and that the mechanism of energy production is more important than its internal organization. Finally, Lotman reminds us that humans, like any and all living organisms, are a 'function of the biosphere' (12).

To understand more precisely Lotman's interpretation of the biosphere and his fundamental differences with Vernadsky, I will examine Vernadsky's contribution as reflected in his works, which were first published in the 1930s and 1940s. Vernadsky begins his essay with the notion that any living organism (живое вещество) is the 'sum total of all of the Earth's organisms present at a particular moment in time' (1989: 139). It is only in the biosphere that organic life may exist. As such, the biosphere contains 'the earth's troposphere, oceans and a thin layer in continental regions not extending deeper than 3 kilometers' (1989: 140). However, Vernadsky notes that mankind is constantly striving to 'increase the size of the biosphere' (140). He differentiates between organic and inorganic matter within the biosphere and lists sixteen major differences between them, as well as certain laws of the biosphere. His points can be summarized as follows (1989: 141-4):

1 Natural living bodies only occur in the biosphere. These living, organic bodies never arise from inorganic ones.

2 Only natural, living bodies can reproduce. Each is a 'singular whole' (единое целое).
3 The physical space occupied by living organisms is divided into asymmetrically defined left and right chemical forms.
4 Natural living organisms can give rise only to living organisms of the same type.
5 Natural living organisms exhibit self-regulated movement.
6 The constant molecular movement between the biosphere and its organisms – including internal and external transfer – is unique.
7 The quantity of living organisms is directly tied to the size of the biosphere.
8 The average mass of living organisms is generally unchanging.
9 The minimum size of living organisms is determined by breathing.
10 The chemical make-up of living organisms is a function of their own characteristics.
11 The quantity of chemical combinations in natural living organisms is connected with the number of individual organisms and reaches many millions.
12 The free energy of the biosphere increases with the nature-based processes of the living organism.
13 Natural living organisms are always mesomorphs.
14 Certain processes in living organisms may lead to critical changes in isotopic combinations.
15 The great majority of living organisms change by evolutionary processes but at very different rates.
16 The creation of living organisms is not reversible in time.

Vernadsky also differentiates another state of the biosphere, which he calls the noosphere (ноосфера). The noosphere is the final evolutionary stage of the biosphere in terms of its geological historical development on earth (1989: 149–50). Vernadsky sees the development of the noosphere as parallel to the growth of democratic ideals in society. For this reason, he is confident about the future of the Earth.[5]

Generally speaking, the preceding list has very little to do with Lotman's definition of the semiosphere. However, we do find the concepts of binarism, asymmetry, and dynamic change – principles essential to Lotman's notion of semiosphere – in many of Vernadsky's principles.

The central concepts that Lotman borrowed from Vernadsky, which lie at the heart of his conceptualization of the semiosphere, are twofold: (1) the *relationship* of living organisms to their natural, physical context where it is precisely the physical context that makes life possible, and (2) the principle of an internal *structure* that defines all developments and changes within the biosphere. However, in Lotman's semiosphere the context is not natural (in the biological sense) but rather human-built, and the semiosphere serves as the fundamental requirement for maintaining and developing human culture.

Energy and Entropy in Semiotic Space

If the study of culture depends heavily on understanding how communication takes place, then we cannot begin to analyse cultural space to any great depth without articulating a view on the essence of the communicative process. Sebeok directly links communication (i.e., 'transmissions ... from one part of a system to another [that] produce change') and entropy, and sees communication as a means to decrease entropy (1991: 22). Sebeok argues that because of the relationship between entropy and information, entropy belongs on the 'margins of semiotics' (1991: 84).

As discussed initially in chapter 3, the definition of entropy changes with the context. In terms of molecules, entropy is the measure of the probability that a particular system state will be realized. The greater the entropy, the more probable a particular system state. The result is that entropy necessarily will increase in any closed system. In communication theory, entropy is defined on the principle of unpredictability of semantic content such that entropic means high information and redundant yields low information (O'Sullivan et al. 1994: 106). In yet another distinct field, called social entropy theory, in which models distinguish between 'internal' and 'imported' entropy, there is the potential for entropy to decrease. As Bailey notes (1990: 71): 'The Prigogine entropy equation shows that, although internal entropy production increases or remains constant within the system, imported entropy can be decreased by importation of energy from the environment, thus resulting in an overall decrease of system entropy or the increase of order.' (Prigogine entropy equation for open systems: $dS = d_eS + d_iS$ [Bailey 1990: 81]) Bailey's fundamental point rests on the fact that most social (and here I would add cultural) systems are open rather than closed, and may not be in equilibrium.

All of the fields of semiotics (anthroposemiotics, cultural semiotics, endosemiotics, biosemiotics, phytosemiotics) model the production and consumption of information either in the human context or in a larger context that is not restricted to human verbal systems. Although Lotman is only interested in the anthroposemiotic sphere, his conceptualization

Figure 4.2

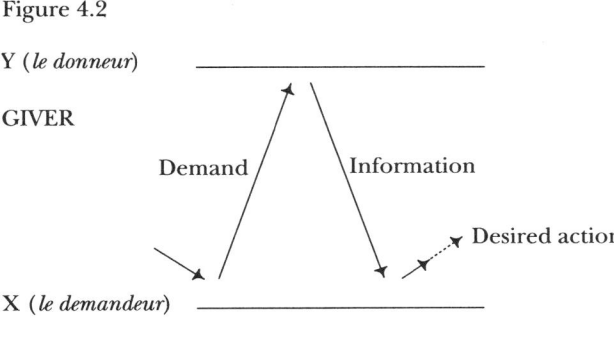

of the semiosphere and its structural principles is clearly supported by Sebeok's work, even though Sebeok, in his later work, became more interested in biosemiotic questions.[6]

In studying communication and information flow, we are ultimately focusing on both input and output, encoding and decoding at multiple levels. We have already seen some of the more interesting semiotic models that demonstrate this principle (Lotman, Sebeok, Jakobson). We might add to these Thom's model, given in figure 4.2, and his comment that it is impossible to reduce information to the content signified; rather, information is the meaning plus intentionality, which allows meaning to continue and grow (1983: 278–82).

If researchers in semiotics continue to view the relationship between information and entropy as mutually implicative, then these two items should be included in the semiotic agenda. Certainly, for Lotman, the notions of information (as a measure of the number of alternative messages available) and entropy are central to his theory of the semiosphere. He makes the following point in defining entropy and the impact of 'self-description' within the semiosphere (1990: 128–9):

> The highest form and final act of a semiotic system's structural organization is when it describes itself. This is the stage when grammars are written, customs and laws codified. When this happens, however, the *system gains the advantage of greater structural organization, but loses its inner reserves of indeterminacy which provide it with flexibility, heightened capacity for information and the potential for dynamic development.*
>
> The stage of self-description is a necessary response to the threat of too

much diversity within the semiosphere: the system might lose its unity and definition, and disintegrate. Whether we have in mind language, politics or culture, the mechanism is the same: one part of the semiosphere (as a rule one which is part of its nuclear structure) in the process of self-description creates it own grammar; this self-description may be real or ideal depending on whether its inner orientation is towards the present or towards the future. Then it strives to extend these norms over the whole semiosphere. ... A list of what 'does not exist,' according to that cultural system, although such things in fact occur, is always essential for making a typological description of that system.

In the final sections of chapters 7 and 8 we will see how Lotman's modelling of entropy within the semiosphere has broader application to the construction of culture texts and verbal texts in the works of Evgenij Zamjatin.

We are now ready to consider semiotic modelling systems that focus more on the biological construction of communication. One of the most powerful models was developed by the biologist Jakob von Uexküll in the early twentieth century.

Uexküll's Semiotic Model

The work of Jakob von Uexküll, a semiotician who worked in behavioural biology at the turn of the last century and founded in 1924 the Institut für Umweltforschung, fits easily into the general Peircean semiotic paradigm: he defines the life process as 'a coherent system in which subject and object define themselves as interrelated elements of a superior whole' (T. von Uexküll 1986: 130). Uexküll's *Umwelt* is the 'self world,' the 'true reality' (*Natur*) that surrounds any living organism as the organism perceives it, 'bubbles that are sharply delineated but invisible to the outside observer' (1982: 3). Uexküll's 'subject' is 'an *interpreter* that receives signals from its environment by way of "perceptual organs" (receptors),' and his 'object' is an '"objective connecting structure" (i.e., ... a link between the operational and the perceptual cue)' (1986: 137). Thus, the *object* is an *open, dynamic cyclic system* that interacts with its environment. In this context he presents the concept of 'species-specific *Umwelt*' defined by the species-specific receptor and effector capacities called *perception* and *operation* (T. von Uexküll 1986: 207; 1992a: 456–61). See Uexküll's functional circle in figure 4.3. For Uexküll, *Umwelt-Forschung* is a 'method of inquiry' that 'researches into the worlds surrounding

Characteristics and Origins of the Semiosphere 61

Figure 4.3

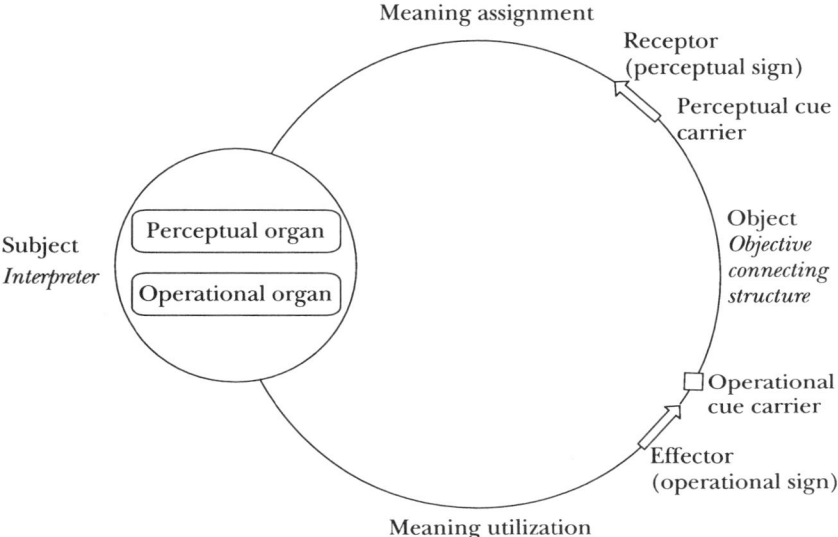

Source: adapted from T. von Uexküll 1986: 207.

animals, as they themselves perceive their own subjective universe' (Sebeok 1991: 71).

Jakob von Uexküll's son Thure notes that two of his father's concepts require clarification: (1) the laws of nature are in no way equivalent to the laws of natural science, since all laws of science are interpretations; and (2) the primary distinction for *Umwelt* theory is between living and non-living organisms, not between nature and humankind (1982: 6–7). Living organisms may respond in a random fashion to stimuli that are only made up of signs; they respond as subjects to external impulses. In Uexküll's theory, a sign 'never exists in its own right; it is always part of a circular process in which a receiver (receptor) receives stimuli, codes them into signs and responds to them as such ... Every sign is ... in the strictest sense of the word "private" – ... There are no objective signs, there are only sign-systems with the same structure and the same code for different receivers of signs' (T. von Uexküll 1982: 8).

In any semiotic theory, sign systems are the components that make up human space. However, different semioticians define that space in different ways. Lotman's theory of the semiosphere is a fully developed formulation of the construction, mechanisms, and dynamic development of complex, culturally based sign texts. Uexküll offers his own version for defining the construction, maintenance, and dynamics of complex biological space. His model, although quite distinct from Lotman's, does demonstrate certain compatabilities between what he calls *types of signs* and what Lotman defines only at the *textual* level, namely, (1) *organizing signs* – signs 'produced by the tactile cells of our skin and the retina cells of our eyes'; (2) *local signs* – projections into surroundings as locations; and (3) *directional signs* – composition of two- and (later) three-dimensional space where muscle activity is required to make the leap from two- to three-dimensional space (T. von Uexküll 1986: 152). However, von Uexküll differs from both Lotman and Vernadsky in that his embedded implicational relationship in space-time is the reverse of Lotman's and Vernadsky's. Specifically, he argues that the living subject is the prerequisite for the existence of space-time, whereas Vernadsky and Lotman talk about how, in nature, space-time is a prerequisite for biospheres and semiospheres to exist (152).

The fundamental assumption of Uexküll's theory is the primacy of humans, not animals, as the target receivers of signs. Only secondarily do we assign a place to other living organisms. Thus, Uexküll's theory is in fact a metatheory, and any interpretations that we as humans make are necessarily interpretations of interpretations, or metainterpretations. The functional circle model emphasizes how these metainterpretations are determinable. As we translate perceptions of privately defined biological or phytosemiotic signs into human language, we clearly move toward the metainterpretation level (1986: 133, 151). No foreign signs may be perceived at all, nor may closed systems be perceived (1986: 130, 151). This final point is exactly in keeping with Lotman's view regarding what may cross over semiospheric boundaries. However, Lotman characterizes what may be perceived over the boundary as a text and not as a sign (1992b: I. 13):

она не может соприкасаться с иносемиотическими текстами или с не-текстами. Для того, чтобы они для неё получили реальность, ей необходимо перевести их на один из языков её внутреннего пространства или семиотизировать факты.

(The semiosphere cannot come into contact with foreign semiotic texts or non-texts. In order for these types of texts to be realized in the semiosphere, it is necessary for them to be translated into one of the languages of semiospheric internal space or for these facts to be *semiotisized.*)

There is an interesting point of coincidence between von Uexküll's theory and Lotman's modelling of the semiosphere: in both, autocommunication must be present for sign interpretation. Lotman's model of autocommunication (see chapter 3) defines the mechanism of meaning generation as a combination of two modelling types: I-I (or auto) communication and I-s/he communication (1990: 21–35). All cultural spaces rely on these modelling systems for the production and transference of information. However, in some cultural contexts one system may dominate the other, though never to the absolute exclusion of the other system. The implications of an asymmetrical application of these two types of communication are dynamic change, a skewing of cultural activity, and hierarchical asymmetries between speakers and receivers (e.g., in I-s/he communication there is a marked differential between the superior source/I and the inferior receiver/s/he) (1990: 35). For Lotman, autocommunication underlies the ability to qualitatively restructure and translate what is never less than a double-version of code and message in the creation of meaningful texts (1990: 22). For Uexküll, the primacy of autocommunication provides the backdrop for any metainterpretations that may be formulated (T. von Uexküll 1982: 9). Given the structure of each *Umwelt*, it becomes clear that in Uexküll's modelling system, all meaning is created through translation – a process that necessarily provides the outcome in the form of a metainterpretation.

Sebeok states the strong version of Uexküll's concept to argue that there is no existence for the organism beyond its *Umwelt*. He also categorizes Uexküll's theory as endosemiotics (a term coined by Sebeok in 1985 to refer to molecular-based sign systems) (Sebeok 1991: 86).

Uexküll's model of semiosis includes an important time structure whereby perception is defined as a 'meaning specifier' but 'meaning-utilization' is only realizable at some future point (T. von Uexküll 1986: 133). For a particular species, the actual length of the moment will vary. Sebeok notes that the *hic et nunc* (the human moment) lasts for three seconds (1990: 134). Since the relationship between subject and object (also read sign and object) is contextually determined, the resulting relationship is realized only through an interpreter. It is the interpreter (like Peirce's interpretant) that can determine whether the relationship is valid or invalid. In such a model, so-called objects exist in the human mind only 'as a coherent whole distinctly definable in space and time ... an abstraction' (T. von Uexküll 1986: 138). Thus, these objects are only knowable as a series of signs, and these signs are 'private' messages understood only by the recipient via its receptors. Probabilities and possibilities are in a reciprocal relationship (ibid.: 138–40). (This formulation can be applied to contemporary models of human memory – cf. chapter 10.)

Because of the hermetic nature of individual messages, we must have access to a code that has a more general competence (e.g., immune cells). In this way, 'biological signs and biological texts write themselves' in a way that is unlike the writing of a verbal text. The overall plan, or 'score,' can be perceived by an 'observer' (implied and essential in Uexküll's theory) only at a higher, synthetic level – not as a sum of parts (1986: 142). And it is in the integration of elements that new qualities and relationships appear that were previously unknown at the individual level (1986: 141–3). Sebeok places Uexküll's words in perspective by reminding us that human beings are semiotic texts (1991: 19). Sebeok's contribution is enormously important in making the link to Peirce's sign categories and theory of interpretants, according to which the immediate and dynamic objects, in application to linguistic systems, necessarily involve not only the linguistic code itself, but also the users.[7] Therefore, in the Uexküll model, the crux of the semiotic problem is the 'sign-theoretical explanation of our mechanistic interpretations' (1986: 148). To differentiate functions, Thure von Uexküll provides three basic types of semiosis: semiosis of information (or signification), symptomatization, and communication. The first two are indispensable in biosemiosis in allowing the observer to 'reconstruct the sign processes of the living beings observed by him/her [but] this reconstruction ... only provides ... the exterior and not the interior structure of biosemiosis' (1986: 150). Only those signs which are a part of the code of an organism's particular Umwelt can be perceived. The semiosis of communication is group-based – both speaker and receiver (or transmitter and recipient) have access to the same set of interpretants. It is here that we find a strong connection between Uexküll's theories and Lotman's work in the semiotics of culture, in which human language plays the central role.

Uexküll's *Umwelt* shares many of the same basic concepts as Vernadsky's principles for the biosphere. However, in Uexküll's system there is a stronger emphasis on defining the communication aspects of the system, not only at the biological level of the individual organism but also at a metalingual level of the observer. And Uexküll places the human organism, not extra-human space-time continua, at the centre of his theoretical foundation.

The Functioning Semiosphere

To complete my presentation of Lotman's theory of the semiosphere, I will look at three aspects of dynamic semiotic space, namely, the roles played by proper names, metatexts, and memory. Because these three phenomena are so important to semiotic theory in general, the discussion will include relevant theoretical contributions from Sebeok and Uexküll.

Proper Names

Lotman begins his discussion of proper names in human semiotic space by assuming a zoosemiotic perspective and using an example from the domestic animal world. Specifically, he claims that if one of several kittens in a litter is switched, the mother will not notice provided the number of kittens remains the same (1992a: 52). In contrast, a child who has seen the kittens will notice if one of them has been substituted or switched. From this he deduces that mother cats perceive at the 'collective' (not individual) level. Here we have a simplistic example of why the animal world is said to be unable to recognize proper names. (I am using the term 'proper name' to distinguish it from the grammatical term for proper noun [имена существительные собственные] and to remain closer to the original Russian [собственные имена]). All of this is connected with an absence of individuation in the animal world. Such individuation – the ability to manifest perceivable behaviours based on individual, conscious choice – is always present in human society and culture. Von Uexküll refers to this ability to react in a individualistic way to external stimuli as the fundamental defining characteristic of living as opposed to non-living nature (T. von Uexküll 1982: 7). What is perhaps even more significant for Lotman is the exclusively human ability to distinguish words in linguistic space from things or objects in exogenous reality (1992a: 56–7). It is this final ability that constitutes the unbridgeable gap between humans and all other animals. The remainder of Lotman's chapter on proper names discusses the differences between proper nouns and other attributes, the tension of unity and conflict in 'I' versus 'others,' and the artistic text (as an experiment in dreaming) that emerges from 'the possibility of increasing the complexity between the first and third persons, i.e. between the pull toward the space of proper names and the objective narrative of the third person' (1992a: 58–63).

In contrast to Lotman, Sebeok (1990: 77–92; [1976] 1985: 139) argues that 'in well-organized vertebrate societies – such as are found in birds and especially mammals – individual members tend to bear a singular proper name (SPN), marking each carrier animal as unique, and that the establishment of this kind of social organization presupposes, among other techniques of mutual co-operation in adults, play.' Sebeok characterizes what these proper names might look like, including 'species, reproductive status, location in space or in time, rank in a social hierarchy ...' (1990: 79). Other examples include the mother hen's cluck (as a proper name) and the baby chick's twitter, which will later become the chick's proper name (1990: 82).

At first blush, Sebeok and Lotman seem to be completely at odds. However, it is more likely that we are dealing with a formal coincidence of nomenclature. Lotman is ultimately making a strong claim about the uniqueness of human language; in that vein he makes reference to one of the most prominent deictic categories in language – proper names and the naming function. The uniqueness of naming is manifested in distinguishing signs – signs that are in us and around us, signs that make up everything we can perceive, signs that make up each human organism, where everything knowable is a sign. Even though Lotman begins his discussion from a zoosemiotic point of view, he is still actually based in anthroposemiotics.

In contrast, Sebeok does not necessarily accept that human language is the central model for all of semiotic theory (although he would continue to argue for the uniqueness of human language as such in the animal kingdom); also, he assumes a more broadly defined zoosemiotic perspective that can be as important as verbal codes. Such a stance allows him to characterize non-verbal and non-auditory signs as proper names. The definitions of human language in Lotman and Sebeok would be compatible.[8] However, Lotman's theory of the semiosphere is clearly restricted to human culture and does not lend itself, as defined, to a broader zoosemiotic model.

Metatexts

Recalling chapters 2 and 3, we have seen that in Jakobson's, Sebeok's, and Lotman's communication models there are at least six factors and/or functions that must be present in any given utterance or speech act.

Characteristics and Origins of the Semiosphere 67

One of these functions, where the focus is on the code, is realized as metalingual. Thus, metalinguistic functions will be represented at one level or another within any given discrete language act. It is both inevitable and logically consistent that Lotman's models of different types of texts provide a place for metatexts. In fact, Lotman discusses the importance of metalingual and metatextual phenomena in a number of contexts.

All types of texts can be placed on a continuum of languages, with artificial languages at one end, natural language in the centre, and artistic language at the other end (Lotman 1990: 14). All forms of artistic texts demonstrate both metalingual and self-referential structures (1990: 16). In fact, according to Lotman's communication model, metalingual structures appear in one form or another in all types of texts. (The necessary presence of metalingual structures in all speech acts is explained in the original Jakobson model, from which Lotman developed his own communication model.) The problem is how to determine whether a text, which is a series of discrete speech acts that manifest at least six factors and functions in different hierarchies, is or is not a metatext. Lotman says it can be both. A particular text can be simultaneously perceived as both a text and metatext (1992b: I. 132):

> ... тот или иной частный текст может выполнять по отношению к культурному контексту роль описывающего механизма, а другой может вступать в дешифрующие и структурирующие отношения с некоторым **метаязыковым** образованием. Наконец, тот или иной текст может включать в себя в качестве частных подструктур и текстовые, и метатекстовые элементы, как в произведении ... Евгения Онегина ... В этом случае коммуникативные токи движутся по вертикали.

(... some texts may fulfill the role of a descriptive mechanism in relation to the cultural context while another might decode and structure the relationship with other *metalingual* formations. Finally, some texts may include in themselves in the form of substructures both textual and metatextual elements like ... *Eugene Onegin* ... In these cases, the communicative charges move vertically.)

At the same time, there is the phenomenon of metainterpretation. Von Uexküll has shown that all our interpretations of the world around us eventually lead to the metainterpretation level. Lotman also claims that all semiospheres move toward higher levels of metalinguistic description – a movement that reduces the degree of energy of the cultural spaces in the semiosphere and leads to higher degrees of entropy.

Finally, because of collective and individual cultural memory, interaction within the semiosphere is transformed through a variety of sociocommunicative textual functions (Lotman 1992b: I. 131). These interactions with texts are primarily perceived based on the specific cultural orientations available at the metalinguistic, metatextual, and metacultural levels. Thus, a text can appear as 'semantically normal' or as 'anomalous, semantically dislocated,' depending on the relationship between the text and other structures that are metaculturally given (Lotman 1990: 46).

In the final analysis, Lotman attributes as much importance to the metatextual level in the semiosphere as von Uexküll does to metainterpretations within the *Umwelt*. From the smallest realization of a communication act to the broadest level of metacultural texts, metalinguistic functions can be found and will necessarily increase as the cultural system moves toward a more entropic state. The phenomenon of metadescription of cultural texts always gives rise to higher entropy, because metadescription leads to 'greater structural organization, but loses its inner reserves of indeterminacy which provide it with flexibility, heightened capacity for information and the potential for dynamic development' (1990: 128–9). Yet the dynamics of the semiosphere guarantee that the tensions of all communication acts will eventually lead to a series of explosions that inject new energy into the cultural space.

Memory

In chapter 3 we briefly considered Lotman's views on the role of collective memory in the maintenance of cultural space, and on different modes of memory construction, including written, linear texts and oral, ritualistic texts (1990: 246–7). Lotman consistently supports the perspective that human language is at the core of all semiotic space and that language plays a central role in the codification of collective and individual memory.

However, Lotman makes a more profound claim about memory as an important function of complex semiotic texts. His argument is straightforward. When a complex artistic text connects itself with the surrounding cultural context (and this happens in a variety of ways, including interaction between addresser and addressee, between the readership and cultural tradition, between the reader and him/herself, between the reader and the text, and between the text and the cultural context), it achieves the 'ability to condense information,' and as a result of this ability develops its own memory, where extratextual information is preserved as well as transformed and new information is created (1992b: I. 131). (In the next chapter I will present a series of analyses of specific realizations of condensation and creation of *culture-textual memory* in Russian literary texts from the twentieth century in the works of Mikhail Bulgakov and Evgenij Zamyatin.)

Lotman's interest in memory is primarily at the collective level. In contrast, Sebeok has examined the importance of memory in the context of the *Umwelt* as providing 'the closest link of the self in nature as well as in culture' (1990: 42). The *Umwelt* is most certainly a modelling system, but it also gives rise to the 'phenomenal worlds' that not only are specified at the species level, but also are uniquely determined for each individual organism (1991: 71). Each *Umwelt*, as a modelling system, requires memory as manifested by some basic form of intelligence and 'rules of logical operation' (71). Thus, Sebeok is able to define the bifurcation of the features and functions of memory as both 'a physical repository and ... social construct' and 'genetic and semiotic' (1990: 42–43). At the level of the self, memory provides the 'internal signposts' that enable humans to see themselves as continuities and to serve as conduits of old information and creators of new information. Here, Sebeok brings to the fore the importance of the semiotic nature of human memory and the fact that memory of signs is the prerequisite for semiosis to occur. Likewise, he reminds us that memory is not a mere construct but a biological, physical fact. Uexküll focuses on the biological aspects of memory and, in a fashion that demonstrates a sophistication that was certainly ahead of its time, points out that memories are not static images but are better described as 'image-formation' processes comparable to 'programs [or schemata] of sequences of impulses' (T. von Uexküll 1982: 16).

In the final chapter of this work, we will look at contemporary theories of human memory in cognitive science and how they can be supported by a semiotically informed model of memory.

PART TWO

The Construction of Semiotic Space in Verbal Texts

CHAPTER FIVE

Lotman, Bulgakov, and Zamyatin

All of Lotman's numerous works on the history of Russian culture and Russian literary texts, from the Old Russian period to the twentieth century, are attempts to show the profound connections between the structural principles that define semiotic space in the context of specific instantiations of verbal (written and oral) and visual mediums of symbolic translation. As we have noted, culture texts for Lotman are sign-based invariant constructs that contribute to a definition of culture. Culture texts include verbal texts (including aesthetic, religious, and poetic text types), but are more broadly defined to encompass a variety of non-verbal texts – visual, musical, or those based on everyday human behaviour. The two major groupings of culture texts are based not on the verbal/non-verbal distinction, but rather on the characterization given by the text itself – either at the level of universal structure and its resulting construction, or at the level of the individual instantiation and its place in the larger semiospheric context.

The first four chapters of this book explicated and analysed the central theoretical semiotic principles crucial to the analysis of any cultural space. These principles embrace not only Lotmanian notions but also important semiotic thought from people working within and beyond the boundaries of anthroposemiotics. In order to test the validity of Lotman's semiospheric principles as presented, I have chosen one of his analyses of Russian artistic culture texts. I will extend his analysis of Bulgakov's *The Master and Margarita* to include other literary texts that he never discussed. In so doing, I will modify his semiotic to be more compatible with Peircean semiotic categories, while reconfirming his universal structural semiotic principles of cultural memory and how internally given patterns of change affect neighbouring bounded cultural spaces. The most marked point of departure will be demonstrated in my extension from Lotman's fundamentally binary model of analysis to an irreducibly triadic model.

Lotman on Bulgakov's *The Master and Margarita*

Lotman's *oeuvre* on Russian culture texts is so extensive that it would be impossible to give a rendering of all of these works.[1] So I will focus here on one of his analyses – specifically, his critical approach to understanding the basic structural principles regarding how semiotic space is constructed in Russian literary texts of the nineteenth and twentieth centuries, especially in his work on Mikhail Bulgakov's *The Master and Margarita*. Lotman's analysis is rather terse; even so, it provides one of the most insightful analyses of Bulgakov's artistry that has been published to date. I will begin with an overview of Lotman's analysis of the concept of home, and develop and extend this analysis to an equally important phenomenon in Bulgakov's work which parallels that of home – namely, the notion of road or path as a central semiotic principle of textual dynamics. Referring to Lotman's work on Nikolaj Gogol' (which is essential for understanding Lotman's subsequent analysis of Bulgakov, the culture-text function of Bulgakov's work, and the specific place of that work in the chain of Russian aesthetic verbal texts), I will show that one can extend Lotman's remarks on the function of the road in Russian literary texts and demonstrate that Bulgakov reclaimed this notion and recast it vis-à-vis his semiotic rendering of a triadic opposition of home-antihome-homelessness.

The Oppositions of Home

Bulgakov's last novel, *The Master and Margarita*, is often considered one of the great works of world literature. Through the author's elegant interweaving of plots, fantastic plot development, allusions to black magic, and retelling of the Book of Matthew, the reader is inexorably drawn into a complex world of conflicting and coincidental semiotic spaces that extend far beyond the verbal text itself. Bulgakov's text is highly complex in form and structure, yet Lotman's analysis of it, though powerful and convincing, is also one of his most succinct.[2]

Lotman begins his analysis by placing the notional opposition of home-antihome in the broader context of world folklore. This opposition in folklore is most often realized as home versus woods (or forests)

(Lotman 1992b: I. 457), and can be understood in the following way:

HOME :: SELF	WOODS :: OTHER
safe, cultured, protected	foreign, diabolic, temporary death, space leading to the afterlife

In the works of Pushkin and Gogol', Lotman finds confirmations of the importance of this opposition. Pushkin focuses on the home as the place of humanity and nurture, of traditions and human individuality, whereas Gogol' focuses on the opposite end of the spectrum, including diabolic antihomes, whorehouses, bureaucratic offices, and homelessness (i.e., the absence of any true home) (1992b: I. 457). At this juncture, Lotman refers to Gogol''s use of the road, which is the primary means of escape from the antihome.

Lotman demonstrates that Bulgakov uses the opposition home-antihome as 'one of the organization principles of all of his work' (1992b: I. 458) by providing convincing examples from a wide selection of Bulgakov's texts (including short stories, novels, and plays). However, Lotman focuses on Bulgakov's use of the 'false home' (ложный дом) in *The Master and Margarita* and the range of its realization. Examples from the novel include communal apartment, apartments in general (note especially the use of the term квартирка [often pejorative in Russian]), the insane asylum (сумасшедший дом), the Griboedov House (Дом Грибоедова), Margarita's stately home (особняк/особнячок), Hell, and Pilate's palace (дворец) in Jershalaim (where the letter j represents phonological 'jot'). The false home is juxtaposed to the 'true home,' the Master's home of eternal rest (вечный дом), any apartments where we hear the sounds of a piano (as opposed to a gramophone), and mere rooms of an apartment where there are books and a fireplace (or stove – печка) (1992b: I. 458–462).[3]

To strengthen his claim that home-antihome is a central structural principle for Bulgakov, Lotman also refers to many of Bulgakov's books and plays, including *Theatrical Novel, Zoja's Apartment, The White Guard,* and *Days of the Turbine Family* (1992b: I. 462–3). All of Lotman's references are convincing and to the point. In the end, he states that one can characterize the Master's journey as 'the search for [a true] Home' (1992b: I. 461).

Lotman concludes his analysis with a general characterization of Bulgakov's last novel (1992b: I. 463):[4] 'А сам этот роман оказывается одновременно и включённым в глубочайшую литературно-мифологическую традицию, и органическим итогом эволюции его автора.' (This novel is simultaneously a part of the deepest forms of literary-mythological traditions, as well as an organic summation of the evolution of its author.)

Lotman briefly refers to 'homelessness' (бездомье) in the context of Gogol''s works as an antipode of the concept of 'true home,' and argues that it is realized in Bulgakov's *Master* as an extension of the 'false home' and 'communal apartment' (1992b: I. 457–8). In this context, Lotman reminds the reader of the name of the only character in the novel who is present throughout, including the beginning and the end – Bezdomnyj (meaning 'Homeless' – the pseudonym of the young poet Ivan Nikolaevich Ponyrjov). Likewise, we have the figure of Jeshua in the Jershalaim story, who is referred to as the 'wanderer,' the one who has 'no permanent residence' (1992b: I. 458).

In order to strengthen the semiotic analysis of Bulgakov's text, I believe we must amplify Lotman's original analysis into a ternary modelling text-organizational system, so that instead of a binary opposition of home-antihome, we have a triadic oppositional relationship (see figure 5.1). Such a structural shift from dyadic to triadic enriches the opposition between the three semiotic spaces, and at the same time gives more weight to the state of homelessness, a theme that permeates the novel and strengthens the ties between the Moscow and Jershalaim stories. But more important, this triadic model supports Lotman's own modelling of semiospheric space better by clearly delineating continuity and discontinuity through ever-present structural tension (see figure 5.2). Furthermore, this shift to triadic structures opens the door for introducing that other organizing principle of Bulgakov's text (also very common in Russian literary and folklore traditions) – the road (дорога and путь). It is precisely through homelessness that the plane of spatial development shifts to the road and its various structural types. Here, Bulgakov's textual space is more of the nature of multiple planes as opposed to points or lines. I will attempt to demonstrate, beginning with Lotman's work on semiotic space in Gogol', that Bulgakov's use of the road is also fundamentally and irreducibly triadic, and that it forms an important dimension of the home-antihome-homelessness textual system, thus exemplifyings Bulgakov's extension of a fundamental principle of artistic textual space (as an equivalent to Lotman's use of the term художественное пространство), that Bulgakov develops in his work.

Figure 5.1

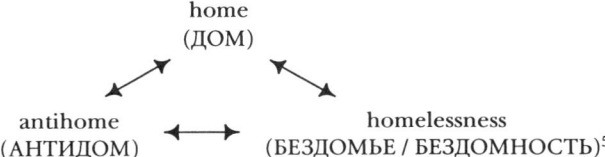

Figure 5.2

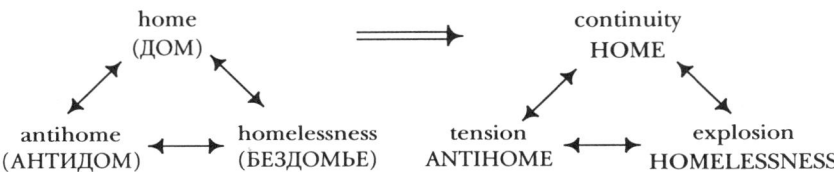

The Artistic Text

In order to introduce Lotman's view of particular structural principles in artistic textual space, we must first recall at least two basic principles of semiospheric organization: (1) all semiospheres are a multiplicity of variegated, potentially hierarchical and multileveled languages and culture texts, and (2) since individual texts and types of texts may be contextualized within the semiosphere in languages that are inadequate for extrapolating meaning, and since the codes correlated with particular texts may sometimes be lost, some texts will always be untranslatable at a particular point in space-time (Lotman 1992b: I. 11–24). With these two principles in mind, we can note that artistic texts (художественный текст) are among the types of texts that generally exist in cultural space.[6] As Lotman reminds us, once such a claim is made this necessarily means there are non-artistic texts as well (1992b: I. 203–4). (Note that Lotman does not make any a priori claims about the status or hierarchical importance of artistic texts, nor does he make artistic/non-artistic the most fundamental difference between culture texts.)

The question Lotman poses at this point is how to distinguish between these two (of many potential) types of texts. He provides two possible answers: (1) Any verbal text 'within the boundaries of a given culture that is able to realize the aesthetic function' is an artistic text (1992b: I.

203) (how the presence of the aesthetic function can be determined is another matter); (2) At the structural level, the text must be organized in such a way that the receiver (or reader) perceives semantic signals that point to the text being artistic (1992b: I. 204–5). In either case, we are dealing with structure, but the structure is defined at different levels – either at the extratextual, cultural level or at the textual level.

Once we know we are dealing with an artistic text (or in this specific context, literary texts), we may become curious as to how these texts develop, how they take on new and unique forms through time. Lotman reminds us that these new forms are the result of the constant interaction between artistic and non-artistic texts within cultural space (1992b: I. 205–15). One example would be a triadic hierarchy of cultural values attributed to these texts in such a way that ethical, religious texts are valued more highly, while artistic texts are given low value and the remaining 'other' textual space is characterized as neutral (1992b: I. 206). Other examples could reverse these values or demonstrate other shifts. Nevertheless, Lotman argues that structurally, the artistic text is always of a different nature than all other potential texts – the other textual types are usually less ambiguous and evaluated in one particular way, whereas an artistic text always presents a complex of conflicting indices as a result of its essence, which is to represent the general principles of a culture's organization (1992b: I. 206–7):

> Художественные тексты ведут себя иначе, чем все остальные. Обычно место текста или его агента ... в общей иерархии культуры обозначено однозначно: сакральный текст или место монаха м.б. святым или презренным, но не может быть святым и презренным одновременно. Юридический текст и свойство быть законником также в каждом типе культуры оценивается однозначно. ... Только художественные тексты могут быть предметом взаимоисключающих аксиологических оценок. Хотя художественным текстам в общей иерархии культуры отводится определённое место, они постоянно проявляют тенденцию к расположению на противоположных концах лестницы, то есть в исходной позиции задают некоторый конфликт, создающий потенциальную возможность дальнейшей нейтрализации в некоторых амбивалентных текстах. ... Внутренняя организация художественной литературы ... изоморфна культуре как таковой, повторяет общие принципы её организации. Литература никогда не представляет собой аморфно-однородной суммы текстов: она не только организация, но и самоорганизующийся механизм. На самой высокой ступени организации

Figure 5.3

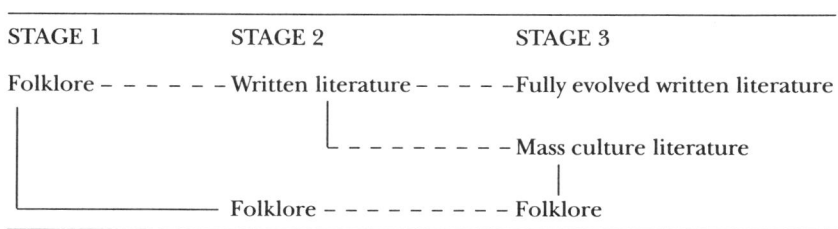

она выделяет группу текстов более абстрактного, чем вся остальная масса текстов, уровня, то есть метатекстов.

(Artistic texts behave differently from others. Usually the placement of the text and its agent are designated unambiguously in the cultural hierarchy: sacred texts and the place of the priest may be sacred or profane, but it would be impossible for them to be both simultaneously. The ability of legal texts to become law is also unambiguously given a value in every type of culture. Only the artistic text may be the object of mutually exclusive axiomatic value. Even though artistic texts in the general hierarchy of culture have a particular place, they are constantly demonstrating tendencies toward movement to the opposite end of the spectrum, i.e., in their initial point there already exists a specific conflict that creates the potential for further neutralization in ambivalent texts ... The internal organization of literature is isomorphic to culture as such and repeats the general principles of [cultural] organization. Literature never presents itself as an amorphous, unilateral sum of texts: It is not only organizing, but a self-organizing mechanism. At the highest level of organization literature selects the group of more abstract texts, that is, metatexts.)

Figure 5.3 shows how Lotman schematizes the diachronic development and increased differentiation of artistic and literary texts (1992b: I. 211). Each of the categories provided includes a range of genres of written literature and may thus be further differentiated.

Returning to our original point, literary texts, as modelling systems for culture itself, require their own artistic space and their own rules for differentiating between different types of artistic spaces, as well as a definition of the role of boundaries in this new type of space. Lotman conducts his most detailed exploration of artistic space in the context of the works of Nikolaj Gogol'. Because Gogol' is not a central topic in this work, I will simply extrapolate the principles of artistic space construction provided by Lotman in his analyses of Gogol', and apply them to Bulgakov's work. The point is to show that Lotman's approaches to defining semiotic space can provide interesting and fundamentally new readings of artistic and literary texts.

Artistic Spaces and Textual Dynamics

Any artistic space represents the author's own modelling system of the world and is represented through a particular type of language of spatial relationships. The space itself is more specifically the author's creation; the language that creates the space is more a product of a particular culture at a particular point in time (Lotman 1992b: I. 414). Lotman suggests that any artistic space can be defined by one of four basic spatial characteristics: *point, line, plane,* and *volume* (1992b: I. 414–21). It is specifically line- and plane-based artistic space that allows for multidirectional movement and directionality. Note that line-based artistic space may or may not demonstrate directionality. Lotman is especially interested in linear artistic space because, unlike point-based artistic space (which is atemporal by definition), it is 'a comfortable artistic language for the modelling of temporal categories ("life path," "road," as a means of character development manifesting itself along the time axis)' (1992b: I. 414). He notes that examples of point space can be found in Russian *byliny* (epic tales), where the fundamental characteristic of point space is its bounded separateness (отграниченность). The presence of both point and linear spaces is demonstrated in Gogol''s *Dead Souls*, in which point space is used for *home*, in contradistinction to linear space used for the *road* (1992b: I. 415–16). The presence of these two fundamental spatial types is seen again in Bulgakov's *The Master and Margarita*.

One other essential difference between artistic space and general semiospheric space has to do with boundaries. The notion and presence of boundaries – perhaps one of the most fundamental defining principles of the semiosphere – is recodified in the context of artistic space in such a way that there will be some spaces whose perception is in no way determined by such boundaries (Lotman 1992b: I. 415). We will see later in this chapter how Bulgakov displaces and destroys textually given spatial boundaries in a profound way. But in order to reach that point in the discussion, the reader will require a developed understanding of directionality in linear or planar artistic space – a notion addressed by Lotman in his formulation of the road.

Space and the Road

In the context of Gogol''s works, Lotman identifies a very important aspect of textual construction. Gogol''s construction of artistic space produces a spatial and character-based directionality that is represented by the symbol of the road (дорога). One of the genre types that grew out of Gogol''s construction of artistic space is 'fantastic realism,' a tradition that is continued in the works of Bulgakov and Zamyatin.[7] The concept of the road is central for Gogol' in that it categorically restricts movement in the direction of *bounded space* in the artistic text.

Gogol''s use of the road reaches its full realization in *Dead Souls*, in which the formal spatial oppositions become the language for extra- or non-spatial categories in plot and character development. The so-called home space in Gogol''s novel becomes restricted to only one type – the antihome – and the fundamental markings of this artistic space become the opposition between bounded-unbounded and directionality-nondirectionality (Lotman 1992b: I. 444). Lotman argues that as Gogolian unbounded space is ambivalent in its definition, within these oppositions, it is precisely the road, demonstrating movement toward a goal, that allows these spaces to be raised to a higher plane (1992b: I. 445). Thus, Lotman claims that 'nondirectionality of space is equivalent to a lack of goal orientation in the existence of the person occupying this space' (1992b: I. 444). This may be true in the context of Gogol''s works, but Bulgakov's *The Master and Margarita* will provide a potentially different interpretation, at least in part, in its conclusion.

One of the final distinctions Lotman draws, which may be applicable in the context of Bulgakov's work, is between the terms дорога (road) and путь (path). Specifically, while дорога (road) is 'a certain type of artistic space,' путь (path) is 'the realization (complete or incomplete) or the non-realization of дорога' (1992b: I. 445). In the case of Gogol''s novel, the road (дорога) is not restricted to one particular type of space; rather, it crosses over and penetrates all spaces (445). Finally, Gogol''s дорога and путь are isomorphic to each other and can lead to 'infinite rising' or 'infinite falling' at both ends of the temporal spectrum (1992b: I. 446). In the final analysis, Lotman characterizes the Gogolian hero as a prophet who 'prophesizes movement into infinity' (1992b: I. 447).

Types of Infinity

In order to set the stage for Bulgakov's textual representations of space-time, it is important to fine-tune our definitions of what infinity might look like in artistic and semiospheric texts. In chapters 3 and 4 I discussed in some detail the construction of boundaries in semiospheric space. I also noted the membranelike, bilingual nature of the outermost boundaries of the semiosphere, and discussed how old and new boundaries are constantly renegotiated within the asymmetrical internal spaces of the semiosphere. Furthermore, we have considered different types of boundaries in the context of the ever-present tensions between continuous and discontinuous dynamics – dynamics that are essential to a functioning semiotic space. In part, these dynamics play themselves out in the languages and codes that facilitate the translation of information across these boundaries. These languages and codes and their descriptions alternate between the poles of continuity and discontinuity in terms of construction, production, and perception. In the context of a more specific realization of semiotic space – namely, as artistic space – the role of boundaries will shift somewhat, in such a way that the dominant characteristic lies in the complex of conflicting indices emanating from the artistic text and will generally be represented by a specific type of spatial design (e.g., point, line, plane, volume). Once the artistic space has achieved a particular level of hierarchical complexity, the role of directionality will increase in significance as an organizing mechanism of the space (including multiple subspaces).

What perhaps requires further explanation here is the shift in artistic space away from semiospheric space in terms of the potential overall unboundedness of the former. It may often be that an author's construction of artistic space strives toward constant movement to infinity (Lotman's characterization of Gogol'). This description fits many authors in the Russian literary tradition, but these authors set up different definitions of infinity. I suggest we keep at least three types in mind when reading Bulgakov's *The Master and Margarita* (see the diagrams in figure 5.4). As these three types illustrate, not all notions of infinity necessarily require accompanying progress (in an evaluative sense); they may require only a dynamic that could result in circular movement and marking time. It is also useful to note that at the linear level, a line in two-dimensional space may continue to infinity and never meet itself (figure 5.4, diagram a), whereas in three- or multi-dimensional space a line may run into itself (as in figure 5.4, diagram b2).

Figure 5.4
(a) Infinity as a mathematical limit, where the functional mapping is moving closer and closer (but never achieving) zero as it goes to infinity:

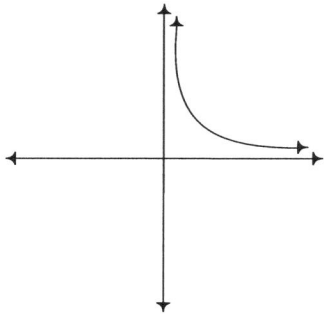

(b) Infinity as a cyclic phenomenon:

1.
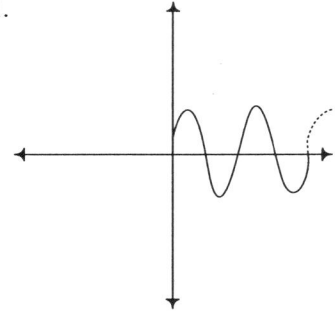

2.
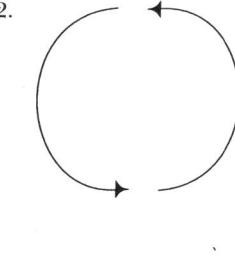

(c) Infinity as a spiral:

1.

2.
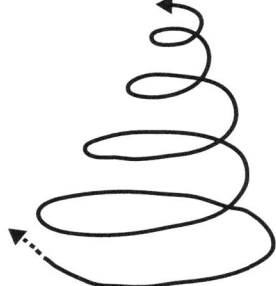

Florensky and Imaginary Space

Pavel Aleksandrovič Florensky (1882–1937), a philosopher, physicist, priest, and literary and art critic, strongly influenced in the theoretical and philosophical thought of many Russian writers at the turn of the last century, including Zamyatin, Bulgakov, and Andrej Bely (to name only three). He was awarded the title of 'Professor of Supreme Artistic-Technical Mastery' (1921–24) at VXUTEMAS (ВХУТЕМАС – Высшие государственные художественно-технические мастерские), later the Moscow Academy of Arts (Академия художеств), where he worked in the same department with Vladimir Favorsky and Vasilij Kandinsky (Byčkov 1996: 309). Florensky's lecture course was titled 'The Analysis of Space in Artistic-Visual Works' (Анализ пространственности в художественно-изобразительных произведениях). In May 1928, Florensky was arrested by the OGPU (Объединённое государственное политическое управление при Совете Народных Комиссаров СССР). He spent the rest of his life in various Soviet prison camps, including Solovki (СЛОН), where he was sentenced to death in 1937 by the NKVD (Народный комиссариат внутренних дел), one of a series of names for the Soviet secret police (Sokolov 1997: 474–7).

Florensky wrote many important works on philosophy and Russian literary and visual arts, including *Ikonostas (Iconostasis)*, *Imena (Names)*, *Stolp i utverždenie istiny (Pillar and Confirmation of Eternal Truth)*, *U vodorazdelov mysli (At the Vodorazdels of Thought)*, *Obratnaja perspektiva (Reverse Perspectives)*, *Xramovoe dejstvo kak sintez iskusstv (Church Ritual as Artistic Synthesis)*, and *Nebesnye znamenija (Heavenly Prophesies)*. One of his books, *Mnimosti v geometrii (Imaginaries in Geometry)* (1922), was one of Bulgakov's favourites. A copy of this work, with copious notes written by Bulgakov in the margins, was found in Bulgakov's archives.[8] Furthermore, Bulgakov and his second wife, Ljudimila Belozerskaja, lived on the same street as Florensky from 1926 to 1927 (M. Levshinskij pereulok, 4) (Sokolov 1997: 478). Sokolov claims that Florensky had a profound influence on Bulgakov, and that he served as a prototype of Fesja, who later became the Master, in *The Master and Margarita* (1997: 478).

If we look to Florensky's book on imaginaries in geometry, we find that Bulgakov probably was not equipped to read at a deep level the complex mathematical arguments. Florensky's goal in his analysis was to take the notions of imaginary (or complex numerical) values and analyse them in the context of plane geometry and later in the context of differential geometry (Florensky 1922: 5). However, Bulgakov probably

Figure 5.5

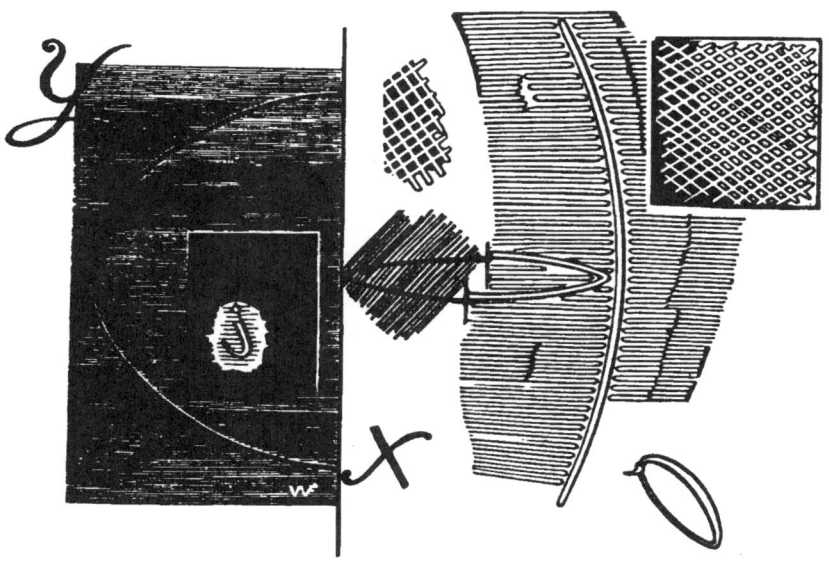

was able to appreciate Florensky's analysis of Favorskij's diagram, which was used on the book's cover (see figure 5.5) and which speaks to the issues of visual perception of transparent bodies between 'something' (нечто) and 'nothing' (ничто) (1922: 59). And probably, as well, he was able to appreciate Florensky's more general statements about the properties of space and spatial constructions and his critique of Dante's construction of multiple spaces (1922: 11, 44–53, 58–65).

The following is an example of one such passage (1922: 53):

> ... можно сказать, что пространство ломается при скоростях больших скорости света, подобно тому, как воздух ломается при движении тел, со скоростями большими скорости звука; и тогда наступают качественно новые условия существования пространства, характеризуемые мнимыми параметрами.

> (It is possible to say that space breaks apart at speeds greater than the speed of light, as air breaks apart in the motion of bodies at speeds greater than the speed of sound; and then come into being qualitatively new conditions of the existence of space that are characterized by imaginary parameters.)

Perhaps more important in the context of Florensky's influence on Bulgakov's construction of artistic space in *The Master and Margarita* is the former's notion of *potential* versus *actual infinity* in his work *Stolp i utverždenie istiny (Pillar and Confirmation of Eternal Truth)* ([1914] 1990: 493–9). *Potential* infinity is expressed as a variable that is always more or less described in terms of movement to positive or negative infinity; in contrast, *actual* infinity is expressed by a constant. But this constant is not determinable as a number; rather, it is available to human perception only as the symbolic effect of something that is greater than any finite entity because such a constant is unknown and 'un-name-able.' Thus, *infinite continuity* is equivalent in some sense to Florensky's *potential infinity*, while *finite continuity* is closer to Florensky's *actual infinity*.

Bulgakov's Journey in Time and Space

Lotman's analysis of *The Master and Margarita* focuses on the construction of artistic space as the fundamental modelling system of the novel. He characterizes Bulgakov's space as determined heavily by the binary opposition of home-antihome. As I have attempted to show, Lotman's initial analysis can provide a richer basis of interpretation if we extend it to a triadic opposition of home-antihome-homelessness. The fundamental difference between these three categories is best represented by a triadic relationship of values: plus (home), minus (antihome), and zero (homelessness). These values clarify that the difference between antihome and homelessness is more complex than presence versus absence.

Figure 5.6

This is, however, only one aspect of Bulgakov's modelling system. Knowing Lotman's important work on Gogol', we can ask ourselves: Given the important similarities between the two authors in their construction of unbounded, linear and planar (for the most part) artistic space, could it be that Bulgakov has developed a modelling system for constructing movement throughout these multiple, uniquely bounded and unbounded spaces? I believe the answer is yes, and I would argue that this model of textual dynamics will be in some ways isomorphic to a triadic modelling of the spaces themselves. In setting up the fundamental oppositions in Bulgakov's novel, I will borrow from Lotman's notion of the defining dynamics of any and all semiotic spaces.

Lotman's conceptualization of road, which allows for plot and character development and for movement between different types of artistic spaces (1992: I. 445), can be divided into three main types in *The Master and Margarita* (see figure 5.6). The relative lack of spatial and temporal boundaries is expressed throughout the novel in a wide variety of ways, including the free movement of characters between clearly discrete units of time and space (e.g., Woland in Moscow on Good Friday in the twentieth century telling Berlioz and Bezdomnyj about his breakfast that very day with Kant; St'opa Lixodeev finding himself one minute in Moscow, the next in Yalta; Jeshua and Pilate meeting on a path in the afterlife; Berlioz reappearing at Satan's Ball after his untimely beheading; the appearance of Levy Matvej on Woland's balcony in Moscow; Master and Margarita finding themselves returned to their cellar apartment). In fact, all the main characters except Bezdomnyj move freely between vastly distinct temporal and geographical spaces, and cross and recross the line separating the living from the dead, this life from the afterlife. Such unboundedness fits nicely with Lotman's expectations of how artistic space can be constructed.

Another (qualitatively different) example of Bulgakov's ability to demonstrate spatial movement between distinct units of time and space in

Master relates to the replicas of verbal text that appear in the Jershalaim and Moscow texts – specifically, Pilate's words: 'O gods, gods ... give me poison, poison' (О боги, боги ... яду мне, яду ...) (ch. 2) . (Only Pilate begs for poison to end his misery. Also, it is only Pilate who uses the archaic form of 'gods' in the early chapters of the novel [chs. 2, 5], while both the Master [ch. 25] and Bezdomnyj [ch. 33] will appeal to the gods in the final chapters.) The same words are uttered in the Griboedov House at midnight but are not attributed to any speaker who is actually present (ch. 5). Through this mirroring of verbal text in the two distinct textual spaces, Bulgakov provides a point of intersection in space-time where the two worlds converge as two planar realizations of the antiworld, or hell. This example is a perfect realization of how Lotman describes the phenomenon of text within a text (1992a: 104):

> ... любая динамическая система погружена в пространство, в котором размещаются другие столь же динамические системы, а также обломки разрушившихся структур, своеобразные кометы этого пространства. В результате любая система живёт не только по законам саморазвития, но также включена в разнообразные столкновения с другими структурами.

> (... any dynamic system is embedded in space where other equally dynamic systems are also found, including broken pieces of dismantled structures, unique comets of that space. Thus, any system lives not only by the laws of its own development, but also includes the variegated encounters with other cultural structures.)

In Bulgakov's model, as described above, it would be interesting to consider the potential directionality of the triadic scheme suggested earlier. In figure 5.7, we see the finite, false road leading to hell (Berlioz's death is final, no afterlife for him), the infinite road of truth allowing Jeshua and Pilate to continue the discussion they initiated at Herod's palace so many centuries ago as they walk toward the light, and the Master's reward of peace (покой), the eternal home that no longer needs access to roads and movement.[9]

If we attempt to coordinate the schematic representations of home space and dynamic space in Bulgakov's novel, we find the points of coincidence shown in figure 5.8. What we see here is that Bulgakov realigns the relationship between the ultimate goal of achievement of home with the desire for an absence of road, a desire for rest to accommodate the Master at the end of the novel. Such a realignment may seem

Figure 5.7

to give rise to a paradox in terms of the construction of continuous and discrete space vis-à-vis the concepts of infinite and finite. In fact, there is no paradox in Bulgakov's construction if it is read in the context of Florensky's work on symbols in infinity. As we have shown earlier, Florensky claims that a distinction must be made between the realization of infinity in potential versus actual terms. In the former, we have quantities that are constantly fluctuating (e.g., one's normal conceptualization of infinity), while in the latter, the quantities are invariant (e.g., any mathematical constant) (Florensky [1914] 1990: 494–5).[10]

The Master's achievement of 'eternal home' is a synthesis of his eternal search for self and truth (signalling infinite internal movement and change) with the actualization of stability and lack of movement around him, his immediate surrounding, including the constant presence of his most deeply loved partner, Margarita. Jeshua and Pilate exemplify a more traditional infinite progression by retaining eternal, infinite movement toward a particular goal (in this case, light) while keeping to the eternal path of truth. Thus, for the Master the realignment of space is not required to accommodate Jeshua or Pilate: for them, the true road is home. Berlioz is the exemplar of the finite, false path leading to a finality of utter destruction, death, the ultimate finite discontinuity. Furthermore, the temporal and geographic boundaries established at the beginning of the novel (for both the Moscow and Jershalaim narratives) explode and break apart into infinity by the end.

When we combine Lotman's notion of semiospheric explosion and tension to this grid, what is of particular interest is the realization that these categories are not unilaterally defined but rather multileveled (неоднородные, многослойные), and subject to refraction into a new configuration of discrete entities (especially in the absence of home and road). If homelessness is primarily defined by explosion, then roadlessness is also initially determined by explosion. However, it is at the end of the

Figure 5.8

Schema for home–antihome–homelessness

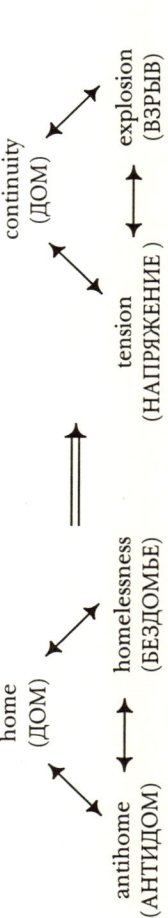

Schema for true road–false road–absence of road

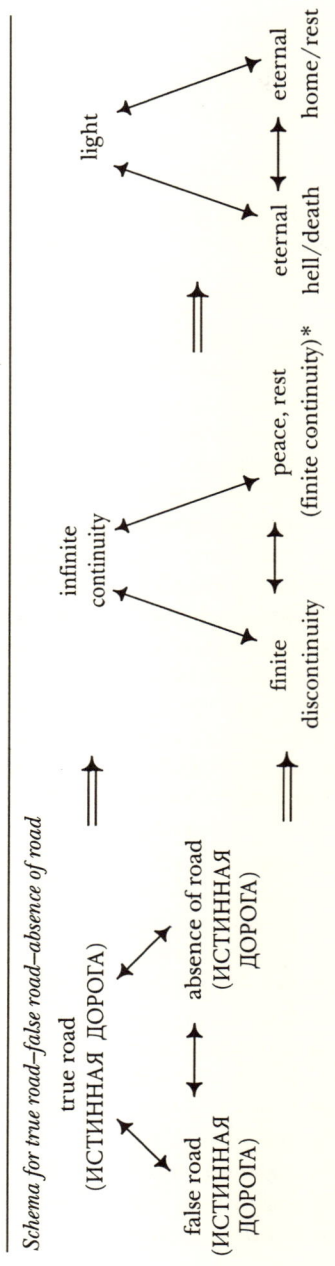

Figure 5.8 (*concluded*)

The Master and Margarita, *stage one*

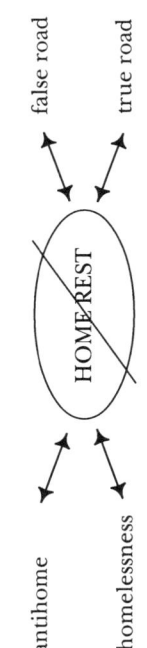

The Master and Margarita, *stage two (end result)*

*continuity as succession (Lotman 1992a: I. 16)

event of explosion (i.e., the terminal boundary) that we reach the potential (but not unlilaterally so) achievement of a state of rest. This was the point desired and achieved by the Master, reflecting no movement on his part to the highest realm. Pilate (and most probably Bezdomnyj) opts for a different realization of the terminal boundary of explosion, which allows him to move on to a higher level of infinite continuity – the eternal road of truth. Thus, my suggested schema for the final alignment of artistic space vis-à-vis home and road reflects the textual dynamic of all of the characters in the novel. Here too, in Bulgakov's *The Master and Margarita*, Lotman's concepts of *doroga* and *put'* are in the same relation to each other as they are in Gogol''s *Dead Souls*. Yet Bulgakov provides an innovation – the option for one of his characters not to be the eternal prophet preaching movement into infinity, at least not in the generic understanding of the concept.

I will now develop the notion of artistic space and its spatial-temporal dynamic by comparing points of textual intersection in Bulgakov and Zamyatin, and by considering how Lotman's theory of the semiosphere shows how artistic texts become more broadly understood as culture texts in the work of Evgenij Zamyatin.

CHAPTER SIX

Bulgakov and Zamyatin

Intertextuality and Revolution

Soviet literature has a unique history – many of its most talented writers found their works forbidden, confiscated, or destroyed. Many Soviet writers were silenced through emigration, through imprisonment, or through death (by execution or suicide). Evgenij Zamyatin (1884–1937) and Mikhail Bulgakov (1891–1940) were two such silenced writers: Zamyatin's works were not published between 1930 and 1988; Bulgakov's prose was not published from the end of the 1920s until 1961. The links between these two writers' works will be discussed in the context of two of their major works – Zamyatin's 'Drakon' (1918) and Bulgakov's *The Master and Margarita* (completed 1940). In the following analysis I unravel the influence of 'Drakon' on chapter 3 of *The Master and Margarita*, in the development of the symbol of revolution in general, and the Russian Revolution, in particular. In order to fully explain such a textual question, I will refer to the biographical and historical facts surrounding the writing of Bulgakov's final novel, and on the crucial theoretical problems evoked by such an analysis. I will use the term *intertextuality* in a distinctly different and broader sense than it has been used by Julia Kristeva. Kristeva's intertextuality is defined mainly in terms of the addressee's role in reproducing and reconstructing the open text (Kristeva 1986: 111); she does not see intertextuality as a 'study of sources' (111). In the following analysis I will demonstrate that a synthetic definition of the text is needed where one finds a constant vacillation of textual boundaries; this yields a perspective of text as both *open* and *closed*, exhibiting the principles of continuous sign functions within the framework of discontinuities. Also, the question of textual *source*, including methodological problems of authorial intention and the constructive function, will play a role in the discussion. Using Lotman's principles of construction of artistic space and artistic texts, and the importance of culture texts in producing and maintaining the semiosphere, I will argue in favour of a redefinition of intertextuality in such a way that boundedness (or discreteness) of culture texts is viewed in a more relativistic, interactive, and dynamic fashion.

Zamyatin and Bulgakov

Evgenij Zamyatin was not only one of the most prominent writers of the twentieth century, but also an important literary critic and theorist. In fact, we find one of the first truly insightful critical reviews of Bulgakov's short story 'D'javoliada' (Diaboliad) in Zamyatin's article 'O segodnjashnem i o sovremennom' (About Today and the Contemporary) (1924):

> The only modern piece in Nedra is Bulgakov's 'Diaboliad.' The author unquestionably possesses the right instinct in the choice of his compositional base – fantasy rooted in actual life, rapid, cinematic succession of scenes – one of the few formal frameworks which can encompass our yesterday – 1919, 1920. The term 'cinematic' is all the more applicable to this work since the entire novella is two-dimensional, done on a single plane; everything is on the surface, and there is no depth of scene whatever. With Bulgakov, Nedra loses its classical (and pseudo-classical) innocence for what I believe is the first time, and as happens so frequently, the provincial old maid is seduced by the very first brash young man from the capital. The absolute value of this piece, somehow too thoughtless, is not so great, but good works can apparently be expected from its author. (Ginsburg 1970: 116).

Following this review, Zamyatin and Bulgakov became friends, and kept in close contact until Zamyatin's death in Paris in 1937. Recent biographical materials and the correspondence of both authors, including their famous letters to Stalin, attest to their close friendship and intertwined fates (Čudakova 1988a; Bulgakov 1989; Bulgakova and Ljandres 1988). Lakšin writes that Bulgakov was at the Belorusskij train station in Moscow to see off Zamyatin when he and his wife, Ljudmila Nikolaevna, left the Soviet Union for good on 14 November 1931.[1] Bulgakov's brother Nikolaj was in Paris prior to Zamyatin's death in 1937 and wrote to Mikhail about Zamyatin's ailing heart (Bulgakov 1989: 371). These two writers were often seen as representative of the bourgeois Soviet writers and were mentioned together in certain critical essays of the day: 'Булгаковы и замятины сожительствовали в Союзе (писателей) рядом с подлинными советскими художниками слова' (*Жизнь искусства*); (Bulgakovs and Zamyatins peacefully co-existed in the writer's union next to authentic Soviet artist of the word. [*The Life of Art*]). And 'Сергеева-Ценского, Замятина, Булгакова называли "писателями новой буржуазии"' (Petelin 1989: 13); (Sergeev-Tsenskij, Zamyatin, Bulgakov were called 'writers of the new bourgeoisie').

Of utmost importance are Zamyatin's critical works on contemporary Soviet literature of his day and its future: 'Zavtra' (Tomorrow, 1919), 'Ja bojus' (I am Afraid, 1921), 'O sintetizme' (About Synthesism, 1922), 'Novaya russkaya proza' (The New Russian Prose, 1923), 'O segodnjashnem i sovremennom' (About Today and the Contemporary, 1924), and 'O literature, revoljutsii, entropii' (About Literature, Revolution and Entropy, 1923) (Zamyatin 1988b). In these works we find an eloquent and precise appraisal of the developmental laws of Soviet literature, as well as the laws of revolution. In many of these essays the theme of the *heretic* is dominant; he sees *hereticism* as the only means for revolution (as a law of nature) to evolve beyond the obligatory periods of entropy. Zamyatin writes in 'The New Russian Prose' that 'heretics are the only (bitter) medicine for entropy in human ideas'; 'Heretics are harmful ... But harmful literature is the best thing of all because it is antientropic' ([1923a] 1988: 447); 'It is the heretic's task to speak heretically today about tomorrow' (447). There can be no revolution without the heretic. And revolution, for Zamyatin, is a force of nature – the law of revolution is a 'cosmic, universal law' (446). Inextricably tied to revolution are 'nations, classes, molecules, stars – and books' (446). In a related essay, Zamyatin coins the term *synthesism* (синтетизм) to describe the 'central point' of Soviet literature in 1923 ([1924] 1988: 433):

Если искать какого-нибудь слова для определения той точки, в которой движется сейчас литература, я выбрал бы слово синтетизм: синтетического характера формальные эксперименты, синтетический образ в символике, синтезированный быт, синтез фантастики и быта, опыт художественно-философского синтеза.

(If one were to look for a single word to define the point toward which literature is moving today, I would choose the word synthesism: synthetic formal experiments, the synthetic image in symbolism, synthesized life, synthesis of the fantastic and daily reality, experiment in artistic-philosophical synthesis.)

It is clear from Zamyatin's biography that he was indeed committed to the ideal of the heretic, regardless of – or in spite of – the regime under which he lived. Many post-Soviet accounts refer to Zamyatin's activities as a Bolshevik prior to the 1917 Revolution and his rejection of the Bolsheviks following his return to Russia in October 1917 (see Zamyatin's biographies, especially [1924] 1988: 476 and Andrews et al. 1994: 98–103).[2] Zamyatin was imprisoned three times, twice before the Russian Revolution (in 1905–6 and 1911) and once after (1922) (Zamyatin 1988b: 475–6). 'Delo Zamyatina,' recently published, contains additional archival data about Zamyatin's imprisonment in 1922 at Shpalernaya Prison in Petrograd (Andrews et al. 1994: 104–9).

Bulgakov in his autobiography reports that he wrote his first short story one fall night in 1919 and that he moved to Moscow at the end of 1921, and there wrote his first book, *Zapiski na manžetax*, which was scheduled for publication in 1923 (Čudakova 1988a: 38–9). Nikolaj Gogol', Anton Chekhov, and Mikhail Saltykov-Shchedrin were the young Bulgakov's favourite authors; all three strongly influenced his later writings (Lakšin 1988: 14–15). Zamyatin also influenced Bulgakov, no less than the Russian writers typically mentioned in Soviet critical and biographical works on Bulgakov. The question necessarily arises: Why is Zamyatin's name missing in contemporary works on Bulgakov (the notable exceptions are Čudakova 1988a and Milne 1990)? I suggest that this is one of many instances of the removal of Zamyatin from Soviet literary history – in this case, not by censorship, but rather through the destruction of the historical context that defines the writer's social milieu. The work of scholars like M. Čudakova has already begun to rectify omissions of this type (Čudakova 1988a, 1988b).

By the end of the 1920s all of Bulgakov's plays had been pulled from Soviet theatres. At this point, Bulgakov wrote his famous letter to Stalin (July 1929) (Bulgakov 1989: 146–9). Stalin answered this letter with a personal phone call, and Bulgakov was soon reinstated at MXAT (Московский художественный акедемический театр, Moscow Artistic Academic Theatre). Zamyatin, who had suffered the same oppression as Bulgakov, wrote his own letter to Stalin, which resulted in his leaving the Soviet Union at the end of 1931. In 1932, while in Leningrad (Zamyatin's home), Bulgakov began to work – after a three-year break – on *The*

Master and Margarita, his 'destroyed novel,' starting with chapter 1 (Čudakova 1988: 372).

On being published for the first time in 1966, *The Master and Margarita* became known as one of the twentieth century's greatest works of fiction. This novel has been analysed often by Soviet, European, and American literary scholars, but these studies have never focused on the theme of revolution. I want to remedy this omission and show how this perspective, or reading, can be connected directly to Zamyatin's story 'Drakon' and to Zamyatin's laws of literary development. I hope to demonstrate, using these two literary texts, that Bulgakov's use of Zamyatin's text was intentional (in Medvedev's sense) and semiotically developmental, and provides an alternative perspective on revolution that attests to the true differences in the philosophies of the two authors.[3] This analysis will support our triadic schematization of road in the construction of artistic space, and confirm the finiteness of the false road taken by the October Revolution. The following analysis will encompass three distinct levels, beginning with a textual analysis of the two works in question, moving on to a comparison of their language and imagery, and concluding with a broader 'semio-cultural' analysis that necessarily broaches theoretical questions about how sign-based functions are realized in language and culture and about the boundaries of the literary (or artistic) text. Lotman's analysis of Bulgakov's novel and definition of a culture text will be central to my conclusions. At the initial level of textual analysis of the two works, we will look for common elements in their language and the resulting imagery.

Textual Links between *Master* and 'Drakon'

The third chapter of *The Master and Margarita* is one of the shortest of the thirty-three chapters of the novel. (The significance of the number 33 has been noted in the context of Bulgakov's use of numerals. For more information, see B. Gasparov [1978] 1994; Kuljus 1998: 65–92.) As often in this book, the opening line of chapter 3 directs the reader's attention back to the closing lines of chapter 2, thus accentuating the spatial and temporal continuum that ties together the many threads of the story. The novel opens on Good Friday evening at Patriarch Ponds. Satan (called Woland) has come to Moscow and has just finished his rendering of the first episode of the Pontius Pilate story (chapter 2). The three characters, Berlioz, Bezdomnij, and Woland, are sitting on a bench in the park; the full moon is in view. The action of chapter 3 focuses on the fulfilment of Woland's prediction – the untimely death of Berlioz. As Berlioz makes his way to call the police to arrest the insane foreigner (Woland), he accidentally (or seemingly so) falls under a tram and is decapitated. At this point the chapter ends.

Written as an interpretative description of the October Revolution (7 November by the new calendar), Zamyatin's short story 'Drakon' depicts Petrograd burning and delirious in the dead of winter. Suddenly, dragon people appear on the scene, temporarily at the tram depot. The trams rush from the 'earth world' to the 'unknown.' The dragon people (soldiers) are the 'escort[s] to the kingdom of heaven' (проводник в Царствие Небесное). With gnashing of teeth and screeching of wheels, the tram rushes into the 'unknown.' Later, one of the very same dragon people is shown as saving the life of a small, frozen sparrow by breathing life into him.[4]

A closer reading of chapter 3 of *The Master and Margarita* reveals a strongly articulated assessment of the October Revolution in the context of the 1930s if one makes the connection to Zamyatin's text 'Drakon.' To build the foundation for such an interpretation, I suggest we look at the lexical items – more substantive than grammatical ones and more salient in the production of semantic information – shared by the two texts under scrutiny (see table 6.1; the grammatical forms are given as they actually appear in the two texts).

The value of table 6.1 depends directly on two textually determined factors: the general frequency of these lexical items in Russian, and their context as provided in each of these two works. Table 6.2 indicates the general frequency of these items (listed in the nominative case form and infinitive) from Zasorina's frequency dictionary of Russian. Substantives and verbs are the two most frequent parts of speech in Russian (Zasorina 1977: 927). The general frequency listing given in Zasorina extends from 1 to 42,854; so the items in these two passages by Bulgakov and Zamyatin are of unusually low frequency.

The mere occurrence of these shared lexical items is not, in and of itself, necessarily significant in the argumentation supporting the view that Bulgakov made use of Zamyatin's 'Drakon.' Nor is the extremely low frequency of these items sufficient to prove deliberate textual borrowing. However, the evidence becomes much more convincing when we view it in light of the contextual and thematic placement in Bulgakov's text itself and in his modelling system in *The Master and Margarita*. To begin, let us briefly recall the historical context surrounding Zamyatin's 'Drakon.'

In the west, 'Drakon' is one of Zamyatin's better-known works, and

Table 6.1

Master and Margarita	'Drakon'
1. воробей sparrow	воробьёныш baby sparrow
2. (вы)порхнул flutter out (perf. past)	(с)порхнул flutter away (perf. past)
3. картузик cap (nom. sing.)	картуз cap (nom. sing.)
4. дьявол существует the devil exists (imperf. pres.)	существовал дракон a dragon existed (imperf. past)
5. вздрогнул/дрогнувшим to jerk, begin to shake (perf. past/participle) (perf. past)	дрыгнул to jerk
6. несущееся rushing (pres. active participle)	в несущемся мире, нёсся трамвай in the rushing-along world, a tram was rushing (pres. active participle, imperf. past)
7. решётку lattice, railing (acc. sing.)	решётки lattice (nom. pl.)

Table 6.2

Lexical item	General frequency[5] (of 42,854)
воробей	29
воробьёныш	0
картуз	12
картузик	3
выпорхнуть	4
спорхнуть	0
дрогнуть	21
дрогнувший	3
дрыгнуть	0
*дрыгать (imperf. of #9)	2
вздрогнуть	22
несущийся	1
нестись	32
решётка	40

perceived as one of his most typical. Mirra Ginsburg's translation of 'Drakon' and other Zamyatin short stories was published in the United States in 1966. However, the Soviet public had no access to 'Drakon' after it was published in Petrograd on 4 May 1918 in *Delo naroda*. 'Drakon' is also conspicuously missing from the two collections of

Zamyatin's work published in the Soviet Union (1929 and 1988). In fact, the 1988 volume of Zamyatin's *Essays* (*Сочинения*), while referring to the fact that many of Zamyatin's repressed works were finally being published (e.g., *We*), made no mention of 'Drakon' – not even in the commentary or lists of publications (1988: 498–575). Čudakova makes one rather cryptic reference to a certain 'short story,' which, however, she fails to name: '"Red, fiery, deadly is the law of revolution" ... these words from the article "About literature, revolution, entropy" could be the epigraph to a story written [by Zamyatin] at that time' (1988: 516). 'Drakon' is only a one-page story of 345 words, so it is hardly likely that space was an issue. This question naturally arises: Why was 'Drakon,' unlike Zamyatin's other works, including *We*, omitted from the collected works published in 1988?

This question is especially important if we bear in mind that Voronskij's letter to Zamyatin (1922), containing a highly critical reaction to both 'Drakon' and *We*, was published in Moscow in *Literaturnoe nasledstvo* (Voronskij 1983: 571).[6] In this letter Voronskij even implores Zamyatin to remember the price they paid for standing up for their beliefs during tsarist rule. In reference to 'Drakon' and *We*, Voronskij writes: 'Could it be that this is all that the October [revolution] inspired you to do ...?' (1983: 571). In 1989 a third collection of Zamyatin's works, *Selected Works* (*Избранные произведения*), was published, and it did include 'Drakon,' but not as part of the *Vereški* cycle of which it was originally a part. The disappearance and readmittance of 'Drakon' to the Soviet literary canon is but one example of the *disruption* (or discontinuities) of normal literary processes that has so often occurred in the Soviet literature. Any attempt to analyse such works requires the researcher to grapple with the additional task of reconstructing organic links among literary texts of the Soviet period – that have been deliberately severed from the context of Soviet literature. Thus, one is faced with the problem of explaining the motivation, to some extent, of each disruption in order to return a given work to its appropriate place in history. Clearly, official Soviet perceptions of 'Drakon' were even more negative than perceptions of *We*.

If we set up a correlation of the two texts through lexical signalling and images, the following schematization becomes possible – a schematization in which we find an inversion and coincidence of symbols in a literal sense, as well as a codification of the topic of revolution from *overt* in Zamyatin to *covert* in Bulgakov. The 'tram' as a symbol of revolution is not unique to Bulgakov and Zamyatin – it is found in other

Russian literary works of the period (cf. Nikolaj Gumil'ev, Vladimir Majakovskij, Boris Pasternak, and others [cf. Timenčik 1987: 135–44]).[7]

According to Lotman, artistic space is multifaceted, and translates into a synthetic whole the author's idiosyncratic modelling system. This translation involves applying the actual languages and codes used to create these dynamic spaces (1992b: I. 414). The languages and codes are always a shared cultural space that is only marginally intersected at the level of actualization of the artistic text. Thus, on the one hand, any and all Russian language texts (artistic and non-artistic) written is what is recognizably Russian will necessarily overlap in many ways. Yet the more that logically consistent structures coincide – especially if they are by definition highly improbable – the higher the probability that there is a goal-oriented trend to be discovered.

Table 6.3 demonstrates that each of the lexical convergences between the two texts is embedded in a deeper structure that serves to intensify the bonding of these two texts. Together, these convergences show that Bulgakov extends Zamyatin's initial concept through imitation and direct *inversion* of images. The interplay of coincidence and inversion of images shared by Bulgakov's and Zamyatin's texts is set out in Table 6.4.

In using 'Drakon' as a textual starting point for chapter 3 of *The Master and Margarita*, we discover a radically different reading than has traditionally been given. In particular, Bulgakov strengthens Zamyatin's characterization of the 'cosmic' nature of revolution by *refracting* the symbolism in 'Drakon.' The fledgling sparrow's life is saved by the dragon, thus demonstrating the humanity of the dragon; however, the sparrow flies away into the unknown. In *The Master and Margarita*, the sparrow, now full grown, wants no contact with Woland and flies away. In conjunction with the image of sparrow is an interesting twist given in Bulgakov that strengthens Zamyatin's image of the 'deranged world' (бредовый мир). Namely, Bulgakov uses the phrase из липы ('from the linden tree'), which is highly unlikely in Russian. Rather, one would expect the preposition с, not из. Subsequent to this usage of the word липа, we find its adjectival form directly following in the text of chapter 3, but in this instance the form липовый is being used strictly in the sense of 'fake, not real' (А ну как документы эти липовые? – 'And if his [Woland's] documents are fake?'). Likewise, it is significant that sparrows do not inhabit linden trees at all; rather, according to the Russian Academy Dictionary, they live 'under the roofs of people's homes' (SSLRJa 1951: 671). Thus, Bulgakov once again deepens the connection between the sparrow in *The Master and Margarita* and 'Drakon.' This image is especially powerful

Table 6.3

Topic	'Drakon'	Master
1. Setting of story	capital (Petersburg)	capital (Moscow)
2. sparrow flies away in fear (воробей/воробьёныш)	baby sparrow end of text	adult sparrow beginning of text
3. sparrow flies away from whom	dragon soldier	Woland (Satan)
4. sparrow flies away from where	deranged world 'из бредового мира'	false world 'из липы'
5. sparrow flies to	unknown	away
6. tram (as revolution) (трамвай)	rushing no rails no driver out of control moves to unknown	rushing newly placed rails driver, Komsomolka out of control comes to a halt
7. escort (проводник)	to Kingdom of Heaven military clothes clothes too big 2 slits for eyes cap – too big simple man Bolshevik	to Hell civilian clothes clothes too small 2 little eyes cap – too small former regent cohort of Satan
8. lattice, railing (решётка)	beginning to fall apart	fallen apart
9. screech, crash (скрежет / грохот)	motion accelerating	motion decelerating

when read in conjunction with the opening of Zamyatin's 'About Today and the Contemporary,' in which the author compares the female sparrow's song to 'truthful' literature; unfortunately, the sparrow's song is regarded in the Soviet period as mere 'chirping' – purposeless and vain ([1924] 1988: 434).

In both Zamyatin and Bulgakov the tram, as the symbol of revolution, antientropic and rushing along, is uncontrollable. (This is how the Revolution is usually seen in the literature of that period.) Yet the degree of destructiveness is different in the two authors' works. Bulgakov fortifies the sense of uncontrollability by adding a driver (not just any driver, but a young communist),[8] newly placed rails, and an explicit warning: Берегись трамвая ('Watch out for trams') (1978: 462). Even with these additions, revolution is nevertheless uncontrollable and – as Berlioz's

Table 6.4

1. Setting	Coincidence: capital city
	Inversion: Petersburg(D) / Moscow(M)
2. *nebyvaloe*	('that which does not occur')
	Coincidence: used in reference to the sun
	Inversion: 'icy' (D) [ледяное] / 'hot' (M) [жаркое]
3. Sparrow	Coincidence: flies away in fear
	Inversion: at end (D) / at beginning (M)
	Baby (D) / adult (M)
4. Tram	Coincidence: symbol of revolution
	uncontrollable (out of control)
	rushing along at great speed
	Inversion: no rails (D) / newly placed rails (M)
	no driver (D) / driven by female Komsomol member (M)
	picking up speed (D) / comes to crashing halt (M)
	Bolshevik at tram depot (D) / communist driving tram (M)
5. Escort	Coincidence: escort from earthly life to the next life
	surrealistic persons: dragon (D) / ghost (M)
	escorts: wearing cap; both remove cap
	reference to escorts' eyes: slits / half-drunk
	Inversion: escort to Kingdom of Heaven (D) / escort to Hell (M)
	military clothes-too big (D) / civilian clothes – too small (M)
	simple man (D) / former regent, aristocrat (M)
	Bolshevik (D) / Cohort of Satan (M)
6. Lattice	Coincidence: no foundation, lattice not attached to ground
	(no place to hide)
	Inversion: directionality of movement changes

D = 'Drakon'; M = *The Master and Margarita*

death demonstrates – cannot be stopped at will, even by the driver. Yet Berlioz's death is the outcome expected once he has chosen the false road – in this case the path corresponding to that of the Revolution.

The escorts to the other world are refracted in a most dramatic way. Both are surreal figures of mythology and fairy tales, and they serve a similar purpose – to lead others from one world to the next. The inversion of their attire and backgrounds accentuates the progression of revolution. Both figures are nameless; both are soldiers at the beginning of the Revolution, and later civilians. (Bulgakov names his escort in *The Master and Margarita* for the first time only in chapter 9, 'Koroviev's Antics.') The forces they represent are part of nature, except Bulgakov disambiguates this cosmic force and focuses on its evil nature.[9] The final common image, that of lattice or railing (решётка), provides a shift in the perspective of direction of movement. For Zamyatin the movement of the Revolution, as related to the image of the lattice, is a destruction of barriers that separate masters from slaves; for Bulgakov, the lattice is dilapidated. There are no functional barriers left – the Revolution is everywhere.

The question of the absence of barriers is strengthened when one examines the differences between 'Drakon' and the third chapter of *The Master and Margarita*. It has been noted recently that as early as his novella *Na kuličkax*, Zamyatin uses the image of an aquarium, which reappears in 'Drakon' and the novel *We* in a metonymic form (Andrews et al. 1994: 48): 'Человечьи кусочки плавали, двигались, существовали в рыжем тумане ... как рыбы в стеклянной клетке какого-то бредового аквариума.' (Human pieces are swimming, moving, existing in the red fog ... like fish in the glass cage of some sort of crazy aquarium [Zamyatin [1913] 1989, ch. 7]); 'Из бредового, туманного мира выныривали в земной мир драконо-люди, изрыгали туман ... – белые, круглые дымки, выныривали и тонули в тумане.' (From the insane, foggy world dragon people emerged onto the earth world and burped fog – white, round puffs of smoke; they emerged and disappeared into the fog ['Drakon']).[10]

The disjointed worlds of Zamyatin's 'Drakon' are isolated in the image of an *antiworld*. When Berlioz and Bezdomnyj are speaking with Woland in chapter 3 of *The Master and Margarita*, they are sitting on a side of the Patriarch Ponds that no longer exists in the *real world*; rather, they find themselves in a different type of 'antiworld' (на всех трёх сторонах квадрата, кроме той, где были наши собеседники – 'on all three sides of the rectangle except for the one where our interlocutors were'). Here the aquariumlike space extends beyond the pond itself and consumes Bulgakov's characters as they become a part of an underworld where squares have a total of three sides, not four. The three-sided square is also connected with theatrical textual space (Lotman 1992b: I. 414–15). Yet, Bulgakov's worlds are not as numerous, nor do they bear the clarity of boundaries found in Zamyatin's 'Drakon.' This difference in representation has a significant effect on how movement is textually constructed by the two authors.

In terms of textual structure, Bulgakov and Zamyatin share an important verbal pattern. Specifically, the predominance of *nu*-suffixed semelfactive perfective verbs in the final passages of each text presents a striking pattern (see table 6.5). Both authors use these verbs to show movement in textual space, focusing especially on the movement of the tram and the accompanying characteristics of sound.

Table 6.5

'Drakon'	The Master and Margarita
trepyx**nul**s'a *flutter*	vskrik**nul** *shout*
dryg**nul** *jerk*	rva**nul**a *jerk*
sporx**nul** *flutter away*	podpryg**nul** *jump up*
zaxlop**nul**is' *slam*	krik**nul** *shout*
	mel'k**nul**a *flash*

In this manner, Bulgakov extends and develops Zamyatin's initial view on the Revolution and provides his own answer to the 'unknown' referred to by Zamyatin. No longer is there any doubt about the outcome of the Revolution. For Bulgakov, the uncontrollable Revolution, led by the communists along a new path, has come to a crashing halt, resulting in death and destruction.[10] Perhaps the 'seventh proof' (the title of chapter 3 of *The Master and Margarita*) of the existence of God, which is discussed in the first three chapters of the novel, is not simply Woland's (or Satan's) existence, nor is it merely the death of Berlioz; rather, it may be the seventh of November – the day of the Revolution – as well.

Lotman has noted the importance of the formal construction of semiotic space in the artistic text, a space in which 'roads' and 'paths' (дорога, путь) play an important role (1992a: I. 417, 445):

> The artistic symbol of the road forbids motion in that direction where space is limited ('go off the track'), and the naturalness of motion where a similar boundary is absent ... There, artistic space becomes a formal system for the construction of various, including ethical, models ... Until now we have used the concepts of дорога and путь as synonyms. It is now time to differentiate them. Дорога is a specific type of artistic space, while путь is the motion of a literary character within that space. Путь is the realization (complete or incomplete) or the non-realization of the дорога.

In the context of Bulgakov's last novel, we have already drawn the parallel between a triadic relationship between different types of *paths* and the construction of the opposition home-antihome-homelessness in chapter 5. In comparing Bulgakov's *The Master and Margarita* with Zamyatin's 'Drakon,' we find once again the salience of the road as a means of constructing continuous semiotic spaces between and among discrete artistic texts. In this particular instance, Zamyatin's infinite, unending, and seemingly *unevaluated path* that leads to the unknown becomes Bulgakov's finite end of the road, culminating in death and destruction for all those who cross it. (Using Lotman's definition of road in the context of nineteenth-century Russian literature – and in particular the works of Gogol' – one might argue that we find the same mark of foreboding [запрет] in Zamyatin's text where the movement is 'off the track' [cf. 'Drakon': Это было уже в соскочившем, несущемся мире ... 'That was already in the world that was rushing along off the tracks']).

There is, however, a deeper relationship between the Bulgakov and Zamyatin texts, reflected in the construction and deconstruction of artistic space. This relationship is revealed when we apply Lotman's categories of artistic space. At the beginning of 'Drakon,' Zamyatin constructs a complex form of linear and planar spaces that ultimately disintegrates into chaos. This chaos is a result of the incessant movement of the characters in diametrically opposed directions to different worlds. Zamyatin calls these seven worlds the 'earth world,' 'delirious, foggy world,' 'off-the-track, rushing by world,' 'human world,' 'humane world,' 'Kingdom of Heaven,' and 'unknown world' (земной мир, бредовый, туманный мир, соскочивший, несущийся мир, человечий мир, человеческий мир, Царствие Небесное, неизвестное). The directionality of movement ('left, right, up, down') is schematized by Zamyatin in the story's third sentence. From there, we have a coordinate system in which to place all subsequent motion in 'Drakon.' (Thus, the dragon people move *up* from the delirious, foggy world into the earth world. From the earth world, the tram and the dragon people move *forward* into the 'unknown,' while sending human dweller *up* to the kingdom of heaven. When the dragon responds to save the sparrow, he moves *back* to the human world. In the end, the dragon turns his back on the humane world and moves *forward* into the unknown. Note that the human and humane worlds are on parallel x-axes that continue on, resulting in the parallel coordinates of the earth and off-the-track, rushing worlds, and ultimately infinity.) As Zamyatin maps out the characters' movements to these different worlds, thus creating a series of discontinuities, his artistic space falls apart and turns into what Lotman calls 'fragmented non-space' (раздробленное не-пространство) (1992b: I. 433). (There is a breakdown of sight and sound in the text [as forms of communication] of 'Drakon' between the multiple worlds. This is an example of how discontinuity can lead to 'non-space.')[11] By resorting to *inversion* and *extension* of the images provided in Zamyatin's 'Drakon,' Bulgakov, in chapter 3 of *The Master and Margarita*, reconstitutes Zamyatin's fragmented non-space as a new, continuous space.

Atemporal Reflections

The first version of *The Master and Margarita* (written in the summer of 1928) opens with the following: 'В час заката на крайней скамейке на Патриарших прудах ...' (At the hour of sunset on a far corner bench at Patriarch Ponds ...) (Čudakova 1988a: 300). The final version, as published in 1966, reads: 'Однажды весною , в час небывало жаркого заката ... когда солнце, раскалив Москву, в сухом тумане валилось куда-то за Садовое кольцо ...' (One spring, at the hour of an impossible hot sunset ... when the sun, having baked Moscow, in a dry fog rolled somewhere beyond the Garden Ring ...) (1978: 423–4). The additions to the final version of the novel, a version begun in 1932 in Leningrad, reflect a interesting doubling of lexemes and images used in the third line of 'Drakon': 'Горячечное, небывалое, ледяное солнце в тумане – слева, справа, вверху, внизу – голубь над загоревшимся домом.' (A fevered, impossible, icy sun in the fog – to the left, to the right, above, below – a dove over a house on fire [Zamyatin 1966: 70]). The two significant images in this passage are related to the word небывало(е), which can be translated as 'impossible' or 'imaginary' but literally refers to something that cannot normally happen. This highlights the extraordinariness of the day being described, as well as the phrase 'солнце в тумане' (sun in the fog), demonstrating the day's fuzzy, dreamlike quality.

It is impossible to prove that Bulgakov's addition of the phrase небывало жаркого to the beginning of his novel was an intentional connector to 'Drakon.' However, the ending of *The Master and Margarita* also seems to reconnect with the third line of 'Drakon': 'Тогда луна начинает неистовствовать, она обрушивает потоки света прямо на Ивана, она разбрызгивает свет во все стороны, в комнате начинается лунное наводнение ...' (Then the moon begins to rave, it brings down streams of light directly on Ivan, it splashes light in all directions and a moon-flood begins in the room) (Bulgakov 1978: 812). Here one finds a direct reference to all four directions, reiterating the light imagery and directionality found in Zamyatin (слева, справа, вверху, внизу). For Bulgakov, sunlight has turned to moonlight, and day to night, and the revolution has ended – for now. Zamyatin, the heretic revolutionary and former Bolshevik, has passed away. Bulgakov, dying, has finished the manuscript he once destroyed and never expected to be permitted to publish. Entropy has returned, but only until the next full moon, for as Zamyatin reminds us, 'there is no final revolution' ([1923] 1988: 516).

I have attempted to demonstrate some of the ways in which discrete texts can interact with each other on a variety of levels, incorporating both 'textual' and 'extratextual' information. As a result of such an interactive schema, one becomes more focused on the dynamic disposition of the text itself, and on how complex a matter it is to determine the constructable boundaries of a given text or texts.

One of the significant aspects of the textual interrelationship between Bulgakov and Zamyatin is Bulgakov's fulfilment of Zamyatin's prophesy concerning the future of the 'new synthetic art' in Russian literature. Zamyatin prescribed the following criteria: 'Movement away from realism and everyday life; fast paced, fantastic topic, deepening of symbolism and colors ...; ... the artistic organism [i.e. the writer] is experiencing the growth of elements of philosophy, and widely generalized conclusions' (1988b: 509, 518). The removal of Zamyatin's 'Drakon' from Soviet literature did not succeed in silencing the text. In *The Master and Margarita*, one finds the embodiment and extension of Zamyatin's philosophy of literature, as well as his artistic space and text. Yet again, the reader is reminded that 'manuscripts don't burn.'

Construction and Intention in the Artistic Text

The theoretical implications of the diachronically determined interrelatedness of Zamyatin's 'Drakon' and Bulgakov's *The Master and Margarita* make a statement about the nature of the literary text as a semiotically determined culture text. Inherent in my discussion of the text is the question of textual boundaries or lack thereof. We have already considered the construction of the artistic texts and their corresponding textual spaces and directionality in Lotman's work on semiotic space. For Lotman, the artistic text is both bounded and unbounded, depending on its coincidental points and planes with other semiotic spaces within a particular semiosphere. Furthermore, Lotman emphasizes the atemporal nature of temporally given phenomena and images in cultural memory such that 'the past contained in it [i.e., culture] does not "depart into the past" as in the natural flow of time; ... it becomes fixed in cultural memory, and acquires a permanent, if background, presence ... The memory of a culture is constructed not only as a store of texts, but as a certain mechanism for their generation ... a mechanism that works against natural time' (Lotman and Uspenskij [1977] 1985: 65).

For Julia Kristeva, as noted earlier, any reading of a text is necessarily a rewriting; this implies a text that is open and unbounded. The unboundedness of the text is a fundamental part of Kristeva's notion of intertextuality. In fact, the concept of the boundless text is generally prevalent in deconstructionism (cf. Jacques Derrida's characterization of *le texte general*, which incorporates the notion of history as a boundless phenomenon [Derrida 1973: 310]). However, to avoid implying a 'study of sources,' Kristeva moves away from the term intertextuality in favour of the term *transposition* (Kristeva 1986: 111). There are two alternatives to the definition of text as unbounded: (1) if the text is not closed, then it is open; and (2) the text is both open and closed. Medvedev espouses the first view, emphasizing the error in viewing a work of art as a 'closed-off unity' (Medvedev and Bakhtin 1985: 23–30, 45). In Medvedev's view, the European formalists require that every attempt at textual interpretation somehow be related to authorial intentionality (ibid.: 47). Medvedev's alternative is to present an outline of a theory of literary analysis that unites literary history with sociological poetics (ibid.: 30–6) where 'poetic language' is seen as a purely social phenomenon and the text is seen as having specific ideological structures that both 'refract' and 'reflect' a range of spheres (from socioeconomics to epistemology [ibid.: 16]). Such a definition displaces any notion of authorial intentionality in any form. I would argue that a semiotic approach to textual analysis would not allow intentionality to become the goal of interpretation. Nor would it imply that intentionality be part of the *method* of analysis. But such an approach does not exclude the category itself.

Here again, Lotman offers a different and more complex perspective that requires a new definition of authorial intention. If authorial intention is only actualized in the creation of the artistic space of the text, then any such realization is determined first and foremost by the author's modelling system and by the languages and codes of the culture at a particular synchronic point on the space-time continuum. We have already shown that the author does not dominate the creation of artistic space – he or she is only one of many creators. This fact becomes even clearer when we recall that any artistic space is only partially captured by a given artistic text (cf. the case in which an author develops her/his model of the world in a number of discrete texts). Ultimately, as all *linear, planar*, and *voluminous* (объёмный) spaces are permeated by directionality and never designated unambiguously as one type or another, then as the text moves up the hierarchy of complexity, it is more likely to be perceived as a by-product of this organization of textual types – namely, a metatext (1992b: I. 206–7, 414–17). The literature of a particular culture will always self-select a subgroup of its artistic texts as metatexts. The most likely candidates for this role are usually the more abstract exemplars that propagate a perpetual tension and conflict in their dynamic unfolding within the act of transmission (see chapters 3 and 4).

The question of whether textual boundaries exist is intimately connected to a more general issue: the interrelation of continuity and discontinuity in a semiotic system. In Peircean and Lotmanian semiotic theory, continuity is fundamental and can only be resolved if there is agreement that a system exists and that within this system there exist perceivable structures. If we accept the definition of text as dynamic structure, or dynamic substructure, then we cannot disregard the boundaries of the text. However, only through discontinuities can we discriminate between semiotic structures. Thus, the structure itself may be continuous in nature, but there will be obligatory membranelike boundaries, or discontinuities, that serve to separate one structure from other structures. It follows that the text can be defined as a relatively autonomous system, where the boundaries are of the nature of discontinuities, allowing for dynamic inflows and outflows (to use Thom's terms). Such a definition implies a synthetic answer on the nature of the text – it is both open and closed.

In defining the literary text in this way, we are no longer obliged to discuss intertextual versus extratextual elements; rather, all the 'extratextual indices' (Corti 1978: 21) (including reader, addressee, and biographical aspects of the author) can be recognized as part of the constructive function of the text itself. Therefore, our definition of a text is necessarily semiotic and implies that the text is a relatively autonomous dynamic subsystem whose potential for multiple functioning is only realized through interaction – interaction with the author, the reader, the addressee, and the social, historical, and cultural space, all of these being parts of the literary *context* and basic to the production of cultural meaning (as described in chapters 2 and 3). In other words, it must be properly embedded in the relevant semiospheric cultural space.

It is the interaction of the semiotically defined system of literary signs, a system that is more narrowly and incisively circumscribed in the development of Russian and Soviet literature, that makes this literature unique. This tradition of continuity in succession in Russian literature has a sociohistorical basis that was, to a large extent, connected to the need to preserve intensely intimate links between works due to censorship – a problem not of the Soviet period alone but of Imperial Russia as well. Because literature was linked in this way, many works that were formally erased from Russian and Soviet literary history survived. Not only that, but the very same 'elements of philosophy, the broad, generalized conclusions' spoken of by Zamyatin played and continue to play a significant role in the progression of Russian literature. In the Soviet context, the axis of *rewriting* has been interpolated from the generic reader-text axis to a *cultural order-text axis*, where the primary interaction has moved away from the reader as an individual, representative of his or her cultural milieu, to a monolithic authority refracting and resplicing information crucial to textual structure and its interpretation. Thus, I would argue that the relevance of the re-establishment of the lost continuity of Soviet literary texts, and their inherent intertextuality, is assigned an entirely different *value* by pre- and post-Soviet Russian readers than by those outside the Russian/Soviet cultural system.

CHAPTER SEVEN

Extending Lotmanian Theory

Lotman has argued, and I think convincingly, that the author of a literary text does not dominate the creation of artistic space – that person is but one of many creators. This shared creativity springs from the unique position that such a text occupies as a 'self-organizing mechanism' that 'repeats the general principles of the culture's organization' (Lotman 1992b: I. 206). Furthermore, any artistic space is only partially captured by a given artistic text (cf. the case in which an author develops her/his model of the world in a number of discrete texts). We have already seen that *linear, planar,* and *voluminous* (объёмный) artistic spaces are permeated by directionality and never designated unambiguously as one type or another. As the text moves up the hierarchy of complexity and abstraction, it is more likely to be perceived as a *metatext* (1992b: I. 207). The literature of a particular culture will always self-select a subgroup of its artistic texts as metatexts. The most likely candidates for this are usually the more abstract exemplars, which propagate a perpetual tension and conflict in their dynamic unfolding. In some instances a text may be selected as a metatext beyond its geographic and temporal cultural context.

The novel *We* is Zamyatin's best-known work. It is also one of the exemplars of twentieth-century world literature. Perhaps because of its contribution to the genre of anti-utopian literature, this work has been extensively discussed over the past sixty years, mainly in the West. It is interesting that even though his works reappeared on the Soviet scene in 1986 with the publication of selected 'tales' in *Literaturnaja Rossija* (no. 52 [26 December]: 19), as well as a collection of novellas (повести) and other short stories, Zamyatin still has not taken his appropriate place in Russian scholarship.[1] He is gradually being invited into the canon of twentieth-century Russian literature, but it is not clear that he is being revisited in terms of the actual depth and breadth of his contribution, not only to individual writers but also to entire movements in the literary and visual arts. At first glance, it is strange that Lotman never wrote about Zamyatin, given their theoretical affinities. This may be because Zamyatin was not published in the Soviet Union for more than fifty years.

One of the more notable textual questions relating to *We* is Zamyatin's prolific use of mathematical formulae, numerical equations, numerals as names, and references to specific mathematicians, and of rich colour imagery. In those critical works which note these aspects of the text, the conclusion is generally drawn that these references are part of the fabric of creating the sense of the fantastic (see Cooke 1988, C. Proffer 1988, White [1966] 1988). I want to argue for a new interpretation of the use of mathematics as mathematical text and numerical text in the fabric of *We*.[2] With the assistance of metatheoretical principles articulated by Lotman in his later works on cultural space and the semiosphere, I hope to demonstrate that Zamyatin was not using mathematics or numerals as imagery or abstract commentary; rather, he was creating distinct types of texts that, when woven together, produced a truly synthetic (Zamyatin's term was синтетический) supertext demonstrating the world view to which he was committed.[3] These texts exist in four primary varieties: verbal, mathematical, numerical, and colour. I will analyse only the first three, to demonstrate that the novel's non-verbal texts conform to a general notion of text definition so that they are more than merely metaphors or abstract points of view, and more than a group of non-integrated symbols.[4] I believe I can demonstrate that one of the fundamental reasons *We* has remained such a powerful phenomenon in world literature relates to Zamyatin's ability to craft a culturally viable model (or even metatext) by creating not merely a text but a fully dynamic, heterogeneous semiotic space. In order to properly contextualize the present analysis, I will consider first the similarities between Zamyatin's and Lotman's views on Russian literature and culture.

Zamyatin and Heresy

In many ways, Zamyatin's notion of heresy and explosion, as explicated in his critical essays and fictional works, parallels the Lotmanian model presented in the preceding chapters. Lotman's theory of the semiosphere is preoccupied with cultural spaces (as opposed to biological/physical spaces) at a multiplicity of levels, including the plane of artistic texts (especially verbal and visual art forms); in contrast, Zamyatin's remarks are more restricted to the sphere of the development of the arts in terms of cultural spaces (Zamyatin 1988a: IV. 282–90) and also more preoccupied with the laws of physics, mathematics, and thermodynamics in the physical universe at a philosophical level and their more general application to culture in the sense of a synthetic model of progress and change (1988a: IV. 291–9). The textual content that guarantees the potentiality of explosion is at the heart of Zamyatin's philosophy of heresy (1988b: 407): 'The world is alive only through heretics: Christ the heretic, Copernicus the heretic, Tolstoj the heretic. Our symbol of faith is heresy: tomorrow is most certainly heresy for today, which has turned into a pillar of salt, for yesterday, which has disintegrated into dust. Today negates yesterday, but tomorrow is the negation of negation.'

Lotman's notion of cultural *explosion* has been considered in detail in the context of the semiosphere. Zamyatin's version of the explosion is equally interesting in its fictional and non-fictional verbal manifestations. In his 1928 essay 'For the Collection about My Book' (Для сборника о книге) (1988a: IV. 298), Zamyatin writes that his books are of the same chemical makeup as dynamite, with one major difference: a stick of dynamite will only explode once, whereas a single book will explode an endless number of times (298). He takes this point further in his embodiment of the exploding text in 'The Story about the Most Important Thing' (Рассказ о самом главном) (1924), in which the worm *Rhopalocera* (Zamyatin's neologism, formed from Greek and Latin roots) represents a stick of dynamite about to explode.[5] In *We*, which Zamyatin characterized in his autobiography of 1922 as his 'most jocular and most serious' work (самая моя шуточная и самая серьёзная вещь) (1988a: III 14), we find textual explosions in a variety of guises, including revolution, executions, and lobotomies.

The Synthetic Texts in *We*

Zamyatin created highly synthesized texts in all his works. However, *We* is an extraordinary example of the level of density that is achievable if the textual material is sufficiently heterogeneous: it includes a variety of texts, including the mathematical, numerical, verbal and colour texts mentioned earlier. Using Lotman's definition of text (i.e., text is a sign-based construct realized by means of a variety of symbolic systems [e.g., language, rituals, visual arts, etc.] that characterize structure, including metalanguage that assigns values to cultural categories, or place an activity of the individual in his/her surroundings), I will show that Zamyatin's texts fulfil this broader definition. Let me begin with the numerical and mathematical.[6]

Numerical Texts

Any text is a generator of meaning, and all texts require at least a communicative context such that there is a code, a message, a context, an addresser, an addressee, and contact (using Jakobson's terms as Lotman does). It follows that we can begin our discussion of Zamyatin's numerical and mathematical texts as examples of texts embedded in another verbal text, or of texts as codes referring to external phenomena beyond the verbal text itself. I believe that both approaches are relevant and that, in fact, Zamyatin demonstrates both. In the first instance, we would need to show that the numerical and mathematical texts intersect and include (or are included in) the verbal text of *We*. In the second case, we would inspect these texts for mappings onto spaces not necessarily embodied in the novel itself. These spaces could be other literary texts, extratextual spaces, and other culture texts (i.e., historical, mythological cultural spaces, including Zamyatin's contemporary sociopoliticocultural space of Petrograd in 1918–20).

Most critical discussions have noted that *We* is permeated with numerals and mathematical references (cf. C. Proffer 1988; Cooke 1988; White [1966] 1988; Heller 1994: 78–96). However, these elements have been treated as abstractions, the forms of which can be interpreted for their graphic value or for symbolic reference to a machinelike futuristic society. In fact, one can argue that these elements form coherent, synthetic texts that are central to the novel's overall shape (Andrews, Lahusen, and Maksimova 1994: 13–103).

When considering the numerical aspects of *We*, we notice immediately that the characters are assigned alphanumeric combinations instead of names: D-503, R-13, S-4711, O-90, 1-330.[7] Furthermore, a series of numbers are used throughout the text to refer to a variety of situations and places – for example, 59, 50, 40, 200, 13, 112, 48.

Many attempts have been made to make sense of the alphanumeric 'names' in Zamyatin's novel. Early critical works noticed the even-odd alternation between female and male characters, but that was the extent of their findings (see Cooke 1988, C. Proffer 1988). When we apply principles of number theory, the Fundamental Theorem of Arithmetic, and basic formulae for geometric figures, the following relationships became apparent:

1. 503 and 13 are prime numbers. 13 is the sixth prime number and 503 is the ninety-sixth prime number. Furthermore, 13 is not merely a prime number, but a *twin prime* (простое число-близнец). R-13 and D-503 are often juxtaposed to each other in the novel as mirror images. Recall that R-13 is characterized as 'having a minus sign.' If we then combine the ninety-sixth and sixth primes (where R-13, as the sixth prime, bears a minus), we get 96 − 6 = 90 − the numerical name of O-90, who is the third member of their love triangle.
2. According to the Fundamental Theorem of Arithmetic, all non-prime numbers can be broken down into their component, prime parts. This means the female characters O-90 and I-330, who are non-primes, can be expressed in terms of a series of prime numbers such that:

    $90 = 2 \times 3 \times 5 \times \mathbf{3}$

    $330 = 2 \times 3 \times 5 \times \mathbf{11}$

    These two numerals differ in only one prime − 3 versus 11. If we take the number at the end of the male characters' names, we see O-90 associated by virtue of the prime number 3, with both D-503 and R-1**3**. Likewise, the character I-330 is associated with S-47**11**. These numerical expressions provide the starting point of the relationship between the main characters of the novel. The numerical text reveals this information before the verbal text does, which denotes the difference in speed between the two textual levels.
3. If we use the Euclidean principle of unlimited prime numbers, we can also imagine S-4711 as the sum of the parts of the numeral itself, yielding 4 + 7 + 1 + 1 = 13. Here, we see from the very beginning of the numerical text that R-13 is related to or involved with S-4711. Their relationship is only revealed in chapter 16 of the novel (Andrews et al. 1994: 19–20). We can also consider other numerical names as the sum of their parts, to arrive at the following relationship, in harmony with the letter names:

Extending Lotmanian Theory 117

D-503: 5 + 0 + 3 = 8

R-13: 1 + 3 = 4

D = 2R is the formula for the diameter of a circle (O); given this, we find that if D = 8 and R = 4, then 8 = 2 × 4, which is a valid equation that reiterates the relationship between D, R, and O. In one instance, they are in a triangular relationship, and in the other, a circular one (Andrews et al. 1994: 27–8).

From these examples, we see that the numerical text of *We* retells the verbal narrative of the novel but at a different *speed*. The reader is provided information about the narrative at different levels of intensity and speed in the numerical, mathematical, and verbal texts, in such a way that both the numerical and mathematical texts register information about character interaction much sooner than the verbal text, and in larger chunks. (Lotman's description of the interactions within semiospheric space [see chapters 3 and 4] is very similar to the type of textual interactions I have noted here.)

This discussion is only a small piece of the overall narrative of the numerical text, which concerns not only the names of characters, but also geometric figures. For example 'Cube Square' [Площадь Куба], the phrase that starts the second paragraph of chapter 9 of the novel and refers to a public square (like Time Square), is also the Russian name for the formula $S = 6A^2$. If we insert the number given by Zamyatin directly following the phrase 'cube square,' namely 66, into the formula for the area of a cube, we get $S = 6(66)^2$, which echoes the biblical number of the Antichrist, 666. This diabolic number appears yet again under the guise of a fraction in chapter 4 concerning the probability of ending up again in the same auditorium $112 - 1,500/10,000,000 = 3/20,000 = 1/6666.6666$).[8] Zamyatin only reduces the fraction to 3/20,000 – it is up to the reader to finish the equation. This principle of textual construction and active reader participation is clearly articulated by Zamyatin in his article 'Zakulisy' ([1929] 1988: 469–70):

> Сегодняшний читатель и зритель сумеет договорить картину, дорисовать слова – и им самим договоренное, дорисованное – будет врезано в него неизмеримо прочнее, врастет в него органически.

(Today's reader and viewer are able to articulate the picture, draw the words – and that which they finish articulating and drawing themselves will be engraved in their memory immeasurably more powerfully; it will become an organic part of their being.)

Zamyatin's principle of textual construction requires the reader to participate actively in the dynamic evolution of the narrative in order to imbue the text with meanings. Most of these mappings of meanings will be polysemic. If the reader fails to take the challenge, the narrative *slows down* and becomes less synthetic and voluminous, as well as more linear.

With regard to the other numerical values used throughout the text, I suggest that each can be mapped onto extratextual space that either is geographically given or that somehow relates to the author's context at that time. To take an example, consider that the number 59 is used in chapter 17 as the x-axis, Prospect 59, which leads to the beginning of the coordinate system. If the x-axis is the horizontal axis, geographically speaking it would be latitudinal, and D-503 claims he is located there. The city of Petrograd (now Saint Petersburg) is located at latitude 59 (more precisely 59°57′). When we recall that Zamyatin was an engineer who built ships (icebreakers to be exact), it should not surprise us that he made numerical references to geographic coordinates.

Another example of numerical mappings on extratextual space is the use of 112, the number of the auditorium where D-503, by a twist of fate, ends up twice (see chapter 4). The descriptions throughout the novel of this 'auditorium,' mentioned for the last time in chapter 40, evoke the image of prison. Zamyatin was imprisoned twice in Shpalernaya Prison in Saint Petersburg/Petrograd. As he notes in his autobiography of 1924, he ended up in the same 'gallery' twice – initially as a Bolshevik, and the second time as an anti-Bolshevik. Boni and Boni, in their book on Russian prisons (1925: 90), tell us that during the early years after the Russian Revolution, Shpalernaya Prison held exactly 112 places for male political prisoners.[9]

Mathematical Texts

Zamyatin's mathematical text is built on a rich system of carefully developed principles involving geometry and calculus. He uses a series of Euclidean geometric figures, principles, and formulae from Euclidean and non-Euclidean geometries, as well as implicit functions, imaginary and irrational numbers, Taylor and MacLaurin series, and integrals. He deftly connects and deepens the content and form of his novel by weaving into the verbal text multiple layers of important mathematical equations. Beyond this, it is the 'Integral' itself that is the central, unifying image of the novel.

THE INTEGRAL

The *Integral* is one of the most synthetic images to be found in *We*, and perhaps one of the most synthetic images in twentieth-century Russian literature. To understand this concept merely as a play on words, or as a spaceship designed to spread the Single State's *final revolution* to the universe, would diminish its force as the central image of *We*. We meet the *Integral* at the very beginning of the novel (Zamyatin 1989b: 549): 'Через 120 дней заканчивается постройка Интеграла. Близок великий, исторический час, когда первый Интеграл взовьется в мировое пространство' (The building of the *Integral* will be complete in 120 days. The great historical hour when the first Integral rises up into world space is very close). In the course of the text, D-503 refers to the *Integral* a total of 19 times (cf. chapters 1 [6 times], 2 [2 times], 10 [1 time], 15 [1 time], 16 [1 time], 17 [1 time], 27 [2 times], 34 [1 time], 36 [4 times]). In most of these cases (14 to be exact) the word *Integral* follows some form of the word 'build' – most frequently references to D-503, one of the main builders of the *Integral* (строитель 'builder,' строить(ся) 'to build,' постройка 'building of').

We know that Zamyatin was an engineer who built icebreakers and that he oversaw the building of the *Alexander Nevsky* (later renamed after *Lenin*) in England (1916–18). Verbal descriptions of the *Integral* spaceship are very similar to descriptions of the kinds of ships Zamyatin built (cf. his article 'About My Wives, Ice Breakers and Russia' О моих жёнах, о ледоколах и о России [1921] 1989: 548–53). Yet it is clear that this central image fits predominantly into the mathematical text of the novel. By following and building the *Integral*, the reader can achieve a deeper reading of the novel's other texts, for the concept of the 'integral' is key to what in English mathematics is called *calculus* (in Russian the term is высшая математика 'higher mathematics').

DEFINITE AND INDEFINITE INTEGRALS

At the beginning of the novel, Zamyatin constructs for the reader a *definite integral*, generally given in textbooks as

$$\int_a^b f(x)\ dx,$$

with all the necessary pieces (via the main characters), and with a specific goal articulated in the verbal text:

1. Boundaries: 0 and 1
2. The integral itself: ∫ (Recall that all references to the character S-4711 refer to him as 'like an S' or 'similar to an S' [see chapters 2, 3, 25, and 32].)
3. The differential: $\mathcal{D}$ [D or D/d]
4. In chapter 1 of the novel, D-503 states that the goal of the *Integral* (space ship) is to 'straighten out the wild curve.'

When we combine these four characteristics, then we have the pieces that are consistent with the textbook definition of a definite integral in calculus (except for some mention of a function):

$$\int_a^b f(x)\ dx$$

Note that the letter *d* of the integral is written as Δ in both the English and Russian mathematical representations of the definite integral as a series, namely

$$\int_a^b f(x)\ dx = \lim_{\|S\| \to 0} \sum_{i=1}^n f(x_i^*)\ \Delta x_i)$$

A definition of integration for laypeople would include one or both of the following: (1) a numerical expression of the area under a curve; (2) a summation or value that consists of a series of infinitely small segments (i.e., segments of infinitesimal magnitude).

It is important to note that the function to be integrated is never explicitly defined by Zamyatin. The only mention of a *function* is found in chapter 37 (1989b: 672–3):

На талонах мелькнуло совершенно незнакомое мне имя. Цифр я не запомнил – только букву, Ф ... на полу в её комнате затоптанные розовые талоны, и на одном: буква Ф и какие-то цифры ... Во мне они – сцепились в один клубок, и я даже сейчас не могу сказать, что это было за чувство ...

(A completely familiar name flashed on the coupons. I didn't memorize the numbers – only the letter: F ... on the floor in her room, trampled rose-coloured coupons and on one of them: the letter F and some numbers ... they latched together into a single lump within me, and I can't even say now what kind of feeling that I was experiencing ...)

Other mentions of the word *function* are in the context of 'implicit functions' (неявная функция – 'In every joke of an implicit function there is a lie' [во всякую шутку неявной функцией входит ложь]) (1989b: 556; cf. also chapters 7 and 12 of the novel).

The lack of definition of the function to be integrated is noted again toward the end of the novel. In his essay 'On Literature, Revolution, and Entropy' ([1923b] 1988: 446–7), Zamyatin refers to this issue in slightly different terms: at some point in the future we will know the exact 'formula' for revolution (we do not know it yet) and it will involve 'numerical values.' This characterization fits also nicely with the context of *We*, since the value of any definite integral is always a numerical value.

If the integral is non-integrable, it is possible to convert it to a Taylor series with its required (ever-present) remainder, R (expressed mathematically as $R_n[x]$). (The importance of the Taylor series to calculus cannot be overestimated. Although I will discuss the Taylor series separately later on, it will be helpful to state here that the Taylor series makes it possible to integrate functions that previously could not be integrated. The strong mathematical condition states that the function to be integrated must be continuous within each interval of integration, including all possible derivatives.)

By the end of the novel the boundaries of the integral have been destroyed or removed (the death of I-330 and the evacuation of O-90) and the remainder has been eliminated (the death of R-13). Only D-503 and S-4711 remain. This yields an *indefinite integral* with no defined boundaries:

$$\int f(x) \, dx$$

If one were to map an indefinite integral, the result would be a 'family of curves' (семейство кривых) (Šnejder et al. 1978: 228) (see figure 7.1). The *indefinite integral* is also often called the *antiderivative* (Riddle 1974: 184).

Once again, through mathematics, Zamyatin is demonstrating that the goals of the Single State are unachievable – because the individual

122 The Construction of Semiotic Space in Verbal Texts

Figure 7.1

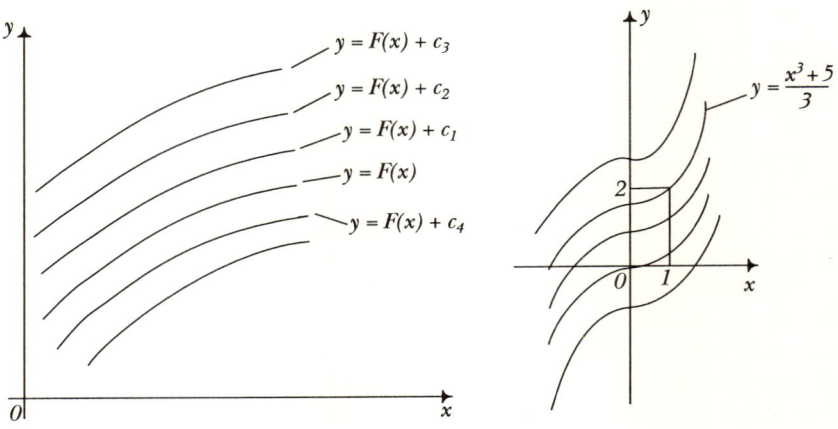

has been destroyed, so too have been destroyed the boundaries of the integral; the geometric result of this is no longer a region of rectangular segments, but rather a series of discontinuous curves. Such a family of curves cannot geometrically cover all the territory required to integrate the universe. At the beginning of the novel there was hope of building the integral; by the end it is mathematically clear that the integral as planned cannot exist – the anti-utopia is, in a sense, the anti-integral. Total integration has become impossible, and the fate of the Single State is doomed to fail. Even if integration of a given function is impossible at first, the Taylor series provides a means of integrating such functions on a term-by-term basis. By destroying individual terms, the Taylor series also becomes dysfunctional and non-resultative. The destruction of R as remainder also makes the potential use of the Taylor series null and void.

At the end of the novel, D-503 states: 'I am certain – we will be victorious. Because reason must win out' (Я уверен – мы победим. Потому что разум должен победить) (1989b: 680). This statement is one of hope. In a world where there *is* a last number (chapter 30 of the novel), where infinity has been negated, where the individual has been destroyed, surely 'reason will be victorious,' not the insanity of the Single State. Note that Zamyatin does not ridicule mathematics as unreasonable; rather, he uses mathematics to achieve a *reasonable* solution, while demonstrating that the leaders of the Single State are misusing mathematics.

There is another aspect of the integral that is also important. Zamyatin has constructed a 'real' integral in the form of a ship/ellipsoid and is utilizing it as the mechanism for bringing together all individuals into a single state. The Single State accepts the integral and is even building a literal embodiment of the integral. However, the philosophy of the Single State creates a paradoxical situation for the *Integral* and integration. Namely, the integration of the universe requires the integral. But the indefinite integral is not a value; rather, it is a family of curves. However, the Single State rejects 'curves' in principle and demands straight lines: '... разогнуть дикую кривую, выпрямить её по касательной – ассимптоте – по прямой. Потому что линия Единого Государства – это прямая. Великая, божественная, точная, мудрая прямая – мудрейшая из линий ...' (... unbend the wild curve, straighten it out along the tangent the asymptote – along the straight line. Because the line of the Single State is straight. The great, divine, exact, wise straight line – the wisest of all lines ...) (1989b: 549).

The rejection of the curve makes the *Integral* superfluous and non-functional in the given context. The *Integral*, then, becomes a paradox as well. The Single State has no need of the indefinite integral that it has created by the end of the novel, since it cannot straighten out curves; all it has achieved is to define families of curves (see figure 7.1).

The Taylor Series

Zamyatin makes repeated reference to Taylor and the Taylor series:

1 Title of Chapter 7: Eyelash. Taylor. Henbane and Lily of the Valley. Ресничный волосок. Тэйлор. Белена и ландыш.
2 'Yes, that Taylor was without a doubt one of the most brilliant of the ancients. It's true that he didn't figure out that he could generalize his method to every aspect of life, to every step, 24 hours a day – he was unable to integrate his system over the full 24 hours. But, nevertheless, how is it that there are entire libraries written about this Kant guy and Taylor is hardly noticed, Taylor the prophet who was able to see ten centuries into the future.' (Да, этот Тэйлор был, несомненно, гениальнейшим из древних. Правда, он не додумался до того, чтобы распространить свой метод на всю жизнь, на каждый шаг, на круглые сутки – он не сумел проинтегрировать своей системы

от часу до 24-х. Но все же: как они могли писать целые библиотеки о каком-нибудь там Канте – и едва замечать Тэйлора – этого пророка, сумевшего заглянуть на десять веков вперед.) (1989b: 567)

3 'I saw it – in Taylor format, measured and quick, in step, like the controls of a huge machine, the people bending and turning below. Their pipes shining in their hands.' (Я видел: по Тэйлору, размеренно быстро, в такт, как рычаги одной огромной машины, нагибались, разгибались, поворачивались люди внизу. В руках у них сверкали трубки.) (1989b: 595)

4 '... and in one and the same second we walk out on our stroll and go into the auditorium, into the hall of Taylor exercises, and go to bed ...' (... и в одну и ту же секунду выходим на прогулку и идём в аудиториум, в зал Тэйлоровских экзерсисов, отходим ко сну ...) (1989b: 555)

5 'Crystal chromatic steps of combining and separating infinite series – and the summation chords of Taylor and Maclaurin's formulas.' (Хрустальные хроматические ступени сходящихся и расходящихся бесконечных рядов – и суммирующие аккорды формул Тэйлора, Маклорена.) (1989b: 558)

6 ' ... chambers of rhythmic Taylor-happiness ...' (... клетки ритмичного тэйлоризованного счастья ...) (1989b: 573)

7 'R – is always the same. According to Taylor and mathematics – he's always at the tail end.' (R – всё тот же. По Тэйлору и математике – он всегда шёл в хвосте.) (1989b: 572)

The reader is repeatedly reminded by D-503 of the value of Taylor and his series. There can be no doubt that these passages refer at least to Brook Taylor, the mathematician, and his work. First of all, the Taylor series is of the utmost importance in integration. Second, the series described is indeed a Taylor series. Finally, the mention of MacLaurin in conjunction with Taylor is one of the strongest confirmations of the source of these references, as the MacLaurin series is a special case of the Taylor series. It is likely that the author of these comments is also alluding to Frederick Taylor, a major figure in the development of optimal systems for engineering human resources. In fact, I would argue that multiple interpretations are valid within this context and that Zamyatin has in mind both Taylors.[10]

What are the more salient aspects of the Taylor series in the context of integral calculus? The Taylor series permits us to integrate functions that

Extending Lotmanian Theory   125

previously could not be integrated, by enabling us to integrate *term by term*. However, the function must be continuous within each interval of integration, including all possible derivatives. This is a *strong mathematical condition*. If the function is discontinuous within the given integral, it cannot be expressed in terms of the Taylor series, which is a *power series*. Zamyatin tells the reader that Taylor himself did not realize the range of application of his own series, where this method would be applied to all of life and to each and every hour of the day ('from one to twenty-four' 1989b: 567). In this statement Zamyatin is telling the reader why the Single State will be unable to integrate the universe, or even itself – it forgot to integrate all twenty-four hours in the day. On several occasions we are reminded that 'personal time' lasts from 16 to 17 (4 to 5 p.m.) and 21 to 22 (9 to 10 p.m.) (1989b: 555). These two time slots have not been integrated into the series and thus represent *discontinuities*, making the series dysfunctional until all twenty-four hours are included. The irony is that Zamyatin is directly pointing out to the reader that the Single State will not be able to implement its vision because there is still 'personal time.' The Great Operation only removes imagination – it is not a complete solution to the ultimate problem of total integration.

The positive outcome of application of the Taylor series for the Single State is the following: the more you integrate each term of the Taylor series, the greater the number of n's (segments integrated) and the less the remainder (R). That is, as the series expands infinitely, the remainder becomes smaller and smaller, moving toward its limit of zero. Note, however, that if R is representative of 'Russian poets' collectively, the implication of applying the Taylor series is that poets will become obliterated as a result of the integration process, just as the imagination is destroyed via the Great Operation.

Decoding of Multiple Texts

When one considers the complexity of Zamyatin's multiple texts and their synthesized integration, one might wonder whether the author ever really intended that his mathematical and numerical texts be decoded (or translated). In his letter to his wife, Zamyatin often used codes (cf. Bučina and Ljubimova 1997: 16–23). He also made stable associations with certain (not all) sounds and letters (e.g., R is loud, bright, red, hot, fast; L is pale, cold, light-blue, light; N is tender, snow, sky, night; D and T are stuffy, heavy, foggy, smelly; M is kind, soft, motherly, sealike;

A is wide, far away, ocean, misty warm air or mirage, breadth of scope; O is high, deep, sealike, natural; I is close, low, pressing [Annenkov 1991: 236]). In each instance, Zamyatin was using coded forms to convey meaning, never to obscure it. These examples, coupled with Zamyatin's avoidance of random, casual images (случайные образы), argue for an aggressive reading of the various and fragmented non-verbal texts that always accompany Zamyatin's verbal texts.[11]

Perhaps the opaqueness of these texts for most twentieth-century readers, Russian or not, is the result of a miscalculation on Zamyatin's part. Since Zamyatin was always anticipating the new curve of the heretical *tomorrow*, especially in terms of literary genres, it is possible that he anticipated a world of readers that had no knowledge of Russian or Soviet culture (even as he wrote his novel, Zamyatin knew that the chances of publication were slim). Being sensitive to the cultural overlay of verbal communication, perhaps he hoped that his message would reach a broader audience that would share, at least, the basic principles of calculus. There was a chance that by relying on the calculus as the basis for one of his texts, he would discover a way of overcoming the language barrier. It would have been reasonable for Zamyatin to hope so, given the importance of calculus in twentieth-century mathematics everwhere in the world. Yet as it turns out, most of Zamyatin's readers are unable to engage with the mathematical and numerical texts.

Zamyatin did not use random elements in his texts; instead, he declared that his goal was to bond multiple space-time images and continua into synthetic superimages that would explode into meaningful form as the reader 'speaks the picture' and 'draws the words' (cf. Zamyatin's articles 'About Synthesism' and 'Backstage'). Considering this, it should not surprise us that a coherent, internally consistent mathematical text weaves into and beyond the other verbal and non-verbal texts of the novel. The answers to the text puzzle are generally multiple and seldom unique; they exist simultaneously on different planes beyond and within the narrative and necessarily support a dynamic, energetic reading. If the answers were necessarily singular, Zamyatin's novel would move rapidly toward entropy, losing its ability for new explosiveness in space-time.

My position regarding a multitextual view of *We* is supported by Zamyatin's articulation of the eternal battle of energy and entropy (1923b) 1988: 446–7:

Революция – всюду, во всем; она бесконечна, последней революции нет, нет последнего числа ... закон революции не социальный, а неизмеримо больше

– космический, универсальный закон – такой же, как закон сохранения энергии, вырождения энергии (энтропии). Когда-нибудь установлена будет точная формула закона революции. И в этой формуле будут числовые величины: нации, классы, звезды – и книги. ... Когда пламенно-кипящая сфера (в науке, религии, социальной жизни, искусстве) остывает, огненная магма покрывается догмой – твердой, окостенелой, неподвижной корой. Догматизация в науке, религии, социальной жизни, в искусстве – это энтропия мысли ...

(Revolution – is everywhere in everything. It is infinite, there is no final revolution, no last numeral ... the law of revolution is not social, but immeasurably larger – a cosmic, universal law – like the law of preservation of energy, the degeneration of energy (entropy). One day there will be an exact formula of revolution. And this formula will have numerical values: nations, classes, stars – and books ... When the flaming, boiling sphere (in science, religion, society, art) cools off, the fiery magma becomes covered in dogma – a hardened, non-dynamic crust. Dogmatization in science, religion, society, and art is entrophy of thought.)

In another essay written in 1923 ('Novaja russkaja proza' 1988a: 268), Zamyatin elaborates that intolerance of multiple artistic philosophies and forms, and the canonization of a particular form in art, is the surest path to entropy and destruction of the art form itself. When a system is believed to have achieved a maximally developed state, then that system moves away from energy and tends toward entropy. Zamyatin urges his readers to battle constantly against entropy, both as readers and as cultural citizens, even if in the end entropy takes over any closed (not open) system for a time – a time that is never unbounded.

As mentioned in chapters 3 and 4 of this work, Lotman makes a very similar point in his definition of entropy and the impact of self-description within the semiosphere (1990: 128–9):

The highest form and final act of a semiotic system's structural organization is when it describes itself. This is the stage when grammars are written, customs and laws codified. When this happens, however, the system gains the advantage of greater structural organization, but loses its inner reserves of indeterminacy, which provide it with flexibility, heightened capacity for information and the potential for dynamic development.

The stage of self-description is a necessary response to the threat of too much diversity within the semiosphere: the system might lose its unity and definition, and disintegrate. Whether we have in mind language, politics or culture, the mechanism is the same: one part of the semiosphere (as a rule one which is part of its nuclear structure) in the process of self-description creates it own grammar; this self-description may be real or ideal depending on whether its inner orientation is towards the present or towards the future. Then it strives to extend these norms over the whole semiosphere ... A list of what 'does not exist,' according to that cultural system, although such things in fact occur, is always essential for making a typological description of that system.

In the end, both Zamyatin and Lotman bring us to the brink of a *boundary*. Whether it be a bounded function, the 'wall' of our cultural-political space, or the boundaries of the semiosphere, these boundaries are always present as dynamic, membranelike structures separating and containing cultural spaces, and act as a summation of 'bilingual translation filters' (Lotman 1992b: I. 13) where what may be 'beyond the boundary or wall' today will return to our cultural space 'tomorrow,' very much like Zamyatin's return to his Russian readership at the end of the twentieth century.

It is precisely the crossing over of internal and external boundaries of multiple, seemingly untranslatable, texts that brings the most profound realizations of new meanings. It may be the very fact that the verbal text seems to be a continuous narration, whereas the other texts are constructed and perceived as fragments or discontinuities that are invading the continuous verbal one, that produces the powerful reaction on the part of the reader. Lotman correctly notes that it is the discontinuities of potentially untranslatable matter that create the most semiotically profound impression on the reader (Lotman 1992b: I. 120–1).

Lotman sums up his conclusions on the source of the power of literary texts and art in his chapter 'The Logic of Explosion' in *Culture and Explosion* (1992: 189):

Искусство расширяет пространство непредсказуемого – пространство информации, одновременно, создает условный мир, экспериментирующий с этим пространством и провозглашающий торжество над ним.

(Art expands the space of the unpredictable – the space of information and, at the same time, creates a hypothetical world that is experimenting with this space and announcing its victory over it.)

It seems that in *We*, Zamyatin unknowingly confirms and restates Lotman's eloquent principle by demonstrating that the artistic culture text can be more than simply a representation of culture. Rather, Zamyatin's text *is* culture. Recalling Lotman's characteristics of artistic space earlier in this chapter, it seems most appropriate to label *We* as a voluminous space. Perhaps it is precisely at what Lotman refers to as the volume-text level that artistic texts begin to merge with more generally determined culture texts, thus manifesting an essential step in their dynamic translation to the metatextual level. Because of its enormous richness of abstraction, its multiple levels, and its fundamentally different rates of information transmission, *We* is a self-selecting candidate for a metatext – a status that has been repeatedly recognized by Soviet censors and readers of many different cultures over the past eighty years. And despite the discontinuities in space-time that separate the semiotic spaces of Zamyatin's novel from his readers, the dynamically given heterogeneous texts of *We* weave an intricate network of signs that culminate in an explosive synthesis of new and familiar cultural forms and meanings at each instance of engagement.

PART THREE

Semiotic Theory as a Cognitive Science

CHAPTER EIGHT

Visual and Auditory Signs in Human Language: Perception and Imagery

It is important to remember that we have no intuitive power of distinguishing between one subjective mode of cognition and another.

Charles Sanders Peirce

Превращение зримого в рассказываемое неизбежно увеличивает степень организованности. Так создаётся текст. (The metamorphosis of the visual into the verbal inevitably increases the degree of organization. This is how texts are created).

Jurij Mixailovič Lotman

Roman Jakobson's article 'On the Relation between Visual and Auditory Signs' articulates and analyses an important set of issues that are central in both the study of semiotics and in imagining technology and neuroscience. Although Jakobson's original study encompassed a wide range of semiotic systems, including language, visual arts, film, and music (all from the anthroposemiotic sphere), I will focus on his conclusions as they relate to linguistic sign systems specifically, and attempt to demonstrate that the structural and perceptual importance of visual signs is no less significant than that of auditory signs in building and maintaining linguistic structures at multiple levels in human language. I will argue for a more interactive relationship between visual and auditory signs in terms of the underlying sign types that necessarily give rise to such a distinction. In my conclusion I will refer to Lotman's work on the question of representational (or pictorial) versus conventional cultural sign texts in the construction of the continuum of the multiple artificial and natural languages that interact in any cultural space.

Jakobson begins his work on visual and auditory signs by stating that the difference between these two sign types lies not in their 'degree of importance' but rather in their 'functional difference' ([1964] 1987: 467). He starts by noting the universality and domination of speech in human language, and the secondary or complementary roles played by visual gestures, reading, and writing (467–8). He qualifies these generalizations in the following way: 'Both visual and auditory perception obviously occur in space and time, but the spatial dimension takes priority for visual signs and the temporal one for auditory signs' (469).

There is no question that spoken language can and does exist in individuals and cultures where there is no equally developed visually based symbolic system. This observation clearly captures the obvious characteristics of communication systems and their production side. Perhaps the structural, coded (significant) side of linguistic signs may demonstrate a relative hierarchical shift in the centrality of visual signs as the individual language user moves from a period of intensive language acquisition to a period of maintenance with marginal growth. In a series of articles and books, Jakobson himself paves the way for entertaining such contingencies by continually pointing out a set of important parameters, including the following: (1) the perceiver's probabilistic disposition in interpreting verbal input (Jakobson and Waugh [1978] 1988: 242); (2) distinct developmental patterns of sensory and motor abilities in perceiving and producing phonemes in speech (ibid.: 251); (3) the difference in the competence of senders and receivers of verbal messages, where the broader competence rests with the receiver ([1972] 1985: 87–8); (4) the importance of the context sensitivity of sound patterns in language (ibid.: 84, 89); and (5) the qualitative changes in an individual's abilities and development of language in terms of his or her temporal evolution ([1977] 1985a: 147).

In an attempt to address the question of semantic coding in linguistic sign systems, I have examined in a series of articles the use of vision categories in the semantic structures of language, using examples from comparative Slavic and contemporary standard Russian (CSR). I will not repeat these findings here; rather, I will summarize certain conclusions related to these analyses as a prelude to presenting some of the more salient features of the functioning human visual cortex in perceiving and analysing visual images into component parts. In doing so, I will challenge Jakobson's claim (1987: 470) that visual images lack oppositional categories similar to those of distinctive features in phonology. I will also reconfirm the Peircean axiom that all meaning – and in particular linguistic meaning – is diagrammatic.[1]

Visual Categories in Semantic Structures

It is generally recognized that language includes semantic fields and lexical items that correspond to some degree to visual categories in exogenous reality (verbs like 'see, observe, watch,' categories of colour, etc.). However, the existence of such categories does not in itself prove that categories of vision, to some degree, organize and reorganize semantic structures in diachrony. In the following section I review some of the potential kinds of vision-related semantic spaces in Slavic and CSR and demonstrate the role they have played in diachronic semantic change. The focal point of the discussion is the importance of visual categories in defining segments of the semantic code in a given synchronic period and determining semantic shifts in diachronic development. Such an argument does not give pre-eminence to vision categories in semantic space, but rather makes an obligatory connection to the underlying guiding principles of iconicity and diagrammatization in defining all semantic space – principles that may overlap to some degree with visually based semantic signs.

In earlier works, I have attempted to demonstrate the systematic structure of diachronic semantic shifts, particularly in the category of vision-based lexemes and verbs of knowing (Andrews 1995b, 1996b). In both these studies I referred to Elizabeth Traugott's work on speech act verbs and epistemic meanings in the historical evolution of English (1989, 1991). Data from Russian support Traugott's findings in English and reinforce what Traugott refers to as 'subjectification' in determining the teleology of semantic shifts in diachrony. To add substance to the present analysis, it would be useful to reconsider some of the relevant data from the historical development of Russian – specifically, the relationship between the lexemes of 'seeing' and 'knowing.'

A distinction between two basic types of 'knowing' is traceable to Indo-European: (a) knowing as fact (*weid– 'see' [perfect *woida 'have seen' > 'know']), and (b) knowing through acquaintance (*ĝenə, *ĝnō–) (Buck 1988: 1,208–9). It is suggested that *weid– yielded a meaning of 'know' in a wide range of languages, including Greek, Germanic, Balto-Slavic, Celtic, and Indo-Iranian, based on the perfect form (Buck 1988: 1,041). Thus, it seems that for many Indo-European languages, the connection between 'seeing' and 'knowing' is the rule rather than an exception. (The relationship between 'seeing' and 'knowing' is not unique to earliest Indo-European; it includes Japanese and some of the languages of Australia and New Guinea [Traugott 1991: 403].) What *is* unique is how each of these descendent languages reinterpreted the relationship between 'knowing' and 'seeing' and expanded the corresponding semantic field.

As early as Common Slavic, a difference in ablaut grade was used to distinguish the lexemes 'knowing' and 'seeing' (cf. Old Church Slavonic and Old Russian – věděti, viděti). In contemporary Russian the verbs 'knowing' and 'seeing' represent a shift to a vowel difference expressible in terms of vowel height; in some cases they also substitute differentiating verbal suffixes to the lexemes in question (cf. *vedat'//videt'/vidat'*). Nonetheless, these two concepts continue to be conceptually related in the Russian speaker's mind – a fact clearly demonstrated by the semantic field of the CSR *ved-* and *vid-* lexical morphemes in word formation, as well as by a large number of proverbs and folk sayings relating the two (Andrews 1995b: 362–70). Simultaneously, modern Russian maintains two verb forms meaning 'know': *vedat'* and *znat'*.

During the period of coexistence of two verbs for 'knowing' in Russian, there has been significant transference of vision-based knowledge to the verbal root that was not etymologically connected to 'seeing.' For example, the verb *uznat'* ('to recognize, find out') clearly indicates a vision category in its meaning 'to recognize' (unless the context prohibits any sort of visual contact – like a phone call), and the verb *oboznat's'a* ('to mistake someone for someone else') almost exclusively refers to visual mistaken identity (e.g., *Izvinite, ja oboznalas'* 'Excuse me, I thought you were someone else'). Reverse semantic transference of this particular type is rather unusual and specifically representative of vision categories. As such, the Russian examples of semantic transference attest to the powerful nature of the association in Russian of knowledge with sight. This includes 'spiritual knowledge' in the guise of confession and profession of faith in verbs with the *ved-* root (e.g., *ispovedovat'/ispovedat'(s'a)*) (Andrews 1995b: 365–6).

Yet Russian demonstrates a similar shift in other vision-related lexemes to confession's alter ego – shame and punishment (cf. *z/r* root: *zret'* 'to see, view,' but *pozorit'* 'to shame,' *pozor* 'shame,' *ozorstvo* 'mischief,' *podozrevat'* 'suspect,' *kaz* root: *kazat'(s'a)* 'show, seem,' *nakazat'* 'punish,' *nakazanie* 'punishment'). It is important to note that a similar semantic shift of the lexemes for 'shame' and 'punishment' is conspicuously missing from the rest of Slavic. The exception is Bulgarian, but here it is highly probable that these forms occur in Bulgarian as a result of borrowing from Russian.[2]

The above data demonstrate that individual language systems experience semantic change over time, and that these changes correspond to vision-based fields of meaning, whether or not these meanings are etymologically codified diachronically.[3] The semantic fields based on spatio-visual categories are *diagrams* of a particular semiotic type (where *diagrams* are one of three iconic subtypes, the other two being *images* and *metaphors* [see Shapiro 1991: 13, 56]). Thus, the evolution of these fields will be driven by a systemic need to reach an even higher degree of *diagrammaticity* (i.e., a greater stability of sign types achieved through inherent similarity). In this instance I would suggest that the need for greater diagrammaticity is driven by perceptual categories that are both neurologically and culturally determined. Thus, the diagrammaticity of any linguistic system is necessarily imperfect, even as it shapes and patterns instantiations of linguistic change from potential to actual (Shapiro 1991: 17, 65–72). In order to pursue such a hypothesis, we will consider the human visual cortex and its relationship to language development and language maintenance.

The Functioning of the Visual Cortex

The human cerebral cortex is divided into four lobes – frontal, parietal, temporal, and occipital. These are determined by the consistent position of certain sulci (or grooves) in the brain. (There is no 'language cortex,' although some neuroscientists are still interested in prospects of a localized language centre in the brain [Calvin and Ojemann 1994: 138, 187–9, 251]). Typical descriptions of the four lobes generally note the following functions: (1) frontal – motor control; (2) parietal – somatosensory and body image; (3) occipital – vision; and (4) temporal – hearing, learning, memory, emotion. It is in the occipital lobe that the primary visual cortex is located. Surrounding part of the primary visual cortex (also called Area 17, striate cortex, OC, and V1) is the secondary visual cortex (also called Area 18). Several aspects of the human visual system are relevant to our discussion of visual and auditory sign perception in the context of language. The underlying hypothesis is as follows: If aspects of language acquisition, language usage, and language change over time are related to and determined by perceptual operations and categories, then understanding the mechanisms of perception and of the storage and retrieval of perceptual information will play a role in elucidating these linguistic phenomena at a fundamental level.[4]

One of the most profound discoveries concerning the functioning of V1 – which is the first cortical area to receive input from the eyes – is that the area is retinotopically mapped and contains multiple representations in any discrete event – that is, spatial structures are literally mapped multiple times in particular layers of area V1 within the first hundred milliseconds after the neuronal firing of convergence zones.[5] This fact has profound implications for questions of diagrammaticity in sign perception because of the iconic structure and retinotopical mappings in parts of V1.[6] It is also important to note that V1 analyses regions of the visual field in units called *hypercolumns* (Kandel et al. 1991: 433). Each hypercolumn contains its own complete set of orientation columns, which allow for perception of placement, orientation, and colour (433). In fact, these hypercolumns parallel in an interesting way the structure of distinctive features in phonology.[7]

Another significant discovery concerning V1 relates to the interrelationship between perception and mental imagery. Kosslyn (1994: 15–16, 53–78) refers to a body of research that argues in favour of a feedback relationship between visual perception and imagery: 'These neuroanatomical features suggested to us that stored visual information might be capable of evoking a pattern of activity in at least some of the retinotopically mapped areas – which would produce a mental image' (1994: 15). In one set of experiments, Kosslyn and his colleagues, using PET scans (positron emission tomography), demonstrated that V1 can be activated in subjects when their eyes are closed and they are imagining how certain alphabet letters look (1994: 17). They also determined that the size of the image affected specific regions of V1: larger objects activated the anterior part of V1, whereas the posterior part of V1 was more active when small sizes were imagined (1994: 18). The experimenters' conclusions support the hypothesis that 'imagery relies on topographically organized regions of cortex, which support depictive representations' (1994: 19). Alternative theories have argued in favour of propositional (i.e., not depictive) representations that specify 'unambiguously the meaning of an assertion' (1994: 5).[8]

Other significant research has raised questions about the nature of visual identification used in the perception of faces and written words. These questions are compounded by studies which support the conclusion that it is inherently more difficult to distinguish visually between animate objects as opposed to inanimate ones (Kosslyn 1994: 64, 113–14; Dudai 1989: 262–4). Some of the reasons postulated for the difference in difficulty are based on curvature and on the similarity of animate objects to one another in contradistinction to inanimate objects. Yet what is perhaps more profound is the conclusion that viewer-oriented representations dominate object-oriented representations (Kosslyn 1994: 127–36). This means that the information encoded in the individual's neural mappings will retain perceptual properties that are defined by the viewer's specific perspective, as opposed to the actual dimensions of the object viewed. The encoding of viewer-centred representations is more complex, but the parameters defining visual memory are sufficiently large that this is not a problem. Furthermore, both the encoded input representations and the subsequent patterns of activation of these representations demonstrate viewer-centred perspectives (128–9). While rejecting extremes, Kosslyn contends that viewer-centred properties in visual representations are typically stored, whereas object-centred properties may also be stored, but as 'routines' (136). One of the most interesting examples of this phenomenon is the viewer-oriented representations found when retinotopic mappings are activated (128).[9] These findings show that the older view of visual perception as operating in a mechanical fashion (like a camera) is no longer valid. Rather, visual perception is transformational (more precisely, semiotic) in nature and requires an evaluation or even re-evaluation of the stimuli being perceived. Finally, the fact that visual imagery and visual perception share 'the same underlying mechanisms' facilitates an understanding of their interactive nature (54–5). This is especially important in the context of the potential interference of visual images in visual perception, where maintenance of a visual image may hinder visual perception. (Kosslyn describes the results of a series of experiments by Craver-Lemley and Reeves where subjects were asked to form visual images [of lines, for example] while deciding about the alignment of other segments. In each of these experiments, the accuracy rate in visual perception diminished by 15 per cent due to the maintenance of visual images.) In this regard, it is interesting that the maintenance of an auditory image *enhances* auditory perception; this is the reverse of what happens in visual perception (55).[10]

My cursory description of the functioning visual cortex, specifically Area 17, presents salient information about the nature of encoding and stored visual perceptions, the coordination of perception and imagery, and the importance of the viewer's unique perspective in the storing of visual stimuli. Visual perception as described above bears interesting parallels to principles of language perception and production in the semiotic framework. We will return to some of these similarities in the conclusion, in which I define more rigorously the importance of visual signs in language.

Language Development and the Absence of Vision

Jakobson identifies 'audible speech' as 'the only universal, autonomous, and fundamental vehicle of communication,' whereas visual signs are either concomitant (e.g., facial expressions, gestures) or substitutive (letters or other written symbols) ([1964] 1987: 467–8). He concludes that 'the universality of music, the fundamental role of speech in human culture, and, finally, a mere reference to the predominance of word and music in radio suffice to prove ... the supremacy of sight over hearing in our cultural life is valid only for indexes or icons and not for symbols' (469). In order to evaluate the importance of visual perception in linguistic symbols, we will consider the question of language acquisition and the problems connected with this phenomenon in blind children. (Note that Jakobson is restricting his reference to human semiotic systems – human language in particular – and is not including non-human species.)

Dunlea (1989: 2) points to the growing evidence that vision is important in 'the emergence of communication,' and to the potential impact of this on blind people's language acquisition and development. Many studies conducted with sighted infants have indicated that visually based strategies play an enormously important role in establishing 'elicited behaviours,' especially those involving specific eye contact (2). Vision and visual signs are important to conceptual development and to establishing referential relationships. It is through such relationships that children are able to abstract from concrete, specific referential names to comprehension and usage of those 'names' on a more general, symbolic level (3).

The congenitally blind child, deprived of visual perception, must learn the world through the remaining senses. Among blind children, touch becomes the primary sense that allows for comprehension of spatial qualities. It is not yet clear whether the haptic representations of the blind share common features with the visual representations of the sighted.[11] In the following discussion I present an overview of some of the language difficulties experienced by blind children. I then contrast these difficulties with those faced by deaf children, and conclude by raising questions about the importance of the visual cortex in imagery and in determining semantic fields.

Blind children often exhibit more difficulties in first language acquisition than their sighted counterparts. These difficulties appear in the realms of phonology, morphology, and semantics. Blind children often stutter. Also, they often have problems learning certain speech articulations (including voicing), and in the initial stages their word production is often delayed (Dunlea 1989: 15–17). In learning to distinguish and produce phonemes, they generally rely more on manner than on place of articulation. This is because they are deprived of the visual similarities involved in articulating specific speech sounds. As such, the acquisition process is somewhat different in terms of its internal hierarchy, and includes different patterns of phonological substitution (Dunlea 1989: 15; Mills 1983; Mills and Thiem 1980). However, these children generally develop normative speech and pronunciation.

Another, perhaps more significant problem arises in the blind child's acquisition of deictic terms. Pronouns and other deictic terms (e.g., demonstratives like 'this' and 'there') are difficult for them to acquire (Dunlea 1989: 16, 18, 46). The reasons for this seem to revolve around the blind child's absence of perspective with respect to the speaker of a given utterance (Dunlea 1989: 18, Mulford 1983).[12] Blind children also demonstrate more errors in self-reference for longer periods of time (Dunlea 1989: 83).

In the realm of semantics and semantic categories, blind children tend to overgeneralize based on categorical grounds, whereas sighted children overgeneralize based on associative complexes (Dunlea 1989: 55). However, underextension is more significant when it comes to differentiating the language of blind and sighted children. In the blind, the semantic space of lexemes is more directly tied to the original context for a longer period of time, with no word mortality (Dunlea 1989: 50, 61–2). In fact, Dunlea points out that blind children often fail to recognize that a word is not part of the referent (1989: 63). If this is true, it seems plausible to characterize this phenomenon as a reduction of the *symbolic* level in the use of language in blind children, accompanied by an increase in the *indexical* level.

Finally, visual-based lexemes are not meaningless in the language of blind children; rather, they have different meanings, which result in a tactic/haptic meaning for verbs such as 'look' and 'see' (Dunlea 1989: 15, 20; Landau and Gleitman 1985).

Deaf children demonstrate high levels of creativity and overextension (both of which are missing in blind children). They also exhibit behaviours more like those of sighted children (Dunlea 1989: 64–5). Information of this nature has often been missing or overlooked in studies comparing deaf to hearing children. In fact, various generalizations regarding language acquisition problems in the deaf have often been used to support the finding that auditory signs are more important than visual signs in the acquisition and production of human language. However, we now have access to a considerable amount of data that demonstrate the affinity of language acquisition in sighted children compared with non-sighted children. In this vein, I would like to argue for a re-evaluation of visual signs and their importance in language.

Returning to Kosslyn's research on the links between visual perception and imagery, I believe we can explain the differences in language acquisition and production in sighted and blind children. If, as Kosslyn argues, stored visual information may be able to trigger activity in certain areas of V1 that are retinotopically mapped, then certain parts of the brain that are used in visual perception are also used in visual mental imagery. This relationship would imply that imagery can affect what one actually perceives – a point that has been demonstrated in terms of visual imagery and visual perception (Kosslyn 1994: 56–75). In fact, if imagery is based to a large degree on viewer-centred representations, we can begin to see why blind children have semantic fields that are less flexible and generally non-changeable over time. The misinterpretation of sign for referent in the blind child is related in part to the disengaged visual cortex (which would necessarily affect imagery and retinotopically mapped areas in sighted speakers), thus reducing the viewer-centred representations in favour of object-centred representations. But would such a relationship as described imply that visual perception and imaging can impact auditory perception? The following section deals precisely with this issue and shows that vision does indeed play a role in auditory perception – a role that modulates over time.

The Relationship between Visual and Auditory Signs

In their paper 'Hearing Lips and Seeing Voices,' McGurk and MacDonald demonstrate quite convincingly that phoneme perception is not restricted merely to auditory signs (1976). Specifically, their work consists of showing a videotape of a subject producing four pairs of phonemes (/ba-ba/, /ga-ga/, /pa-pa/, /ka-ka/) to 103 subjects (21 preschool children [3 to 4 years old], 28 primary school children [7 to 8 years old], and 54 adults [18 to 40 years old]). Besides the tape on which lip movements and sounds were coordinated, another set of tapes using synchronized voice-overs was made that demonstrated a divergence in lip movement and sound produced while maintaining voiced/voiceless oppositions, resulting in the following: (1) ba–voice, ga–lips; (2) ga–voice, ba–lips; (3) pa–voice, ka–lips; (4) ka–voice, pa–lips.

The results of this study show that visual input, especially when it does not integrate with the auditory cue, plays a significant role in auditory perception, especially in adults. Thus, 98 per cent of adult speakers claim to have heard /da-da/ in context 1, and 81 per cent of adult speakers claim to have heard /ta-ta/ in context 3 (1976: 747). Children's responses mirror the adult ones, except that the percentages are 81 per cent and 64 per cent respectively in context 1. Note that the responses to contexts 2 and 4 did not produce the perception of alveo-dentals (t, d), but rather combinations of the original points of articulation (cf. gabga, bagba, baga, gaba; kapka, pakpa, paka, kapa) (747).

The authors interpret their findings as follows: (1) visual perception, especially perceived lip movements, plays a distinctive role in auditory perception of speech, and (2) adults rely more heavily than children on visual cues (as opposed to auditory cues) of articulation (ibid.). These findings seem to be generally reproducible (cf. Massaro 1987; O'Neill 1954; Mills 1983; B. Johnson and Spaulding 1994 [unpublished research]). They also provide empirical evidence that even in the perception of speech production, visual signs may play a significant, distinctive role.[13] One could argue that this type of experiment is artificial, and thus produces results which may not be meaningful in a more general context. I suggest that such experiments *can* be interesting if appropriated carefully. I propose the following points for consideration: (1) Visual stimuli, including lip and mouth movements, may be processed and interpreted by the brain more rapidly than the accompanying sound waves. (2) There are clear differences in reliance on visual cueing based on age; adult speakers seem to rely more heavily on visual cues (the explanation may be found in the powerful multiple mapping ability of the visual cortex). (3) The presence or absence of meaningful units of sound plays a significant role in the perceiver's ability to decode the utterance.

There is a significant body of literature, based predominately in experimental psychology, that confirms that vision plays a functional role in speech perception. In this context, it is not surprising that studies including non-sighted and sighted deaf and hearing children show that these groups acquire phonology in distinct ways, with sighted children first acquiring phonemes with 'visible articulation distinctiveness' (Massaro 1987: 39). In the case of sighted children, labial and labiodental consonants are more readily acquired (39).

144 Semiotic Theory as a Cognitive Science

Mills and Thiem (1980) conducted experiments with German speakers that were similar to those of McGurk and MacDonald and Massaro. Even in examples where auditory /ð/ occurred, speakers never selected such a response. The lack of any phonemic status for /ð/ in German clearly plays a determining role in conjunction with visual and auditory perception. Preliminary studies with Russian speakers show that they never select /ð/ or /θ/, neither of which occur phonemically or phonetically in Russian. Furthermore, when Russians are tested with English pronunciations of labial and dental stops, they consistently select voiceless consonants for voiced consonants. This result is explained by the presence in English of aspiration in the pronunciation of labial and dental stops that is missing in Russian.

A completely independent project on the integration of visual and linguistic information in speech suggests that addressees process auditory speech *incrementally* (Tanenhaus et al. 1995: 1632). By monitoring eye movements with a special Applied Scientific Laboratories camera mounted on a helmet, investigators were able to record eye movements in response to verbal cues (Tanenhaus et al. 1995: 1632-4). From the perspective of the present discussion, one of the most interesting results obtained in this study was that subjects visually identified the object spoken in speech before the actual lexeme was completely pronounced (1633). If there were two objects visually present that had similar phonological shape (cf. 'candle' and 'candy'), the eye movement to the correct object extended from 145 milliseconds to 230 milliseconds (1633). The researchers were interested in establishing a cause-effect relationship between information in the visual field and linguistic syntactic processing; even so, their initial experiments supported the claim that visual cues play a significant role in speech comprehension. In some cases the visual cue, especially when it was referentially part of a meaningful set of forms, was registered before the lexical cue had been completely enunciated. These findings support the kinds of results reported by McGurk and MacDonald (1976), and indicate that visual perception does indeed play a role in auditory speech perception and comprehension and does so in a fashion that has generally been overlooked by phonologists as well as by linguistics proper.

Brain, Language, and Culture: The Construction of Meaning

The interrelationship between visual and auditory signs at multiple levels in the structure and production of human language accentuates the obligatory interaction and implied necessity of both types of sign in the encoding and decoding processes of dynamic language and its perception in communication. My primary goal is to demonstrate the importance and unavoidability of the activation of multiple perceptual networks at all levels of language, including speech production and semantics. Each of these networks is involved in the temporal development of the individual organism in such a fashion that hierarchies may (and generally do) shift in time. Ultimately, we return to the Peircean notion of *diagrammatization*, where the set of linguistic signs coexists in a dynamic determined by inherent asymmetry, in which the sign complex incessantly modulates from plateaux of greater or lesser stability. The force of iconicity is the dominant factor in defining and redefining diagrammatic relations by activating ever-changing relationships between the 'final interpretant and its corresponding immediate and dynamic interpretants. The embedding of visual categories in linguistically determined interpretants is motivated by the parameters of human perceptual ability in building meaningful relationships between functioning signs in semiosis.

The connection between brain and language is even more viable at the beginning of the twenty-first century, a time of rapid expansion of neuroscience's knowledge of the human brain. Here again, Jakobson is at the forefront of a movement. As early as 1980, with the publication of 'Brain and Language,' he was articulating the direction of development of this particular scientific paradigm:

> At present, those governing functions of the brain which are connected with the output of speech and with its input lend themselves to an attentive examination, and it seems as if the joint efforts of linguists and neurologists are summoned to suggest and open even deeper insights both into the structure of language with reference to the brain and into the structure of the brain with the help of language. ([1980] 1985: 177)

What is missing from Jakobson's statement, and from most contemporary studies of the brain and language, is a strong statement regarding what types of information the linguist and the cognitive scientist will acknowledge as central to the construction of *meaning* and *meaningful categories* in language. It seems impossible to imagine any theory of linguistic meaning that fails to take into account *reference*. And reference inevitably leads to a range of overlapping and discrete extralinguistic signs, signs that are always bound in semiospheric space-time. Thus, we must also question how culture, as well as the cultural context, becomes codified in human language. There are two fundamental ways that cultural information is coded and communicated within speech communities – in the creation of *texts* (using Lotman's definition), and in the creation of individual and group *memory*. The latter point will be the focus of the final chapter; the former has been the focus of each of the preceding chapters.

Lotman provides one of the clearest methods for reconciling these two aspects of codification by constantly reiterating the intimate relationship between any manifestation of the text and the actualization or condensation of cultural memory (1990: 16–18). In all these statements, Lotman retains the complexity of a multifaceted communication event (see chapters 2 and 3) that obligatorily has multiple functions in any given instance:

> ... the spectrum of texts which fill the space of culture can be represented as if they are disposed along an axis, one pole of which is formed by the artificial languages and the other by artistic ones. Other languages are disposed at points along the axis closer to one or other pole. We should bear in mind, however, that the poles of this axis are an abstraction unrealizable in actual languages: just as artificial languages are impossible without some rudimentary synonymity and other 'poetic' elements, so languages with an observable tendency towards 'pure' poetism must have metalingual tendencies. We should also bear in mind that the place of the text on the above – mentioned axis is a moveable one ... (1990: 16)

Beyond this, Lotman reminds the reader that one of the primary functions of language is to create memory through texts (be they verbal or pictorial) in order to generate new meanings and condense pre-existing ones (e.g., the I-I and I-s/he models of chapter 3). The movement from individual to cultural group is essential if human cultures are to continue to exist. This movement is guaranteed by any semiotic text's ability to 'preserve the memory of its previous contexts' (1990: 18).

As we move along the continuum of different kinds of languages (artificial, natural, artistic), we encounter an important correlation between iconic, indexical, and symbolic forms. It is, therefore, a universal of human culture that the meaningful texts will always be both representational (pictorial) and symbolic (conventional), including hybrids of each type (Lotman 1990: 124). And it is precisely this diversity of textual modes that guarantees the dynamic mechanism for maintaining and multiplying meaning in the cultural and biological spheres of human existence.

CHAPTER NINE

The Language of Memory in the Memory of Language

> Memory is a particular, rather specialized form of adaptation to experience, itself a general property of living organisms ... to understand the mechanisms of memory, of plasticity, it is also necessary to understand the mechanism of specificity ... Ordered and restrained variance can only make sense against a largely invariant background.
>
> Steven Rose, *The Making of Memory*

> ... losses at the event-specific level can be turned into 'gains' at the general-event level.
>
> Daniel Schacter, *Searching for Memory*

Peircean semiotic theory has repeatedly shown that the interaction of signs in semiosis is neither linear nor homogeneous. In fact, any activated sign becomes determinable and makes the transition from a merely potential sign to an actual functioning sign complex via multiple levels of interpretants. The modulation between the different kinds of interpretant types is determined by the degree of completeness of interaction – that is, whether or not we are dealing with a 'third of thirds' or something less developed (Peirce 1931–58: 8.315; Savan 1980: 257–60). The implications of such variability in sign development are clearly articulated by Peirce himself when he draws attention to the fact that signs can be false or unrealized (Short 1981: 200). In the next sections I present current research in the area of human memory and demonstrate that recent discoveries and perspectives are enriched and supported by Peircean sign theory and by semiotic theory in general. The discussion includes (1) the encoding/decoding process, (2) priming and cues, and (3) different types of memory: long- and short-term memory, declarative and procedural memory, source memory, and episodic and semantic memory. I show that the Peircean model of semiosis and sign categories provides an adequate metalanguage for describing current models of human memory and also may provide valuable insights for the scientific study of memory.

Encoding and Decoding: Learning and Retrieval

It is true that encoding and remembering are very closely related and often 'virtually inseparable' (Schacter 1996: 52); however, it is also true that achieving a deeper understanding of the mechanisms of memory requires that these two related processes be analysed as relatively autonomous, in such a way as to recognize that one can only remember that which was encoded in the first place. This acknowledgment does not imply direct, conscious awareness of the encoding process.

There are many paradigms available for studying human memory, reflecting the enormous achievements of the past twenty years in cognitive science, neuroscience, and psychology. But these approaches are not always compatible, especially when the researchers are neurobiologists as opposed to cognitive psychologists or developmental or social psychologists. (For a stimulating collection by scholars from different disciplines researching memory, see Solomon et al. 1989. For an overview of learning and memory complete with a comprehensive bibliography, see Johnson and Hasher 1987.) The controversies that arise in these different approaches often revolve around which distinctions and categories are most significant. By way of introduction to this research, I will summarize some of the more generally acknowledged methods of defining memory, particularly human memory, and contextualize the discussion with encoding and decoding foci.

Steven Rose (1992: 24, 136) constructs his theory of memory by beginning with a rigorous definition of learning. He explains that the human and animal forms of memory are related and shows how research in animal memory is important in discovering important principles of human memory. The validity of generalizing from animal to human memory has been hotly debated. However, Rose as a biologist has committed himself to showing the relevance to humans of discoveries made in animal learning and retrieval. He is sensitive to the position that only humans have 'verbal memory' and can learn and remember without particular behaviours (if speech is excluded as a behaviour), but he also states that the cellular principles at work in non-human declarative memory may also be operating in human verbal memory (326). Obviously, animals cannot articulate in speech their particular ability to remember or their remembrance of specific memories. Thus, learning must be viewed as a behavioural modification that demonstrates three behavioural properties: (1) it is a direct result of experience, (2) it is reliable, and (3) it is adaptive (136). When we start with this definition of learning, we can define remembering as 'the expression of the modified behavioral response at some time subsequent to the initial learning' (136). Rose goes on to make an important distinction between recall and recognition (318). Embedded in this distinction is the belief that the 'retrieval of memories' is the central issue, not the actual storage of memory (following Tulving 1972, 1983, 1985). In distinguishing recall from recognition, scientists can attribute further differences to these categories, including the feature of saturation.[1] Finally, Rose's position carries with it the explicit consequence that memory is not directly observable or measurable; rather, it is always inferred to exist. Rose reminds us that although brain-imaging technologies, including PET, MRI, and fMRI, provide fascinating results, the observation that brain activity has increased in a particular region does not constitute proof that memory resides in that section of the brain (133): 'The store might be somewhere quite different, somewhere that doesn't need a great flurry of glucose utilization to activate it; we might be looking at the peripherals to the engine rather than the engine itself ... And, even more importantly, at the less mechanistic level, they cannot tell us about meaning, about the translation rules between mind and brain.'

One common approach in memory research has been to study subjects with memory disorders, including forgetting and various forms of amnesia. The literature in these areas is extensive. Amnesiacs may demonstrate deficits in both encoding and decoding/retrieval. Furthermore, 'amnesic symptom can be simulated in normal subjects'(Mandler 1989: 100–1). Forgetting is a natural, adaptive part of memory. In fact, the inability to forget can create difficulties for the functioning social being (cf. Schacter 1996: 81, 318, and Rose 1992: 100–3 for the story of Shereskevskij, originally given in Luria 1968).[2] Forgetting, like remembering, is an 'active process' and not just the 'mere erasure of stored information' (Rose 1992: 320). And different types of memory are forgotten in qualitatively different ways (procedural memory, for instance, is forgotten differently than declarative) (320).

It is essential at this juncture to be familiar with the distinctive categories of memory that are commonly spoken of in the fields of cognitive psychology, neuropsychology, and neurobiology. One major distinction in memory-based research is the difference between long- and short-term memory (LTM and STM). This important distinction, made initially by Hebb (1949) and based on durable changes in the neural structure of the brain involving protein synthesis and synaptic growth, has served as the fundamental premise for a great deal of research. In this context, perhaps the biggest question has been the exact relationship between these two forms of memory and how they interact or fail to do so (Baddeley 1989: 108–9). Once we make the distinction between STM and LTM, we encounter further significant subdivisions that serve as a framework for discussing different types of LTM in particular.

Squire (1987: 134–74) provides an excellent survey of the types of STM and LTM that have been posited, and critically examines their utility in the field. In his discussion he focuses on the reception and analysis of information rather than on retrieval and retention. Some of the more interesting types of STM include William James's distinction between *primary memory* ('information that forms the focus of current attention and that occupies the stream of thought' [Squire 1987: 135]) and *secondary memory* ('knowledge of an event, or fact, of which we have not been thinking, with the additional consciousness that we have thought or experienced it before' [Squire 1987: 136, quoting James]), and the notion of *working memory* ('a collection of temporary capacities intrinsic to information-processing sybsystems' [1987: 137]). Besides these potential types of STM, some researchers argue for an additional distinction between *immediate* and *short-term memory* (143). Declarative memory, although discussed mainly in the context of LTM, is also possible in the context of STM (242).

In neurobiology, memory is analysed at the cellular level (as opposed to the broader, system level). From this field, there is strong evidence to support a qualitative difference between STM and LTM. In LTM, protein synthesis occurs and changes the neuronal synaptic connections. When cerebral protein synthesis is blocked, permanent memories are not formed (Squire 1987: 145–7). Nevertheless, Squire is clear that STM and LTM are most useful when taken as 'behavioral categories' (150).

Squire's discussion of LTM focuses on *declarative* versus *procedural memory* and then subdivides declarative memory into *episodic* and *semantic* (151–72). However, he notes that the literature makes many possible distinctions among LTM categories (see table 9.1). Declarative memory is generally understood to be (1) 'memory that is directly accessible to

Table 9.1

Fact memory	Skill memory
Declarative	Procedural
Memory	Habit
Explicit	Implicit
Knowing that	Knowing how
Cognitive mediation	Semantic*
Conscious recollection	Skills
Elaboration	Integration
Memory with record	Memory without record
Autobiographical memory	Perceptual memory
Representational memory	Dispositional memory
Vertical association	Horizontal association
Locale	Taxon
Episodic	Semantic*
Working	Reference

Source: Squire 1987: 169.
*'Semantic memory' occurs twice under 'skill memory' to show different associations with 'fact memory.'

conscious recollection ... It deals with the facts and data that are acquired through learning, and it is impaired in amnesia' (Squire 1987: 152); and (2) storage of information that includes space-time parameters as 'explicit knowledge' (162, 242). Procedural memory is defined as almost the opposite of declarative memory: 'memory that is contained within learned skills or modifiable cognitive operations ... spared in amnesia' (152). These two types of memory are acquired in different ways and generate distinct types of representations and neural organization; only declarative memory can be consciously perceived, and only it is available through all modalities, whereas procedural is slower, almost automatic (161–2). Although some researchers in cognitive psychology and AI (artificial intelligence) have moved away from this distinction on the basis that 'knowledge' cannot be clearly divided into procedural versus declarative, and that information can be represented as both (160), Squire argues that this distinction is very important because it represents 'how the brain itself actually stores information' (160). Squire notes that declarative and procedural memory may or may not be stored in separate areas of the brain (166).

Regarding subtypes of declarative memory, Tulving originally suggested *episodic* versus *semantic*, where episodic is actually experienced by the individual and semantic is factual information without the 'temporal landmarks' (Tulving 1972, Squire 1987: 169). In the context of the present analysis, it is especially important to note the placement of so-called semantic memory as a 'skill-based,' automatic phenomenon that is in opposition to episodic memory, which by definition is conscious and non-automatic (Mandler 1985: 93; 1989: 93). Obviously, from a linguistic-semiotic point of view, it would be difficult to argue that semantic knowledge can ever be automatic or context-free, as opposed to episodic memory, which is 'context dependent and "remembered"' (1989: 94).[3] (I will return to the question of semantic memory in the next section in the discussion on priming.) I suggest that in the literature, one of the fundamental errors committed in the general placement of semantic memory arises from two fundamentally false assumptions about human language: (1) the belief that humans learn their first language without conscious effort, and (2) the notion that there can be semantic meaning (or linguistic meaning) that is devoid of context and purely formal in nature. As I will demonstrate in the final section of this chapter, a Peircean perspective can make important additions and corrections to the analysis of language as it is manifested in relation to human memory.

I conclude this section by noting that neuroscientists like Rose (1992: 91), who are very articulate in their opposition to brain/computer metaphors, refer specifically to the distinction between *information* and *meaning*: for them, meaning 'implies a dynamic of interaction ... a process which is not reducible to a number of bits of information.' Such a distinction brings to the fore the important view that memory is not a static phenomenon whereby engrams are permanently imprinted on a particular part of the cortex; rather, any given memory is always modified in any instantiation. As Rose correctly ascertains: 'Our memories are recreated each time we remember' (91).[4] This distinction is reminiscent of the Peircean notion of knowledge as 'observed facts' versus 'practical knowledge' (Buchler 1955: 150–1). It is only through inferences that knowledge (and this necessarily involves memory) can be activated for future behaviour and decision making. And that which Schacter refers to as explicit remembering is diagrammatically determined: 'Explicit remembering always depends on the similarity or affinity between encoding and retrieval processes' (1996: 60).[5] In this vein, we now begin to see that memory, like language, 'is not confined to a small set of neurons at all, but has to be understood as a property of the entire brain, even the entire organism' (Rose 1992: 322).

Semantic Memory and Priming

Perhaps the terms 'semantic memory' and 'priming' in the title of this section should be reversed, given the history in psychology of the development of perspectives on semantics in psychology. Initially, researchers were struck by the repeatable experimental results that amnesic patients demonstrate influence due to recent experiences while having no conscious recollection of those experiences (Schacter 1996: 166–71; Weiskrantz and Warrington 1979: 187–94; Dudai 1989: 260). The notion of priming is defined in the context of presenting subjects with word lists that 'prime' their ability to provide at higher rates of speed the correct solutions to word fragments with which they are confronted after having the opportunity to study the appropriate lists. The results showed that subjects were able to benefit from priming not only in testing that occurred an hour after studying word lists, but even after a week (Schacter 1996: 167). However, the subjects had less accurate 'conscious memory' of what they had studied. Furthermore, amnesic patients also benefited from these priming experiences although they were completely or almost completely deficit in episodic memory (which allows one to remember specific episodes and experiences from the past). These results led Schacter, Tulving, and others to posit a different kind of memory beyond the already established episodic memory system – semantic [or reference] memory (which is typically defined as 'knowledge that is independent of events in the individual's life' [Dudai 1989: 264]) (Schacter 1996: 169).[6] As the debates continued throughout the 1980s, still more types of memory systems were proposed. For example, a distinction was made between implicit and explicit memory (171). Another important aspect of these debates focuses on the perspective of encoded events, whether they are propositional or iconically based. The central question is whether these events are coded based on viewer-orientation (or self) or object-orientation (which may be the inanimate object or, in the case of animate objects, the other speaker) (Kosslyn 1994: 127–35; Johnson et al. 1996: 135–56).[7]

Theories of priming have become quite developed. Two of the more prominent types of associative priming are (1) *spreading activation* – during memory retrieval an internal representation is activated, which then 'spreads to associated concepts, and residual activation accumulating at concepts facilitates their retrieval' (McNamara 1994: 507), and (2) *compound cue* – 'memory is searched with a cue that contains information about the target item and the context in which it occurs' (507).[8]

In more recent experiments, the populations studied for priming effects have included patients with Alzheimer's disease. In these groups, unlike with amnesic patients, priming has little or no effect, though motor skill acquisition is still viable (Schacter 1996: 187). Studies of this nature support the separation of acquisition of motor skills (or procedural memory) from effective priming for perceptual skills.[9]

It is essential to question whether motor-based verbal or written responses in experiments of the kind described above ought to be conflated with semantic knowledge of a particular language. Clearly, the language-based knowledge of a given individual is not necessarily represented by articulated verbal or written responses. In fact, perhaps it is the specific distinctive properties of these systems that explain certain phonological and morphological acquisition issues in first and second languages. I would argue that it has become essential to include linguists in discussions of memory and other trends in cognitive science if we are to achieve the same level of sophistication inherent in the individual disciplines studying cognition as human language becomes more and more central in verifying their hypotheses about the codification and retrieval of memory.

Source Memory

Questions about veridical remembering have become central to the study of human memory. Clearly, the reliability of courtroom witnesses is directly connected to their ability to accurately remember events under scrutiny. Research has demonstrated that one of the most important aspects of veridical remembering is the subject's ability to identify the source of the information remembered. This point – coupled with important discoveries in the neurobiological structure of the brain, which highlight the importance of plasticity and the dynamic nature of remembering (viz., all memories are dynamically reconstructed when retrieved) – poses critical issues for judging the reliability – and at the same time, the organism-specific subjectivity – of the encoding/retrieval process.

Johnson and colleagues (1993: 3) define *source* as:

> a variety of characteristics that, collectively, specify the conditions under which a memory is acquired (e.g., the spatial, temporal, and social context of the event; the media and modalities through which it was perceived) ... A central claim of the source-monitoring approach is that people do not typically directly retrieve an abstract tag or label that specifies a memory's

source, rather, activated memory records are evaluated and attributed to particular sources through decision processes performed during remembering ... Source monitoring refers to the set of processes involved in making attributions about the origins or memories, knowledge and beliefs.

One of the distinctions made in source monitoring is between internal and *external* sources. So, for example, memories bearing singularly verbal information may not have the same level of certainty of external source monitoring as memories of events that are heavy with spatial and temporal cues (Johnson et al. 1993: 4). The matching of memory to source may seem effortless (i.e., 'automatic') or more deliberate (i.e., 'controlled') (cf. Hasher and Zacks 1979). Because so much of this research focuses on the encoding and retrieval of language-based information, the importance of sophisticated knowledge of language structures and the structure of the linguistic sign is essential if researchers are to draw relevant conclusions. Lotman's work on the semiosphere and his modelling systems of communication are important in this connection, since they add invaluable conceptual depth to studies of human memory, including collective memory (Lotman 1992a, 1992b, [1992] 1995).

Collective Memory

No book on memory can avoid crossing the boundary between the individual and the collective.

Steven Rose, *The Making of Memory*

Steven Rose notes early in his monograph on the making of memory that neuroscience has fundamentally ignored the importance of the 'subjective meanings of memory' (1992: 7). He adds that given the fact that the human mind and brain are by definition open systems, the study of these systems must involve research at the collective level that cannot be reduced to individual organisms. One might argue that the collective level of memory is even more important in the contemporary world, because of the enormous capabilities for archiving cultural, social, and individual histories in ever-expanding media and linguistic forms and technologies. Rose insists that the principles of the structure of memory are not definable only at the individual level: 'Individual our memories may be, but they are structured, their very brain mechanisms affected, by the collective, social nature of the way we as humans live' (1992: 60). Human language is one of the central symbolic systems facilitating the encoding, decoding, recall, and recognition of various types of memory. And language is never predominantly the property of the individual; rather, language is a shared code between one or more speech communities that is embedded in a more broadly defined cultural *milieu*.[10]

As discussed in chapters 2 and 3, the speakers of a given language must assimilate a significant amount of information and behaviours in order to be recognized as full-fledged members of a particular linguistic community. This aspect of language learning depends on mastery of a norm that is determined a priori to the individual speaker's existence in the framework of a dynamic system that presupposes the participants of the speech event (including addresser and addressee, context, contact, code, and message). For this communicative system to begin to operate, it must be initially contextualized and immersed in semiotic space (Lotman 1990: 124). For Lotman, there can be no 'language' or 'memory' without the guarantee of semiosis in the broader form of the semiosphere.

In the context of the semiosphere, language is a complex set of functional relations that map between relatively autonomous heterogeneous, asymmetrical semiotic spaces (Lotman 1990: 125–6). The asymmetry of the semiosphere can be locational (centre/periphery), or it can involve different velocities, speeds, and rates of change or different time frames. The semiosphere may seem to be a semiotic unity at its highest level, but in fact it is a conglomerate of boundaries defining ever-changing internal and external spaces (Lotman 1990: 127–30). Thus, Lotman contends that there can be no 'language' or 'memory' without the guarantee of semiosis in the form of the semiosphere. Lotman's view strongly parallels Rose's point on the importance of collective memory in the construction of memory at the individual level.

One of the ways that cultures and languages maintain their identity is by utilizing collective memory, which creates mechanisms for self-preservation and propagation. Lotman identifies writing as one of the most important means of preserving information of discrete, even anomalous events (1990: 246–7). Writing as memory sets up the potential for linear (cause-and-effect) relationships, and for an increase in 'the quantity of texts' and information in general (247). The other central means of self-preservation is oral culture, where the focus is not on the generation of new texts, but rather on the regular, ritualistic, law-based nature of existence (246–7). Both forms of collective memory rely predominantly on language. It is important to note that writing, as opposed to oral culture, shifts the burden of 'memory' from the individual to an externally given symbolic system that is collectively maintained, whereas oral culture is more determined by the accuracy of individual memory. In essence, language becomes the symbolic 'condenser' between different levels of semiosis and different segments of the time axis (110).

If language itself necessarily exists within and beyond the individual speaker, and requires both individual and collective memory, it follows that texts, as codifications of moments between past and future in an asymmetrical fashion, become meaningful in the undeterminedness of the future (Lotman 1992a: 27–8). And culture, in Lotmanian analysis, necessarily includes not only collective memory, which allows for the preservation and transfer of knowledge and information through time, but also collective intellect, which guarantees the potential actualization of coded information in the present and the production of new information in the future (1992b: 200).

Interpretants and Memory

Any semiotic method is essentially a theory of perception. When semiosis is the focus of inquiry, we are necessarily examining how sign complexes organize and align themselves into meaningful units and categories. In Lotmanian theory the focus is at the category level as a collective phenomenon, whereas in Peircean theory the focus is on the functioning interpretant and the creation of sense at the local, individual level (Peirce [1931–58] 2.228): 'The interpretant creates in the mind ... an equivalent sign, or perhaps a more developed sign.'

As the interpretant necessarily follows from the sign (which excludes the possibility of the sign following from the interpretant), we see the unequivocal importance of the interpretant in initiating and sustaining the process of semiosis (see Peirce 4.127). The Peircean definition of *interpretant* helps explain the central question in the study of memory in defining the relationship between encoding and recall and the construction of *meaning*. If memory, as Schacter states, is one way the human brain creates structure in the external world, it is not surprising to imagine that there are no 'objective,' universal criteria for articulating what is necessarily encoded by the individual (Schacter 1996: 52). In Schacter's words: 'Encoding and remembering are virtually inseparable. But the close relationship between the two can sometimes cause problems in our everyday lives. We remember only what we have encoded, and what we encode depends on who we are – our past experiences, knowledge, and needs all have a powerful influence on what we retain' (52).

What becomes *meaningful* for the individual, and thus worthy of memory coding, is a product of both the semiosphere (cultural space) in which the individual exists and the individual's goals at a particular point in time. These categories are represented by and derived from interpretants – that is, signs that allow for potential retrieval, translation, and modification in usage.

In Peirce's system we can explain with more precision the different types of interpretant types involved in any encoding process. In the case of human memory encoding, it seems pertinent to consider the immediate-dynamic-final interpretant triad as one means of understanding why encoding and remembering are so intimately related. Specifically, the immediate interpretant is a 'first of thirds,' where all interpretants are representative of thirdness and immediacy is a category of firstness. As Savan points out, the immediate interpretant is 'an incipient habit, a propensity to replicate the same interpretation in further circumstances of a like kind' while being uncritical and non-articulated (Savan 1980: 257). The next step in the precise realization of a bounded, finite event is rendered possible by the dynamic interpretant, which is 'whatever interpretation any mind actually makes of a sign' (Peirce 1931–58: 8.315). As dynamic interpretants occur repeatedly, they tend to move toward final interpretants in the mind of the user, where the final interpretant is 'that which would finally be decided to be the true interpretation if consideration of the matter were carried so far that an ultimate opinion were reached' (ibid.: 8.184). The final interpretant is goal-oriented and exhibits control over the observer (ibid.: 8.372). In other words, the final interpretant is the result of the 'successive dynamic interpretants exhibiting a regularity or law' (Savan 1980: 259).

In order to fill in the remaining pertinent sign types, we need a definition of *immediate* and *dynamic object*. These two types of 'object' signs in Peircean theory are required in order to establish tangible relationships between the parts of the functioning sign. Thus, the *dynamic object* is, in fact, *a set of interpretants*, whereas the *immediate object* is *a subset or sampling of the dynamic object*. And it is the sign-dynamic object relationship that may then be characterized as iconic, indexical, or symbolic. Through this process, the human sign user becomes a dynamic object and is centrally involved (and placed) in the encoding process. Kosslyn's viewer-oriented encoding is an example of this phenomenon (1994: 127–36). The inclusion of not only perceived objects but also the perceivers themselves as sets of interpretants is perhaps one of the most powerful and underexplored aspects of Peircean theory, and it is precisely this point that provides fruitful correspondences to the functional circle of Uexküll's *Umwelt* and Lotman's *text*.

Memories, like signs, never occur in isolation; rather, they include both paradigmatic and syntagmatic contexts. Even what we choose to 'remember' is determined by a series of spatial and temporal factors that frame the interpretation of the event for both present and future reference. A semiotic theory of memory would begin by considering a set of different types of memory (long-term, short-term, working, viewer-oriented, object-oriented, topographic/iconic, propositional), how those types interact (or fail to) with one another, and distinct modes for encoding, recall, recognition, and explicit decoding and reconstruction. The areas of interaction between different types of memory are among the more complex and interesting trajectories for future research. One such model for interactive memory is given by Kosslyn (1994: 73, 214–23, 380–1) and is called *associative memory*.[11]

If we recodify Schacter's remark provided at the beginning of this section in the context of Peircean interpretants, we find that 'what we are' is, after all, the constellations of interpretants which then serve as the baseline for whatever encoding/translating process the human is engaged in. This observation becomes more profound when viewed from the perspective of recall and the retrieval process. If explicit remembering is dependent 'on the similarity or affinity between encoding and retrieval processes,' then it is the dynamic object that will determine the level of iconicity in the instantiation of semiosis of the sign. The more developed the relationship between the dynamic object and the immediate and dynamic interpretants, the more complex and expanded the potential final interpretant may become. Such a generalization supports how encoding (i.e., instantiation of the dynamic interpretant) and retrieval (i.e., construction of the final interpretant via the dynamic object) are related in semiosis.

Most researchers studying memory recognize the need to include investigations made in the fields of neurobiology, cognitive science, and psychology; however, they often fail to notice that linguists may have an equally important contribution to make to these discussions. Given the high degree of reliability accorded to empirically measurable behaviours that are embedded in language, it is essential for us to recognize the importance of linguistic phenomena as relatively autonomous bearers and generators of meaning and not merely as formal representations. I suggest that linguistic and semiotic models support a framework of the study of memory in which (1) distinctions such as declarative and procedural memory would be viewed in a more interactive fashion in terms of speech events and textual construction at the level of addressers, addressees, and general participants of the speech and narrated events, and (2) episodic and semantic memory would be in a clear feedback relationship and not treated as distinct, autonomous entities. In such a model, short- and long-term memory potentials would be realizable vis-à-vis specific types of speech and narrated events. The weakest link at this time is precisely in the modelling of the construction and reconstruction of the *message* that is to become a part of memory. Only in grappling with the source of the creation of meaning and meaningfulness can the study of human memory begin to bridge the gap between the individual memory system and collective memory.

My plan has been to acquaint the reader with the more salient aspects of the study of human memory in order to begin to establish a deeper understanding of the nature and role of language in memory. In this vein, I have highlighted Peircean sign categories and Lotmanian models that may play a central role in articulating the interaction between these two phenomena. Although one would not claim that there can be no memory without language, there is certainly no language without the ability to encode and retrieve verbal signs. And if language-based categories of meaning are indeed tied to perceptual categories, then further analysis of the dynamic, functioning triadic sign will lead to profound discoveries in the areas of linguistics and human cognition. As we pursue a more semiotic model of human memory, we will be able to fuse the individual and collective levels into a robust theory of perception.

Notes

Introduction

1 The term 'structuralism' is generally used in American scholarship to refer to the Bloomfield school of linguistics. The use of the term 'structuralist' in the European intellectual context includes both linguists and literary theorists.
2 The relationship between Bakhtin's and Lotman's approaches to the study of language and literature is complex. Several studies have addressed this question, including Jegorov 1999b; Bethea 2000; Mandelker 1994; Shukman 1977: 4, 172 and 1988: 65–78; and Lachmann 1987 and 1997: 101–13.

Ivanov (1998a: 683–4, 1998c: 740–7) discusses Bakhtin's contribution in the broader context of Russian and Soviet semiotics and does not attempt to set up a relationship directly to Lotman. Bethea (2000: 15–16) notes specific differences in the text theories presented by Bakhtin and Lotman. Shukman (1988: 75) argues that Lotman's approach to defining semiotic space is 'more strictly scientific' than that of Bakhtin. Jegorov (1999b: 244–8) is quite critical of the works written on this topic to date and gives a series of differences between the two thinkers. All of the works noted above take different stances as to the degree of similarity, difference, and influence between the two thinkers. Lotman's sister Lidija Mixailovna Lotman, a noted Russian literary scholar in her own right, in personal conversation with me, was very clear about Lotman's deep respect for Bakhtin and his work, but was reluctant to acknowledge any direct impact of Bakhtin's work on Lotman's theories of modelling systems and semiotic space.

I would direct the reader to the following passages from Lotman himself as an additional point of information about the relationship between Bakhtinian and Lotmanian thought (these references do not include all passages in Lotman's work where Bakhtin's name is mentioned): 'Сюжетное пространство русского романа XIX столетия' (1997a: 712–29), 'К проблеме пространственной семиотики' (1998b: 442–4), 'Текст в тексте' (1992b: I.152), 'Язык театра' (1998a: 603–8), 'Литературоведение должно быть наукой' (1997a: 756–65), 'О содержании и структуре понятия "художественная литература"' (1997a: 774–93), 'Динамическая модель семиотической системы' (2000: 543–56), 'Культура как коллективный интеллект и проблемы искусственного разума' (2000: 557–67), 'New Aspects in the Study of Early Russian Culture' [with B.A. Uspenskij] (1984b: 36–52 [English translation]).

Note also Lotman's references to Bakhtin in his personal correspondence (1997c: 255, 330–3, 371–2, 473, 512–13, 682–3, 720). In a letter to one of his graduate students, Larisa Ljvovna Fialkova, Lotman gives a clear articulation of the two major semiotic trends in terms of their definition of space (1997c: 270): 'И в современной семиотике существует два совершенно различных понимания пространства, которые разнообразные популяризаторы сначала писавшие доносы на подозрительное новшество пространственного анализа (Кожинов и др.), а затем ухватившиеся за модное слово, не отличают. Бахтин идёт от идей физики (теории относительности) и рассматривает пространство и время как явления одного ряда (в перспективе это восходит к Канту). Мы же (полагаю, что первыми стали исследовать эту проблему С. Неклюдов и я) исходим из математического (топологического) понятия пространства: пространством в этом смысле называется множество объектов (точек), между которыми существует отношение непрерывности. ... С этой точки зрения пространство – универсальный язык моделирования.' (In contemporary semiotics that are two absolutely different conceptualizations of space, which various popularizers, who at first wrote denunciations against suspicious new forms of analyzing space [Kožinov and others] and then jumping on the bandwagon [when these ideas became fashionable], were unable to distinguish. Bakhtin uses notions from physics [the theory of relativity] and sees space and time as the same type of phenomena [this perspective goes back to Kant]. We, however [I think that S. Nekljudov and I were the first to research this problem], start with a mathematical [topological] conceptualization of space: in this sense, space is a set of continuous objects [points] ... From this point of view, space is the universal language of modelling systems.)

3 Some of Lotman's most noted publications in English are a series of articles published in *The Semiotics of Russian Cultural History* (Nakhimovsky and Nakhimovsky 1985), his monograph *The Structure of the Artistic Text* (1971), and eight articles authored or coauthored by Lotman on semiotic modelling systems in the collection *Soviet Semiotics* ([1977] 1988). Of the above-

mentioned works, the best known is perhaps one that Lotman co-authored with Uspenskij, 'Binary Models in the Dynamics of Russian Culture (to the End of the Eighteenth Century)' ([1977] 1985).

In addition to the excellent three-volume collection of Lotman's works on culture, literature and the semiosphere published in Tallinn, there is a new St Petersburg series of seven volumes of Lotman's work on Russian culture and Russian literature: *Ob iskusstve* (On Art) (1998), *O russkoj literature* (On Russian Literature) (1997), *Besedy o russkoj kul'ture* (Conversations on Russian Culture) (1994), *Puškin* (1995), *Karamzin* (1997), *O poetax i poezii* (On Poets and Poetry) (1996), and *Semiosfera* (The Semiosphere) (2000) (published in St Petersburg by Iskusstvo). Most of these articles focus on Russian life, traditions, and literary works in the eighteenth and nineteenth centuries. One of the issues that arises in some of the volumes noted above is the failure to note the original publication date of many of the articles. Where available, I give the original date as well. In internal references, I list the volume and page numbers but do not list each article individually by name.

4 There are many different definitions of cognitive science today. Given the broad range of fields that this term potentially encompasses (including neuroscience, neurobiology, psychology [neuropsychology and cognitive psychology], computer science, artificial intelligence, anthropology, linguistics, philosophy, semiotics, cybernetics, rhetoric, and others), it is not a trivial endeavour to provide a definition. Howard Gardner's *The Mind's New Science* (1985: 6) gives a good working definition: 'a contemporary, empirically based effort to answer long-standing epistemological questions – particularly those concerned with the nature of [human] knowledge, its components, its sources, its development, and its deployment.' For other definitions of cognitive science, see Frawley (1997: 35–120).

1: Lotman's Contributions to the Semiotics of Culture

1 This particular essay was translated in 1978 (*New Literary History*, no. 9) and is referenced in one of the best-known English translations of Lotman and Uspenskij, 'Binary Models in the Dynamics of Russian Culture (to the End of the Eighteenth Century)' ([Rol' dual'nyx modelej v dinamike russkoj kul'tury] in Nakhimovsky and Nakhimovsky, 1985: 30–66).

2 B. Gasparov (1985: 27) defends Lotman's use of binary typology and argues that evidence of counterexamples to a binary approach is not sufficient in and of itself to reject Lotman's semiotic. I would make the stronger claim that Lotman's binarism is perhaps the weakest theoretical aspect of his semiotic but that he makes significant progress in moving to a more complex

notion of oppositions in his work on continuity and discontinuity, especially in *Culture and Explosion* (1992a) and in *Semiosfera* (2000), which contains the aforementioned *Culture and Explosion*, as well as the original Russian version of Shukman's outstanding translation *Universe of the Mind* and a series of articles and documents on the typology of culture and cultural semiotics. More will be said about Lotman's binarism in the following chapters in the broader semiotic context, by comparison with Peirce and Jakobson.

3 One cannot overestimate the importance of what Soviets called 'xarakteristika' (or a letter of support) in order to find employment. At a time when outstanding military service was highly valued, the absence of such a recommendation most certainly raised questions in any employer's mind.

4 Toporov notes that three major events directly affected the development of semiotics and structuralism in Moscow from the perspective of the Moscow semioticians: (1) Roman Jakobson's visit to Moscow in 1956; (2) the mandate to create in a certain academic institutions of higher learning a division devoted to structural linguistics in 1960; and (3) the Moscow Symposium of 1962 (Jegorov 1999a: 98). At the same time that these important events occurred in Moscow, Lotman began his serious study of the works of Trubetzkoy and Jakobson in combination with his interest in cybernetics and information theory (as represented most significantly in the works of Wiener and Ashby) (Jegorov 1999a: 103).

5 It is quite remarkable that Jakobson and Pomorska eventually received official permission to travel to Tartu once they had arrived in Moscow. The condition was that they must have an official Soviet escort, who, ironically, turned out to be Vjacheslav Ivanov. Ivanov, one of the participants of the Tartu summer school, had been released from his position at MGU (Moscow State University) in 1958 in connection with his defence of Boris Pasternak and his alleged connection with the 'American spy' Roman Jakobson (Jegorov 1999a: 96–7, 131–2).

6 Although Tartu was a closed city to foreigners during those years, the school organizers smuggled in Thomas Sebeok and Jean Umiker Sebeok for one day to the fourth and final summer school. Thomas Sebeok, who had organized the first major American conference devoted to semiotics at Indiana University in May 1962, was an important addition to the auspicious group of scholars representing Soviet semiotics (which included Boris Gasparov from the time of the third summer school) at the 1970 Tartu meeting. Sebeok looks back on the experience as among the most memorable of his career (Sebeok 1977: v–viii).

7 Persecution included a search of the Lotmans' apartment and their personal belongings and papers (in January 1970 by ten KGB agents), as well as being

followed by the KGB when moving about the small town of Tartu. This situation was exacerbated by negative comments made by Lotman and Zara Mints, his wife, concerning the Russian invasion of Czechoslovakia in their publications of 1969 (Jegorov 1999a: 165). Lotman was unable to continue as department chair after 1977.

8 A culture text is broadly conceived to include not only artistic (aesthetic) forms of literary and visual arts texts, but also simple speech acts and other meaning-based symbolic systems.

2: The Structure of Cultural Semiotic Systems

1 Eco (1985) provides a very interesting discussion on the age-old search for the perfect language and the contemporary side effects we find in scholarly theories and practices (*The Search for the Perfect Language* [Oxford, UK: Blackwell] 1985: 12–19).

2 The tension between a given usage of a sign in a speech event and the field of possible meanings potentially represented by that sign (in a broader, more abstract context) is at the heart of Lotman's terminological distinction. However, in order to avoid confusion, it is important to note that for most theoreticians who work with speech and communication events, the term 'code' is used to refer to 'language' and includes *de facto* the cultural/historical context.

Code, as a variable, plays an essential role in Lotman's (I–I) autocommunication systems, where an 'original message is recoded into the elements of its structure' via a second code, resulting in a new message (1990: 22; 2000: 165). In I–s/he communication, the code and message are constants and the addresser and addressee are variables. Texts, according to Lotman, can be interpreted (or misinterpreted) as a code or a message. When a text fails to convey new information, but converts existing meanings into a new system, that text is being used as code – this is the essence of autocommunication. Signals to perceive the text as code (and not message) include rhythmical systems and repetitions (1990: 30; 2000: 172–3).

Frawley (1997: 69–75) discusses the importance of *inner code* for all cognitive science approaches. From a representationalist perspective, inner code is defined as symbolic or 'languagelike,' while from a connectionist's point of view inner code is a 'network of nodes and connections.' Furthermore, definitions of computation are intimately connected to viewing inner code as 'neural information' (given by neuronal firing patterns) (1997: 82–3). Finally, inner code is structured and 'the locale of [the] knowledge' (1997: 72–3).

3 In Peircean terms, any performance of a speech act, which is by definition finite and bounded, would necessarily involve *dynamic interpretants*. Peirce's definition of the dynamic interpretant further specifies it as 'whatever interpretation any mind actually makes of a sign' (8.315). The importance of dynamic interpretants in language change through time is also significant. (For more on this topic see Shapiro 1988: 125 and Savan 1980: 258.)
4 For a series of discussions of the controversy concerning Saussure's influence on Lotman and Soviet semiotics, see Bethea 2000; Mandelker 1994; and Ivanov 1998a: 641–791.
5 I have argued elsewhere (Andrews 1990: 44–80, 1994, 1996a: 2–33) that the Peircean sign types that are essential to the study of semantics in natural languages necessarily include a wide array of interpretants (including the triads of immediate/dynamic/final and emotional/energetic/logical) and immediate and dynamic objects. The fact that Lotman never refers to these sign types is not surprising, in that his level of analysis is generally more focused on the system level, as he himself noted, and not on the individual sign level.

3: Introduction to the Semiosphere

1 We will see in later sections how Lotman's description of communication systems and information production shares similarities with contemporary models of human memory, especially as shown in Gerald Edelmann (*The Theory of Neuronal Group Selection* [New York: Basic Books, 1987]) and Israel Rosenfield (*The Invention of Memory* [New York: Basic Books, 1989]). One can find in Lotman's scholarship discussions of phenomena such as 'textual memory' and asymmetry of the brain's hemispheres (e.g., 'Brain – Text – Culture – Artificial Intelligence' (Мозг – Текст – Культура – Искусственный интеллект) 1992a: 25–33; 2000: 580–9), but Lotman's modelling systems are always based in cultural, not biological, space.
2 Lotman's semiosphere may share certain characteristics with the Peircean notion of ground in that the ground is an essential component of the functioning sign that is given within the sign complex itself and is, by definition, a general attribute (C.S. Peirce 1931–58: 1.551, 1.558, 2.228). What may be of particular relevance in terms of similarity with the semiosphere is that Peircean ground, like Lotman's semiosphere, guarantees the potential existence of invariant meanings. For more on this point, see Andrews (1994: 11–13). Sebeok (1991: 20–41) provides an important view of the role of Lotman in the development of semiotic studies and his conception of the semiosphere.
3 One of the primary defining characteristics of the boundary involves translat-

ability across and within said boundaries. The importance of translatability parallels the Peircean notion of translatability as the defining property of the interpretant and its role in the sign complex. Lotman (1990: 11–19; 1992a: 8–17) most specifically addresses the question of translatability in the context of tension in discourse in terms of (1) a desire to achieve understanding while (2) attempting to increase the value of the message.

4 For a more detailed discussion of Peircean and Thomian perspectives on continuity, and in particular Thomian catastrophe theory, see Andrews (1990: 87–93; 1995b) and Thom (1975, 1983).

5 Perhaps the sense of Lotman's characterization of continuity and discontinuity becomes clearer in the context of his discussion of the 'moment of explosion,' which is a point of higher charged information of the entire system, where any element from within the system or from another system may become the dominant element following the explosion (Lotman 1992a: 28). The inception of the explosion (or discontinuity) is first and foremost the beginning of a new stage in the semiotic system's development (Lotman 1992a: 32). But this new stage must be viewed not as a linear development, but more in terms of a cyclical alternation similar to a sine curve. (For more discussion of the cyclical nature of culture, see Lotman 1990: 144–5.)

6 The difference between самоназвание ('self-naming') and самоописание ('self-description') of cultural space is quite significant in Lotmanian thought (1992a: 26–8; 1990: 128–30, 144; 2000: 254–6, 269). Although both are metalinguistic phenomena, they are distinct in their role in semiosis. Specifically, the term 'self-naming' is introduced by Lotman in a chapter titled 'Continuity and Discontinuity' and refers to a *mechanism* of the structural organization of semiotic space that defines the dynamics of each level (in terms of density, speed, etc.). These semiotic processes (which are constantly occurring in all parts of the semiosphere) may attribute to themselves 'false self-names,' that is, characterize the space based on characteristics that belong to a different part of the semiosphere. 'Self-description,' which is discussed in his chapter on semiotic space, is the *result* achieved when the semiosphere reaches its 'highest form of structural organization.' The 'process of self-description' may create either 'realistic' or 'ideal' mappings of semiotic space and is necessary to maintain balance in hybrid semiotic spaces. The degree of realist or idealist self-description depends on the orientation of the space itself where past-orientation is more 'realistic' and future orientation is more 'idealistic.' Finally, both self-naming and self-description facilitate the perception of unity within the semiosphere – a unity that may mask the most interesting struggles (discontinuities) that co-exist within any synchronic layer of dynamic semiotic space.

4: Characteristics and Origins of the Semiosphere

1 In considering Lotman's definition of dialogue, where the 'value' of the discourse is not determined by the intersecting space but by the non-intersecting spaces, it becomes clearer that Lotman does indeed have a more sophisticated sense of sign interaction that requires a third element (in this case, the non-intersecting spaces) in any cultural act, all of which are necessarily translations (1992a: 15–16). Lotman clearly states that the overlap (общность) of different cultural codes is imaginary (мнимая) (1992a: 15).

2 William Frawley, in his fascinating book *Vygotsky and Cognitive Science,* makes an important contribution to defining the relationship between consciousness and communication. Frawley convincingly argues for consciousness to become an object of study within the field of cognitive science, and demonstrates Vygotsky's importance in developing a theory of metaconsciousness (осознание), as opposed to non-conscious and conscious processing (1997: 6–7, 28–9). Vygotsky's *private speech,* 'self-directed language for metaconscious control,' provides the basis for metaconsciousness and, as such, can be seen as the 'language for thought.' Here, language becomes a mediator between the code and the sociocultural context, 'mediating the progress of mental-computational activity' (7). Such a view is complementary to Lotman's view of language, especially in the form of autocommunication.

It is useful to note here, as well, Vygotsky's three distinctions for different types of 'meaning': предметная отнесённость ('object relatedness'), смысл ('understanding'), значение ('intension') (Frawley 1997: 28–9, 247, 253–6).

3 For more information on modern-day applications of the biosphere and noosphere, see Shirkova-Tuula 1998.

4 Perhaps it was during his high school studies that Lotman, who wanted to become a biologist until the year before entering university, first came into contact with Vernadsky's theory. In any case, Lotman's definition of semiotic space is based not on biological organisms, but rather, as Lotman himself states, on a mathematical conceptualization of space in which the artistic text may be resurrected at any time (1997c: 720; 1990: 127; 2000: 253–4).

5 Vernadsky's noosphere is considered to be the final evolutionary stage of the biosphere. However, this does not mean there is an end of evolution in sight. In fact, Vernadsky has opted to put the question in a different way. Instead of anticipating an end to existence, he asks rather whether life in the universe had a beginning: Was it eternal at the front end, as it seems to be at the back end (1993: 310–47, esp. 315–20)?

6 Mandelker describes Lotman's later works on the semiosphere as a 'metaphor

based on principles of cell biology, organic chemistry, and brain science, to map cultural dynamics' (1994: 385). I suggest that Lotman's proposed theory of cultural space, like his earlier work, is fundamentally defined by anthroposemiotic principles and categories. As Sebeok states in his discussion of a possible analogy between endosemiotic and anthroposemiotic codes, the important point is that 'both are productive semiotic systems' (1991: 86).

7 I have come to the same conclusion as David Savan in his analysis of the use of abduction in human language, where the immediate objects are perceived linguistic forms and the dynamic objects are the speakers themselves (Andrews 1994: 22–3; Savan 1980: 252–62).

8 Sebeok provides many examples of how humans assign proper names to animals and the importance of this phenomenon as an example of iconicity at work (Sebeok 1990: 90). T. von Uexküll (1982) claims that humans view other mammals as abstractions and does not broach the subject of naming (Jakob von Uexküll 1982: 25–73).

5: Lotman, Bulgakov, and Zamyatin

1 The following volumes by Lotman are either entirely devoted to analyses of Russian literature or have large sections devoted to them: *Izbrannye statji II* (1992b), *Izbrannye statji II* (section one, 1992b), *Ob iskusstve* (On Art) (1998), *O russkoj literature* (On Russian Literature) (1997), *O poetax i poezii* (On Poets and Poetry) (1996), *Puškin* (1995), and *Karamzin* (1997 – historical biography of cultural context). All of the ten volumes of Lotman's works published since 1992 include important analyses of Russian literature (see Introduction, note 3).

2 There exists an excellent body of criticism about Bulgakov's work in general and about *The Master and Margarita* specifically. Some of the major criticisms on Bulgakov include works by Ellendea Proffer (1984), Marietta Čudakova (1974, 1976, 1988a), Boris Gasparov ([1978] 1994), David Bethea (1989, 1996), Leslie Milne (1990, 1995), J.A.E. Curtis (1991), Svetlana Kuljus (1998), Laura Weeks (1996a, 1996b), Colin Wright (1978), Andrew Barratt (1987), and special editions of the journals *Russian Literature Triquarterly* (1978) and *Canadian-American Slavic Studies* (1981). It is worth noting that Proffer's seminal monograph on Bulgakov and his works continues to be the central critical work on Bulgakov today.

3 When reading Lotman's description of the characteristics of the 'true home' in Bulgakov, one is struck by the profound similarities between Bulgakov and Zamyatin. See chapter 6 for another aspect of common textuality in Bulgakov

and Zamyatin – namely, that of revolution and cyclic development. Also in the context of home-antihome, we see a similar evaluation of the persons who inhabit the true versus false homes – namely, the 'living' (what Zamyatin calls живые-живые 'the living-living') and the 'pseudo-living' (Lotman 1992b I: 460) (Zamyatin's живые-мёртвые 'living dead'). For an in-depth discussion on the use of home-antihome in the works of Zamyatin, see Baak (1981) and Maksimova (1994, 1998). Bulgakov uses terms for homes and antihomes, including 'building' (здание, зданьице) and 'basements' (подвал, подвальчик), in a particular way. Specifically, buildings are neutral in the context of the novel (or in the worse case, ambiguous), involving such edifices as the Jershalaim cathedral or a house in the woods where Margarita finds the Master in her dream. The use of basements is often associated with home, the haven where the Master and Margarita spent some of their more intimate moments, and the place where the Master wished to die (see chapters 13, 19, 24, 27, and 30 of the novel). Specific lexical evidence supporting the basement as home include such word combinations as 'comfortable' (уютный подвальчик) (ch. 30) and 'in the basement safe haven' (в подвальном приюте) (ch. 13).

I have deliberately omitted page numbers from my references to Bulgakov's novel in favour of chapter numbers due to the extraordinarily large and varied limited editions of this work published in the Soviet Union and, later, Russia.

4 It is interesting that both of the Russian printings of this article, originally written by Lotman in 1986, end with this quote (1992b: I. 463; 1998: 748–54). However, the English translation (1990: 185–92) includes the following two additional paragraphs at the end: 'In Bulgakov the home is an eternal, closed space, the source of security, harmony and creativity. Beyond its walls lie chaos, destruction and death. A flat, and especially a communal flat, is chaos masquerading as home and making a real home impossible. The home and the communal flat are antipodes: this means that the common feature they share – being a dwelling place, living quarters – loses its significance, and all that remains are the semiotic qualities. The home becomes a semiotic element of the cultural space.' Here we have an example of an important principle in human cultural thinking: real space is an iconic image of the semiosphere, a language in which various non-spatial meanings can be expressed, whereas the semiosphere in its turn transforms the real world of space in which we live into its image and likeness.

5 Although Lotman uses the Russian word бездомье for homelessness, a more generally accepted Russian term is бездомность.

6 I have opted to translate Lotman's use of the phrase художественный текст

as 'artist text' in most cases and 'literary texts' in those contexts where it is absolutely unambiguous. Artistic texts include not only literary texts but others such as theatrical, operatic, and cinematic.

7 The importance of Gogol''s influence on both Bulgakov and Zamyatin has been noted by many critics besides Lotman, and acknowledged by the writers themselves. Zamyatin notes in his multiple autobiographies the influence of both Gogol' and Dostoevsky on his development as a writer. The difference between 'fantastic realism' and the use of the fantastic in other ways is a fundamental one. In Gogolian and later Bulgakovian fantastic realism, the fantastic elements are used to demonstrate and explain everyday phenomena. For more on this topic see Lotman 1997: 694–8, 710–29.

8 Inspired by Čudakova's remarks (1974) about the importance of Florensky's book to Bulgakov, many scholars have written about Florensky's influence on Bulgakov (cf. Milne 1990: 251–6; Sokolov 1997: 474–86; Bethea 1989: 201–5, 1991; Edwards 1982: 205; Beatie and Powell 1981: esp. 251–3). Florensky had a profound impact on philosophical thought in twentieth-century Russia. For general discussions of Florensky's importance, see Clark and Holquist 1984: 120–5, 135–8, Xoružij 1990: vi–xvi, Byčkov 1996: 285–332, and Vjacheslav Vsevolodovich Ivanov 1998b.

9 Note that the Russian word покой is also used to mean 'rest' (as opposed to 'movement') in physics terminology, and was used throughout the nineteenth century to mean 'room' – specifically, any internal rooms in a house or apartment other than the corridor, bathroom, and kitchen.

10 Although Florensky was a Russian Orthodox priest and was persecuted by the Soviet authorities for his religious beliefs and affiliations, he played a significant role in the Russian gnostic movement of his day, especially as it was represented in the works of Vladimir Solov'ev and Father Sergej Bulgakov. For more information on understanding the roots of Florensky's gnostic heresy, see Carlson 1996: 49–67.

6: Bulgakov and Zamyatin

1 There is some controversy over the exact date that Zamyatin left the Soviet Union. Lakšin mentions 1932 (1988: 29), while Čudakova states that Zamyatin left 'no later than the end of November' of 1931 (1988a: 357). According the Zamyatin's letter to Bulgakov, Zamyatin intended to be in Moscow on 4 or 5 November and expected to leave the country on 14 November 1931 (Čudakova 1988a: 357).

2 In a letter from N. Nikitin to A. Voronskij (1922), Nikitin characterizes

Zamyatin as 'oppositionary by nature' ['оппозиционер по природе'] (Voronskij 1983: 561).

3 Although they do not connect Bulgakov's novel to Zamyatin's fiction, Beatie and Powell (1978: 219–52) make three points that I would generalize as supporting my claim that the philosophy and works of these two writers are connected: (1) the use of Goethean inversions (225); (2) the use of heresy as a 'motif-complex' of the novel (235); and (3) the classification of *The Master and Margarita* as most of all a work of 'ironic fiction' (238). It is in connection with the third point that we recall Zamyatin's well-known quote from his 1922 autobiography about his novel, *We:* 'самая моя шуточная и самая серьёзная вещь' ('my most serious and most playful work'). I would add that it is precisely in this type of comparison that we also see the profound impact of Gogol' on the narrative structures of both Zamyatin and Bulgakov. The importance of Gogol' for these two writers is another reason Lotman's work (1992b: I. 416–63; 1997a: 548–711) is so nicely applicable to Zamyatin's fiction (see chapter 7). (For a discussion of Gogol''s influence on Bulgakov and Nabokov, see Bethea 1991: 189–96.)

4 Propp notes that the original Russian 'drakon' was always 'vodyanoj' ([found in] water, aquatic) and usually named 'zmej' (snake) in early fairy tales (Propp 1986: 217–19). Also, 'zmej' is strongly connected with fire, is often able to fly, and serves as a border guard. This description fits the image of dragon found in Zamyatin's 'Drakon' and connects the image to a more fully developed 'zmej-drakon' in the novel *We*, in the character S-4711. For more information on Zamyatin's use of folklore and Old Russian literary traditions, see Maksimova 1994.

5 The 1977 *Russian Word Frequency Dictionary* includes the following breakdown in textual percentage types that served as the source for determining word frequencies (Zasorina 1977: 9):

Literary texts – prose	25.4%
drama	27.2
Scholarly and publicistic texts	23.6
Newspaper and journal texts	23.8

In terms of total word usages, 39,268 different lexical entries were derived from 1,056,382 texts (1977: 27).

6 Ironically, in the annotated notes to Voronskij's letter to Zamyatin, all of Zamyatin's works mentioned explicitly by Voronskij are listed with place and date of publication, except 'Drakon' (Voronskij 1983: 572).

7 In Gumil'ev's highly praised cycle *The Pillar of Fire* (Огненный столп),

published in 1921 (the year of his untimely death by execution), one of the most noted poems is devoted to the image of tram as revolution (Заблудившийся трамвай, 'The Lost Tram'). One of the more remarkable elements of Gumil'ev's poem is the reference to decapitation and the decapitated head's slippery box (cf. В красной рубашке, с лицом, как вымя, Голову срезал палач и мне, Она лежала вместе с другими Здесь, в ящике скользком, на самом дне.' 'In a red shirt, with a face like an udder, the executioner cut off my head and it was lying together with others here, in the slippery box at the very bottom').

The word трамвай ('tram') occurs a total of 39 times in *The Master and Margarita*. Of these, 22 refer specifically to the tram's role in Berlioz's death. Almost all of the remaining entries are connected with the cat Begemot (also called Behemoth in English).

8 The word 'tram driver' (вожатый/вожатая) also means 'Young Pioneer leader.'
9 As Berlioz is falling to the ground, he sees the 'gilded moon' (позлащённая луна). The Russian form for 'gilded' here is the non-pleophonic Church Slavonic form, not the expected Russian form (позолоченная). This particular usage of the Church Slavonic form could be: (1) an accentuation of the *supernatural* glow of the moon and (2) the ambiguous meaning of the root -z/l- (зло/зла), meaning 'evil.'
10 Zamyatin, with rare exception, appropriates images from his earlier works to use in later ones. However, his re-evocation of a particular image may occur without explicit mention of the name of the image itself. Thus, instead of stating the lexeme 'aquarium' in 'Drakon,' Zamyatin presents a verbal picture of an aquarium (cf. the use of the verb выныривать ['dive up from the water'] can only be used in the context of water).
11 Lotman (1992b: I. 432–6) discusses the importance of continuity to the construction of artistic space, the perversion of the observer's perspective in textual space, and the mechanism of conversion of continuous space into discontinuous 'non-space' in the works of Gogol'. Although all of Lotman's examples relate to Gogol', I believe they fit quite naturally in our discussion of Zamyatin. Gogol''s profound impact on both Zamyatin and Bulgakov is undisputed in the critical literature.

7: Extending Lotmanian Theory

1 For a complete listing of Zamyatin's publications through 1995, see Galuškin (1997).
2 The following remarks take into account interpretations offered in Andrews

et al. (1994), but the present work recontextualizes these previous findings into a semiotic model of culture.

3 Zamyatin most eloquently describes his notions of the synthetic text in two essays, 'On Literature, Revolution and Entropy' ('O literature, revoljucii i entropii,' also titled 'O literature, revoljucii, entropii i pročem ...' ([1923] 1988a: 446–51) and 'On Synthesism' ('O sintetizme') ([1922] 1988a: 412–19).

4 Heller (1994: 80–2) refers to Zamyatin's numerical and geometrical imagery as 'commentary' but seems dissatisfied with this classification, and in the case of colour makes the following statement: 'Color is so important that on occasion it defines the movement of narrative' (1994: 82).

5 The etymology of Zamyatin's neologism *Rhopalocera* is rhopalo < Greek ῥόπᾰλο(ν) – 'club, stick' and cera < Latin cēra – 'wax; component used to make explosives.'

6 A discussion of the colour text is beyond the scope of this work. However, for interesting discussions of the colour text in Zamyatin's *We*, see Connolly 1979; Proffer 1988; Hoisington and Imbery 1992; Andrews, Lahusen, and Maksimova 1994; and Andrews and Maksimova [forthcoming]. Some of the more salient aspects of the colour text vis-à-vis the other texts are its extended polysemy, enhanced metonymical structure, and reduced narrative speed.

7 The various Russian editions of *We* give the name of the female character from MEFI as 1-330 or I-330 (Arabic or Roman numerals). Given the absence of a definitive signed copy of the author's original manuscript, all remarks will take into account both these interpretations. In the body of this book, only 1-330 will be written.

8 For more *diabolic* numerical references and discussion of MEFI, see Andrews et al. 1994: 86–90. Also note that Russian numerical notation uses a period where English notation uses a comma or space (e.g., Russian 20.000 = English 20,000 or metric 20 000).

9 For a complete discussion of the numerals in *We*, see Andrews et al. 1994: 73–97.

10 For a thorough review of the debate over Zamyatin's references to Taylor, see Andrews et al. 1994: 69–71. Besides Brook Taylor and Frederick W. Taylor, there is also the Cambridge mathematician Henry M. Taylor, known for his contribution to modern elementary geometry. H.M. Taylor is remembered for his definition of a special case circle that is related to the Tucker and Lemoine circles (Cajori 1919: 300).

11 For a discussion of the evolution of specific synthetic images within and across Zamyatin's writings, see Maksimova 1994: 72; 1998: 192–3. For syn-

thetic evolution between Zamyatin and other writers, see Andrews 1992: 75–82.

8: Visual and Auditory Signs in Human Language

1 Eisele comments on Peirce's definition of diagrammatic meaning and reasoning by specifying that diagrammatic includes verbal expressions, algebraic formulae, and diagrams proper (1992: 257).
2 Note the generalization of vision to emotion-related verb forms in Russian (e.g., nenavidet' 'to hate;' l'ubovat's'a 'to admire visually' [< l'ubit' 'to love']).
3 Besides standard, semantic shifts, one also finds examples of confusion of *ved-* and *vid-* root forms in diachrony: (1) ved (< věd) > vid: svědetel' > svidetel' (Sreznevskij [1902] 1955, III: 676); (2) vid > věd: spravědlivost' (15th c. Ruthenian text, Gumec'ka 1978: 373) < въд [as in правъда].
4 There are many different approaches to defining the essence of human language. I am very sympathetic to Frawley's presentation of Vygotsky's contributions to cognitive science and would mention here the notion that human language can be seen as operating on the boundary between 'logical form' and 'social practice' (1997: 62). In particular, this leads to the formulation of a distinction between a 'language for thought,' and not a 'language of thought' (1997: 96–7).
5 For detailed information on the structure of V1, see Tootell et al. 1982, 1988; Kosslyn 1994; and Damasio 1994.
6 For more information on hypercolumns, see Calvin and Ojemann 1994: 208–17.
7 For more specific information on hypercolumns in the visual cortex, see Calvin and Ojemann 1994: 208.
8 Kosslyn (1994: 6) further explains that the debates are not whether proposition and depictive representations are used in cognition – all agree that both are used. Rather, the argument is over the degree of importance of depictive representations versus propositional ones. It is also worth noting that the question of iconic memory has taken on a new look as researchers have become more committed to dynamic as opposed to static models (see Greene 1992: 7–15).
9 Studies of visual memory have determined that as many as 51,180 pictures per second may be stored and searched in long-term memory, while short-term memory demonstrates a recall rate of 986,300 from 1 million if tested immediately. For more information, see Kosslyn 1994: 129–30.

176 Notes to pages 139–52

10 For information on the studies conducted on the relationship between visual and auditory images in perception referred to in Kosslyn's analysis, see S.J. Segal and V. Fusella 1970: 458–64. For details on visual imagery and perception experiments, see Craver-Lemley and Reeves 1987.
11 For more on the question of imagery in blind subjects, see Kosslyn 1994: 334–5 and Kidwell and Greer 1973. The cause of blindness will be significant in determining the degree of imagery, if any, that is functional. This includes a difference in recalling 'high-imagery' words (Kosslyn 1994: 335).
12 Mulford's research demonstrates that blind children do in fact use spatial deictic terms, but only for locations that did not require sensitivity with respect to the position of the speaker (1983: 89–107).
13 Other studies have demonstrated similar findings to McGurk and MacDonald (1976, 1978) but with some interesting differences, including: (1) /d/ and other alveolar or velar stops are less affected by conflicting visual cues (Repp et al. 1983), and (2) auditory /ba/ and visual /ga/ give a greater variety than merely /d/, including /va, ta, fa, la, pa, ða, θa/ (Johnson and Spaulding [unpublished data]).

9: The Language of Memory in the Memory of Language

1 Rose argues that the major question of memory research in the future will be a focus on retrieval, not learning. Discussions of saturation of recognition (as opposed to recall) memory can be found in Rose 1992: 318 and Kosslyn 1994: 129. In Kosslyn, there are very provocative data concerning enormous visual memory potential for both short-term and long-term memory. In the experiments provided in Kosslyn the representations are viewer-centred, not object-centred.
2 For a more in-depth discussion of forgetting, see Riccio et al. 1994: 917–26.
3 It is relevant that Mandler (1989: 93) does state that even in automatic processing, the 'final product is, of course, a conscious content.' Nevertheless, this type of characterization of semanticity remains controversial.
4 It is important to note Rose's distinction of three 'languages' of memory in the brain: morphological – mappings in space; biochemical – gives compositional description; physiological – 'essentially dynamic, describing events occurring in time' (1992: 321). Rose insists that we need at least these three levels of meaning in order to begin to discuss memory. Squire also makes a strong case for a dynamic view of LTM, where LTMs change over time based on other behaviours and events that have nothing to do with the initial learning process (1987: 205).

  A recent study of H.M.'s language ability conducted in February 2000 sheds additional light on the relationship between LTMs and language ability (comprehension and production) (see Skotko et al. forthcoming). For a good survey of the role of memory in language learning, see Fabbro 1999: 89–102.

5 This principle is called the 'encoding specificity principle' from Tulving and Thompson (1973).

6 Dudai gives a good example of episodic versus semantic memory: 'memory of a visit to Jerusalem is episodic, but the fact that Jerusalem is the capital of Israel is semantic' (1989: 264). Note also that Kosslyn is a major proponent of the notion that aspects of episodic and semantic knowledge may be encoded and/or decoded by a dual, interactive code – one propositional, the other image-based (1980, 1994). For more information on cognitive models of memory, see Conway 1997. For a discussion of vision and memory in aphasiacs, see Fabbro 1999: 121–2.

7 Also embedded in these questions are issues which suggest that faces and written words may involve mechanisms not generally used in other forms of identification (Kosslyn 1994: 64).

8 For more information on theories and types of priming, see McNamara 1992, 1994, and McKoon and Ratcliff 1992.

9 Schacter (1996: 333 n 50) mentions special problems associated with the priming of new semantic associations in amnesic patients that do not give results on a par with experiments with priming by familiar lexical items.

10 Frawley (1997: 114–74) provides an excellent discussion of Vygotsky's views on the importance of the 'culture-mind interface' and the role speech plays in this equation.

11 Kosslyn's associate memory (AM) is a subsystem offered by his theory of perception that receives information from 'all sensory systems' and contains associations between 'perceptual representations' as well as abstract, language-based categories (1994: 73). The function of AM as a distinct structure is to store 'associations among individual perceptual representations' and to 'organize "conceptual" information that may not be directly derived from the senses' (1994: 215). AM would be distributed throughout the brain but with prominent placement in the temporal-occipital-parietal junction and the posterior superior temporal cortex (1994: 223, 381). These structures would be similar to semiotic texts in their ability to condense information and build translation circuits for activation. Note that such a system would integrate language-based memory in a way that is potentially more rewarding than the traditional view of semantic versus episodic memory.

References

Andersen, H. 1973. 'Abductive and Deductive Change.' *Language* 49 (4): 765–93.
Andrews, E. 1990. *Markedness Theory: The Union of Asymmetry and Semiosis in Language.* Durham, NC: Duke University Press.
– 1992. 'Vzaimosvjaz' tvorčestva Bulgakova i Zamjatina.' *Vestnik SPBgU*, s.2, vyp.2, no. 9: 75–82.
– 1993. 'Interpretants and Linguistic Change: The Case of -*x* in Contemporary Standard Colloquial Russian.' *Journal of Slavic Linguistics* 1 (2): 199–218.
– 1994. 'The Interface of Iconicity and Interpretants.' *The Peirce Seminar Papers* 2: 9–28. Providence, RI: Berghahn Books.
– 1995a. 'Seeing Is Believing: Vision Categories in Russian.' *Meaning as Explanation: Advances in Linguistic Sign Theory,* edited by E. Contini-Morava and B. Sussman Goldberg, 361–77. Berlin: Mouton de Gruyter.
– 1995b. 'The Semiotics of Catastrophe: Interpretants and Linguistic Change.' *Semiotics around the World: Synthesis in Diversity,* edited by I. Rauch, 361–77. Berlin: Mouton de Gruyter.
– 1996a. *The Semantics of Suffixation.* Munich: Lincom Europa.
– 1996b. 'The Shift of "Shame" in Slavic.' *International Journal of Slavic Linguistics and Poetics* 39–40: 299–312.
– 1999. 'Lotman's Communication Act and Semiosis.' *Semiotica* 126 (1/4): 1–15.
Andrews, E., T. Lahusen, and E. Maksimova. 1994. *O sintetizme, matematike i pročem.* Saint Petersburg: Sudarynja.
Andrews, E., and E. Maksimova. Forthcoming. *Nonlinear Modes of Reasoning: The Integration of Color and Verbal Texts in Zamiatin's WE.*
Annenkov, Ju. 1991. *Dnevnik moix vstreč. Cikl tragedij.* Leningrad. Iskusstvo.
Anttila, R., and S. Embleton. 1989. 'The Iconic Index: From Sound Change to Rhyming Slang.' *Diachronica* 6 (2): 155–80.

Baak, J.J. van. 1981. 'Zamjatin's Cave: On Troglodyte versus Urban Culture, Myth, and the Semiotics of Literary Space.' *Russian Literature* 10: 381–422.
Baddeley, A. 1989. 'The Uses of Working Memory.' *Memory: Interdisciplinary Approaches*, edited by P.R. Soloman, G.R. Goethals, C.M. Kelley, and B.R. Stephens, 107–26. New York: Springer-Verlag.
Bailey, K.D. 1990. *Social Entropy Theory*. Albany: State University of New York Press.
Barratt, A. 1987. *Between Two Worlds: A Critical Introduction to* The Master and Margarita. Oxford: Oxford University Press.
Barthes, R. 1966. *Critique et vérité*. Paris: Seuil.
– 1974. *S/Z*. New York: Hill and Wang.
Beatie, B.A., and P.W. Powell. 1978. 'Story and Symbol: Notes Towards a Structural Analysis of Bulgakov's *The Master and Margarita*.' *Russian Literature Triquarterly*: 219–52.
– 1981. 'Bulgakov, Dante and Relativity.' *Canadian-American Slavic Studies* 2–3 (15): 250–70.
Berdnikov, G.P., ed. 1983. *Literaturnoe nasledstvo: Iz istorii sovetskoj literatury 1920–30–x godov*, edited by D.D. Blagoj et al. Moscow: Nauka.
Bethea, D.M. 1989. *The Shape of the Apocalypse in Modern Russian Fiction*. Princeton: Princeton University Press.
– 1991. 'Bulgakov and Nabokov: Toward a Comparative Perspective.' *Association of Russian-American Scholars in USA* 24: 187–209.
– 1996. 'History as Hippodrome: The Apocalyptic Horse and Rider in *The Master and Margarita*.' *The Master and Margarita: A Critical Companion*, edited by Laura D. Weeks, 122–42. Evanston, IL: Northwestern University Press.
– 2000. 'Iurii Lotman in the 1980s: The Code and Its Relation to Literary Biography.' *Reconstructing the Canon: Russian Writing in the 1980s*, 9–32. Amsterdam: Harwood Academic.
Boni, A., and C. Boni. 1925. *Letters from Russian Prisons*. New York: Albert and Charles Boni.
Borges, J.L. 1964. *Other Inquisitions*. Austin: University of Texas Press.
Brown, G.S. 1969. *Laws of Form*. London: George Allen and Unwin.
Buchler, J., ed. 1955. *Philosophical Writings of Peirce*. New York: Dover.
Bučina, L.I., and M. Yu. Ljubimova, eds. 1997. *Rukopisnoe nasledie E. Zamjatina* (vypusk 3, čast' 1). Saint Petersburg: Rossijskaja nacional'naja biblioteka.
Buck, C.D. 1988. *A Dictionary of Selected Synonyms in the Principle Indo-European Languages*. 2nd ed. Chicago: University of Chicago Press.
Bulgakov, M.A. 1978. *The Master and Margarita*. In *Romany* 421–812. Leningrad: Xudožestvennaya literatura.
– 1989. *Pis'ma: Žizneopisanie v dokumentax*. Introduction by V.V. Petelina, commentary by V.I. Loseva and V.V. Petelina. Moscow: Sovremennik.

Bulgakova, E.S., and S.A. Ljandres. 1988. *Vospominanija o Mixaile Bulgakove.* Moscow: Sovetskij pisatel'.
Byčkov, V.V. 1996. 'Filosofii iskusstva Pavla Florenskogo.' *Svjaščennik Pavel Florenskij: Izbrannye trudy po iskusstvu.* Moscow: Izdatel'stvo Izobrazitel'noe iskusstvo.
Cajori, F. 1919. *A History of Mathematics.* New York: Macmillan.
Calvin, W.H., and G.A. Ojemann. 1994. *Conversations with Neil's Brain: The Neural Nature of Thought and Language.* Reading, MA: Addison-Wesley.
Carlson, M. 1996. 'Gnostic Elements in the Cosmogony of Vladimir Solov'ev.' *Russian Religious Thought,* edited by R. Gustafson and J. Kornblatt, 49–67. Madison: University of Wisconsin Press.
Černov, I.A. 1997. 'Opyt vvedenija v sistemu Ju. M. Lotmana.' *O russkoj literature Ju. M. Lotman,* 5–12. Saint Petersburg: Iskusstvo–Saint Petersburg.
Clark, K., and M. Holquist. 1984. *Mikhail Baktin.* Cambridge, MA: Belknap Press of Harvard University Press.
Connolly, J.W. 1979. 'A Modernist's Palette: Colors and Their Function in *We.*' *Russian Language Journal* 33: 82–98.
Conway, M.A., ed. 1997. *Cognitive Models of Memory.* Cambridge, MA: MIT Press.
Cooke, L.B. 1988. 'Ancient and Modern Mathematics in Zamiatin's *We.*' *Zamiatin's* We: *A Collection of Critical Essays,* edited by G. Kern, 149–67. Ann Arbor, MI: Ardis.
Corti, M. 1978. *An Introduction to Literary Semiotics.* Bloomington: Indiana University Press.
Craver-Lemley, C. and A. Reeves. 1987. 'Visual Imagery Selectively Reduces Vernier Acuity.' *Perception* 16: 533–614.
Čudakova, M. 1974. 'Uslovija suščestvovanija.' *V mire knig,* 12:79–81.
– 1976. 'Arxiv M.A. Bulgakova.' *Zapiski otdela rukopisej,* 37:25–151.
– 1988a. *Žizneopisanie Mixaila Bulgakova.* Moscow: Kniga.
– 1988b. 'Eretik, ili matros na mačte.' *Sočinenija,* 498–523. Moscow: Kniga.
Curtis, J.A.E. 1991. *Manuscripts Don't Burn: Mikhail Bulgakov, A Life in Letters and Diaries.* London: Bloomsbury.
Damasio, A.R. 1994. *Descartes' Error: Emotion, Reason, and the Human Brain.* New York: Grosset/Putnam Books.
Deltcheva, R., and E. Vlasov. 1996. 'Lotman's *Culture and Explosion:* A Shift in the Paradigm of the Semiotics of Culture.' *Slavic and East European Journal* 40 (1): 148–52.
Derrida, J. 1973. 'Avoir l'oreille de la philosophie.' *Écarts: Quatre essais à propos de Jacques Derrida,* edited by L. Finas et al., 301–12. Paris: Fayard.
Dudai, Y. 1989. *The Neurobiology of Memory: Concepts, Findings, Trends.* Oxford: Oxford University Press.

Dunlea, A. 1989. *Vision and the Emergence of Meaning: Blind and Sighted Children's Early Language*. Cambridge: Cambridge University Press.

Eco, U. 1979. *The Role of the Reader: Explorations in the Semiotics of Texts*. Bloomington: Indiana University Press.

– 1985. *The Search for the Perfect Language*. Oxford: Blackwell Publishers.

– 1990. Introduction. In *Universe of the Mind: A Semiotic Theory of Culture*, by Ju. M. Lotman, trans. A. Shukmann. Bloomington: Indiana University Press.

Edwards T.R.N. 1982. *Three Russian Writers and the Irrational: Zamiatin, Pil'nyak and Bulgakov*. Cambridge: Cambridge University Press.

Eisele, C. 1992. *Studies in the Scientific and Mathematical Philosophy of Charles S. Peirce*. The Hague: Mouton.

Fabbro, F. 1999. *The Neurolinguistics of Bilingualism*. East Sussex, U.K.: Psychology Press.

Florensky, P.A. [1914] 1990. *Stolp i utverždenie istiny*, tom I. Moscow: izdatel'stvo Pravda.

– 1922. *Mnimosti v geometrii*. Moscow: izdatel'stvo Pomorje.

– 1996. *Uzbrannye trudy po iskusstvu*. Moscow: Czdatel'stvo Izobrazitel'noe iskusstvo.

Frawley, W. 1997. *Vygotsky and Cognitive Science*. Cambridge, MA: Harvard University Press.

Galuškin, A. 1997. 'Vozvraščenie E. Zam'atina. Materialy k bibliografii (1986–1995).' *Novoe o Zam'atine*, edited by L. Heller, 203–324. Moscow: izdatel'stvo MIK.

Gardner, Howard. 1985. *The Mind's New Science: A History of the Cognitive Revolution*. New York: Basic Books.

Gasparov, B. 1985. 'Introduction.' *The Semiotic of Russian Cultural History*, edited by A.D. Nakhimovsky and A.S. Nakhimovksy, 13–29. Ithaca, NY: Cornell University Press.

– [1978] 1994. 'Iz nabljudenii nad motivnoj strukturoj romana M.A. Bulgakova, *Master i Margarita*.' *Literaturnye motivy: Očerki russkoj literatury XX veka* 28–82. Moscow: Nauka.

Gasparov, M.L., ed. 1995. *Lotmonovskij sbornik*. Moscow: izdatel'stvo IC-Garant.

– 1996. 'Ju. M. Lotman: Nauka i ideologija.' *O poetax i poezii*, Ju. M. Lotman, 9–16. Saint Petersburg: Iskusstvo–Saint Petersburg

Geertz, C. 1995. *After the Fact. Two Countries, Four Decades, One Anthropologist*. Cambridge, MA: Harvard University Press.

– 1999. *A Life of Learning. Charles Homer Haskins Lecture for 1999*. American Council of Learned Societies Occasional Paper, 45.

Ginsburg, Mirra, ed. and trans. 1970. *A Soviet Heretic: Essays by Yevgeny Zamjatin*. Chicago: University of Chicago Press.

Greene, R.L. 1992. *Human Memory: Paradigms and Paradoxes*. Hillsdale, NJ: Lawrence Erlbaum.

Gumec'ka, L.L., and I.M. Kernic'kij, eds. 1978. *Slovnik staroukrains'koj movi XIV–XV st.* Kiev: Naukova dumka.
Gumilev, N.S. 1991. *Sobranie sočinenij v 4-x tomax.* Moscow: Terra.
Hardwick, C.S. 1977. *Semiotic and Significs.* Bloomington: Indiana University Press.
Hasher, L., and R.T. Zacks. 1979. 'Automatic and Effortful Processes in Memory.' *Journal of Experimental Psychology: General* 108: 356–88.
Hebb, D.O. 1949. *The Organization of Behavior.* New York: Wiley.
Heller, L. 1994. *Slova Mera mira.* Moscow: MIK.
– ed. 1997. *Novoe o Zamjatine.* Moscow: MIK.
Hofstadter, D.R. 1985. *Metamagical Themas: Questing for the Essence of Mind and Pattern.* Toronto: Bantam Books.
Hoisington, S., and L. Imbery. 1992. 'Zamjatin's Modernist Palette: Colors and Their Function in *We*.' *Slavic and East European Journal* 36 (2): 159–71.
Ivanov, V.V. 1998a. *Izbrannye trudy po semiotike i istorii kul'tury, t. l.* Moscow: Jazyki russkoj kul'tury.
– 1998b. 'Svjaščennik Pavel Florenskij: simvoličeskij vzgljad.' *Izbrannye trudy po semiotike i istorii kul'tury, t. l.*, 706–39. Moscow: Jazyki russkoj kul'tury.
– 1998c. 'O Baxtine i semiotike.' *Izbrannye trudy po semiotike i istorii kul'tury, t. l.*, 740–7. Moscow: Jazyki russkoj kul'tury.
Ivanov, V.V., J.M. Lotman, A.M. Pjatigorskij, V.N. Toporov, and B.A. Uspenskij. [1973] 1998. *Theses on the Semiotic Study of Cultures* (Tartu Semiotics Library 1). Tartu: University of Tartu.
Jakobson, R.O. [1960] 1987. 'Linguistics and Poetics.' *Language in Literature*, edited by K. Pomorska and S. Rudy, 62–94. Cambridge, MA: Belknap Press of Harvard University Press.
– [1964] 1987. 'On the Relation between Visual and Auditory Signs.' *Language in Literature*, edited by K. Pomorska and S. Rudy, 466–73. Cambridge, MA: Belknap Press of Harvard University Press.
– 1971. *Selected Writings II: Word and Language.* The Hague: Mouton.
– [1972] 1985. 'Verbal Communication.' *Selected Writings 7*, edited by S. Rudy with a preface by L.R. Waugh, 81–91. Berlin: Mouton de Gruyter.
– [1975] 1985. 'A Glance at the Development of Semiotics.' *Selected Writings 7*, edited by S. Rudy, 199–218. Berlin: Mouton de Gruyter.
– [1977] 1985a. 'The Grammatical Buildup of Child Language.' *Selected Writings 7*, edited by S. Rudy with a preface by L.R. Waugh, 143–9. Berlin: Mouton de Gruyter.
– [1977] 1985b. 'A Few Remarks on Peirce, Pathfinder in the Science of Language.' *Selected Writings 7*, edited by S. Rudy, 248–53. Berlin: Mouton de Gruyter.
– [1980] 1985. 'Brain and Language: Cerebral Hemispheres and Linguistic

Structure in Mutual Light.' *Selected Writings 7,* edited by S. Rudy with a preface by L.R. Waugh, 163–80. Berlin: Mouton de Gruyter.
- 1980. *The Framework of Language.* Ann Arbor: Michigan Studies in the Humanities.
- 1981. *Selected Writings 3: Poetry of Grammar and Grammar of Poetry.* The Hague: Mouton.
- 1984. *Russian and Slavic Grammar: Studies 1931–1981,* edited by L. Waugh and M. Halle. Berlin: Mouton de Gruyter.
- 1985. *Selected Writings 7,* edited by S. Rudy. Berlin: Mouton de Gruyter.
- 1987. *Language in Literature,* edited by K. Pomorska and S. Rudy. Cambridge, MA: The Belknap Press of Harvard University Press.
- 1990. *On Language,* edited by L. Waugh and M. Monville-Burston. Cambridge, MA: Harvard University Press.

Jakobson, R.O., and L.R. Waugh. [1978] 1988. *The Sound Shape of Language. Selected Writings 8,* edited by S. Rudy with a preface by L.R. Waugh, 242–51. Berlin: Mouton de Gruyter.

Jegorov, B.F. 1994. 'Polveka rjadom s Ju. M. Lotmanom.' *Ju. M. Lotman i tartusko-moskovskaja semiotičeskaja škola,* edited by A.D. Košelev, 475–85. Moscow: Gnosis.
- 1995. 'Ličnost' i tvorčestvo Ju. M. Lotmana.' *Puškin,* Ju. M. Lotman, 5–19. Saint Petersburg: Iskusstvo–Saint Petersburg.
- 1997. 'Biografija duši.' *Karamzin,* Ju. M. Lotman, 5–8. Saint Petersburg: Iskusstvo–Saint Petersburg.
- 1999a. *Žizn' i tvorčestvo Ju. M. Lotmana.* Moscow: Novoe literaturnoe obozrenie.
- 1999b. 'Baxtin i Lotman.' *Žizn' i tvorčestvo Ju. M. Lotmana,* 243–58. Moscow: Novoe literaturnoe obozrenie.

Johnson, B., and A. Spaulding. 1994. Visual and Auditory Cues in Speech Perception. Unpublished work.

Johnson, M.K. 1988. 'Reality Monitoring: An Experimental Phenomenological Approach.' *Journal of Experimental Psychology: General* 117: 390–4.

Johnson, M.K., and L. Hasher. 1987. 'Human Learning and Memory.' *Annual Review of Psychology* 38: 631–8.

Johnson, M.K., S. Hashtroudi, and D.S. Lindsay. 1993. 'Source Monitoring.' *Psychological Bulletin* 114 (1): 3–28.

Johnson, M.K., S.F. Nolde, and D.M. De Leonardis. 1996. 'Emotional Focus and Source Monitoring.' *Journal of Memory and Language* 35: 135–56.

Kandel, E.R., J.H. Schwartz, and T.M. Jessell. 1991. *Principles of Neural Science.* Norwalk, CT: Appleton and Lange.

Kern, G., ed. 1988. *Zamiatin's We: A Collection of Critical Essays.* Ann Arbor, MI: Ardis.

Kidwell, A., and P. Greer. 1973. *Sites, Perception and the Nonvisual Experience: Designing and Manufacturing Mobility Maps*. New York: American Foundation for the Blind.
Kosslyn, S.M. 1980. *Image and Mind*. Cambridge, MA: Harvard University Press.
– 1994. *Image and Brain: The Resolution of the Imagery Debate*. Cambridge, MA: MIT Press.
Kristeva, J. 1970. *Le texte du roman*. The Hague: Mouton.
– 1986. 'Revolution in Poetic Language.' *The Kristeva Reader*, edited by T. Moi, 89–136. New York: Columbia University Press.
Kuljus, S. 1998. *Esoteric Codes in M. Bulgakov's Novel*, The Master and Margarita. Tartu: Tartu Ülikooli Kirjastus.
Lachmann, R. 1987. 'Value Aspects in Jurij Lotman's Semiotics of Culture/Semiotics of Text.' *Dispositio* 12 (30–32): 13–34.
– 1997. *Memory and Literature: Intertextuality in Russian Modernism*. Translated by Roy Sellars and Anthony Wall. Minneapolis: University of Minnesota Press.
Lakšin, B. Ya. 1988. 'Sud'ba Bulgakova: Legenda i byl.' *Vospominanija o Mixaila Bulgakove*, 7–37. Moscow: Sovetskij pisatel'.
Landau, B., and L. Gleitman. 1985. *Language and Experience: Evidence from the Blind Child*. Cambridge, MA: Harvard University Press.
Lotman, Ju. M. 1971. *Struktura xudožestvennogo teksta*. Introduction by T. Winner. Providence, RI: Brown University Press.
– 1975. 'On the Metalanguage of a Typological Description of Culture.' *Semiotica* 14(2): 97–123.
– 1990. *Universe of the Mind: A Semiotic Theory of Culture*. Translated by A. Shukman, introduction by U. Eco. Bloomington: Indiana University Press.
– 1992a. *Kul'tura i vzryv*. Moscow: Gnozis.
– 1992b. *Izbrannye statji v trex tomax*. Vols. 1 & 2. Tallinn: Aleksandra.
– [1992] 1995. 'Ne-memuary.' *Lotmonovskij sbornik*, edited by M.L. Gasparov et al., 5–49. Moscow: izd. IC-Garant.
– 1993. *Izbrannye statji v trex tomax*. Vol. 3. Tallinn: Aleksandra.
– 1994a. 'O prirode iskusstva.' *Ju. M. Lotman i tartusko-moskovskaja semiotičeskaja škola*. Moscow: Gnozis.
– 1994b. *Besedy o russkoj kul'ture*. Saint Petersburg: Iskusstvo–Saint Petersburg.
– 1995. *Puškin*. Saint Petersburg: Iskusstvo–Saint Petersburg.
– 1996. *O poetax i poezii*. Saint Petersburg: Iskusstvo–Saint Petersburg.
– 1997a. *O russkoj literature. Statji i issledovanija (1953–1993). Istorija russkoj prozy. Teorija literatury*. Saint Petersburg: Iskusstvo–Saint Petersburg.
– 1997b. *Karamzin*. Saint Petersburg: Iskusstvo–Saint Petersburg.
– 1997c. *Pis'ma: 1940–1993*. Compiled by B.F. Jegorov. Moscow: Škola 'Jazyki russkoj kul'tury.'

- 1998a. *Ob iskusstve.* Saint Petersburg: Iskusstvo–Saint Petersburg.
- 1998b. 'K probleme prostranstvennoj semiotiki.' *Ob iskusstvo,* 442–6. Saint Petersburg: Iskusstvo–Saint Petersburg.
- 1999. 'Vospominanija.' *Žizn' i tvorčestvo Ju. M. Lotmana,* edited by B.F. Jegorov, 271–354. Moscow: Novoe literaturnoe obozrenie.
- 2000. *Semiosfera.* St. Petersburg: Iskusstvo.

Lotman, Ju. M., and B.A. Uspenskij. 1971. 'O semiotičeskom mexanizme kul'tury.' *Uchenye zapiski Tartuskogo gosudarstvennogo universiteta* (UZTGU) 284, Trudy po znakovym sistemam V. (*Scholarly Notes of Tartu State University,* UZTGU 284, Studies in Sign Systems V).

- [1977] 1985. 'Binary Models in the Dynamics of Russian Culture (to the End of the Eighteenth Century).' *The Semiotics of Russian Cultural History,* edited by A.D. Nakhimovsky and A.S. Nakhimov-sky, 30–66. Ithaca, NY: Cornell University Press.
- 1984a. 'The Role of Dual Models in the Dynamics of Russian Culture (up to the end of the 18th century).' *The Semiotics of Russian Culture,* edited by A. Shukman, translated by N.F.C. Owen, 3–35. Ann Arbor: Michigan Slavic Contributions.
- 1984b. 'New Aspects in the Study of Early Russian Culture.' *The Semiotics of Russian Culture,* edited by A. Shukman, translated by N.F.C. Owen, 36–52. Ann Arbor: Michigan Slavic Contributions.

Lucid, D.P., editor and translator. 1977. *Soviet Semiotics: An Anthology.* Baltimore, MD: Johns Hopkins University Press.

Luria, A.R. 1968. *The Mind of a Mnemonist: A Little Book about a Vast Memory.* New York: Basic Books.

MacDonald, J., and H. McGurk. 1978. 'Visual Influences on Speech Perception Process.' *Perception and Psychophysics* 24: 253–7.

Maksimova, E. 1994. 'Tradicii drevnerusskoj literatury v tvorčestve Zamjatina: Simvolika Doma-Antidoma v romane Zamjatina "My."' *Avrora* 10: 70–6.

- 1998. 'Polemika o polemike: "Peščera" E.I. Zamjatina.' *Russian Literature* 44: 185–95.

Mandelker, A. 1994. 'Semiotizing the Sphere: Organicist Theory in Lotman, Bakhtin, and Vernadsky.' *Publications of the Modern Language Association* (May): 385–96.

Mandler, G. 1985. *Cognitive Psychology: An Essay in Cognitive Science.* Hillsdale, NJ: Lawrence Erlbaum Associates.

- 1989. 'Memory: Conscious and Unconscious.' *Memory: Interdisciplinary Approaches,* edited by P.R. Soloman, G.R. Goethals, C.M. Kelley, and B.R. Stephens, 84–106. New York: Springer-Verlag.

Massaro, D.W. 1987. *Speech Perception by Ear and Eye: A Paradigm for Psychological Inquiry.* Hillsdale, NJ: Lawrence Erlbaum Associates.

McGurk, H., and J. MacDonald. 1976. 'Hearing Lips and Seeing Voices.' *Nature* 264: 746–8.
McKoon, G., and R. Ratcliff. 1992. 'Spreading Activation versus Compound Cue Accounts of Priming: Mediated Priming Revisited.' *Journal of Experimental Psychology* 18(6): 1155–72.
McNamara, T.P. 1992. 'Priming and Constraints It Places on Theories of Memory and Retrieval.' *Journal of Experimental Psychology* 99(4): 650–62.
– 1994. 'Theories of Priming: II. Types of Primes.' *Journal of Experimental Psychology* 20(3): 507–20.
Medvedev, P.N., and M.M. Bakhtin. 1985. *The Formal Method in Literary Scholarship*. Translated by Albert J. Wehrle. Cambridge, MA: Harvard University Press.
Mills, A.E., editor. 1983. *Language Acquisition in the Blind Child*. London: Croom Helm.
Mills, A.E., and R. Thiem. 1980. 'Auditory-Visual Fusions and Illusions in Speech Perception.' *Linguistische Berichte* 68(80): 85–108.
Milne, L. 1990. *Mikhail Bulgakov: A Critical Biography*. Cambridge: Cambridge University Press.
– ed. 1995. *Bulgakov: The Novelist-Playwright*. Luxembourg: Harwood Academic.
Mulford, R. 1983. 'Referential Development in Blind Children.' *Language Acquisition in the Blind Child*, edited by A. Mills, 89–107. London: Croom Helm.
Nakhimovsky, A.D., and A.S. Nakhimovksy, eds. 1985. *The Semiotic of Russian Cultural History*. Ithaca, NY: Cornell University Press.
O'Connor, N., and B. Hermelin. 1981. 'Coding Strategies in Normal and Handicapped Children.' *Intersensory Perception and Sensory Integration*, edited by R.D. Walk and H.L. Pick, Jr, 315–46. New York: Plenum.
O'Neill, J.J. 1954. 'Contributions of the Visual Components of Oral Symbols to Speech Comprehension.' *Journal of Speech and Hearing Disorders* 19: 429–39.
O'Sullivan, T., J. Hartley, D. Saunders, M. Montgomery, and J. Fiske. 1994. *Key Concepts in Communication and Cultural Studies*. New York: Routledge.
Ostrom, T.M. 1989. 'Three Catechisms for Social Memory.' *Memory: Interdisciplinary Approaches,* edited by P.R. Soloman, G.R. Goethals, C.M. Kelley, and B.R. Stephens, 201–20. New York: Springer-Verlag.
Peirce, C.S. 1931–58. *Collected Papers of Charles Sanders Peirce, 1–8*. Cambridge, MA: Harvard University Press.
– 1957. *Essays in the Philosophy of Science*. New York: Liberal Arts Press.
Petelin, V.V. 1989. 'O 'Pis'max M. Bulgakova i o nem samom.' *Pis'ma: Žizneopisanie v dokumentax* 5–28. Moscow: Sovremennik.
Pipes, R. 1990. *The Russian Revolution*. New York: Alfred A. Knopf.
Portis-Winner, I. 1979. 'Ethnicity, Modernity, and Theory of Culture Texts.'

Semiotics of Culture, edited by I. Portis-Winner and J. Umiker-Sebeok, 103–48. The Hague: Mouton.
- 1987. 'Cultural Semiotics vs. Other Cultural Sciences.' *A Plea for Cultural Semiotics,* ed. by A. Eschback and W. Koch, 4–22 (Bochum Publications in Evolutionary Cultural Semiotics 2). Bochum: Brockmeyer.
- 1994. *Semiotics of Culture: The Strange Intruder.* Bochum: Universitätsverlag Brockmeyer.

Proffer, C.R. 1988. 'Notes on the Imagery in Zamiatin's *We.' Zamiatin's* We: *A Collection of Critical Essays,* edited by G. Kern, 95–105. Ann Arbor, MI: Ardis.

Proffer, Ellendea, 1984. *Bulgakov: Life and Work.* Ann Arbor, MI: Ardis.

Propp, V. Ya. 1986. *Istoričeskij korni volšebnoj skazki.* Leningrad: Leningradskij universitet.

Repp, B.H., S.Y. Manuel, A.M. Liberman, and M. Studdert-Kennedy. 1983. 'Exploring the "McGurk Effect."' Paper presented at the 24th meeting of the Psychonomic Society, San Diego, California. *Bulletin of the Psychonomic Society* 358.

Riccio, D.C., V.C. Rabinowitz, and S. Axelrod. 1994. 'Memory: When Less Is More.' *American Psychologist* 49 (11): 917–26.

Riddle, D.F. 1974. *Calculus and Analytic Geometry.* Belmont, CA: Wadsworth.

Riffaterre, M. 1978. *Semiotics of Poetry.* Bloomington: Indiana University Press.

Rose, S. 1992. *The Making of Memory: From Molecules to Mind.* New York: Anchor Books.

Rudy, S. 1986. 'Semiotics in the USSR.' *The Semiotic Sphere,* edited by T.A. Sebeok and J. Umiker-Sebeok, 555–82. New York: Plenum Press.

Savan, D. 1976. *An Introduction to Peirce's Semiotics.* Toronto: Victoria University.
- 1980. 'Abduction and Semiotics.' *The Signifying Animal,* edited by I. Rauch and G. Carr, 252–62. Bloomington: Indiana University Press.
- 1986. 'Response to T.L. Short.' *Transactions of the Charles S. Peirce Society* 22 (2): 125–44.

Schacter, D.L. 1996. *Searching for Memory.* New York: Basic Books.

Sebeok, T.A. [1976] 1985. *Contributions to the Doctrine of Signs.* Lanham, MD: University Press of America.
- 1977. 'Foreword to the Paperback Edition of Soviet Semiotics.' *Soviet Semiotics: An Anthology,* edited and translated by D.P. Lucid, v–viii. Baltimore, MD: Johns Hopkins University Press.
- 1990. *Essays in Zoosemiotics.* Toronto: Toronto Semiotics Circle.
- 1991. *A Sign Is Just a Sign.* Bloomington: Indiana University Press.
- 1999. 'The Estonian Connection.' *Sémeiótiké* 26.
- [in press]. 'Biosemiotics: Its Roots, Proliferation, and Prospects. *Semiotica* 131.

Sebeok, T.A., and J. Umiker-Sebeok, editors. 1986. *The Semiotic Sphere.* New York: Plenum Press.
Segal, S.J., and V. Fusella. 1970. 'Influence of Imaged Pictures and Sounds on Detection of Visual and Auditory Signals.' *Journal of Experimental Psychology* 83: 458–64.
Shapiro, M. 1983. *The Sense of Grammar: Language as Semeiotic.* Bloomington: Indiana University Press.
– 1988. 'Dynamic Interpretants and Grammar.' *Transactions of the Charles S. Peirce Society* 24 (1): 123–30.
– 1991. *The Sense of Change: Language as History.* Bloomington: Indiana University Press.
Shirkova-Tuula, I. 1998. 'On the Concept of Ecological Optimism.' *Paideia* (web publication, The Paideia Project, Boston University).
Short, T.L. 1981. 'Semeiosis and Intentionality.' *Transactions of the Charles S. Peirce Society* 17: 197–223.
– 1986a. 'What They Said in Amsterdam: Peirce's Semiotic Today.' *Semiotica* 60 (1/2): 103–28.
– 1986b. 'David Savan's Peirce Studies.' *Transactions of the Charles S. Peirce Society* 22 (2): 89–124.
Shukman, A. 1977. *Literature and Semiotics: A Study of the Writings of Yu. M. Lotman* (Meaning and Art 1). Amsterdam: North-Holland.
– ed., 1984. *Ju. M. Lotman, B.A. Uspenskij. The Semiotics of Russian Culture.* Ann Arbor: Michigan Slavic Contributions.
– 1988. 'Semiotic Aspects of the Work of Jurij Mixailovič Lotman.' *The Semiotic Web 1987,* edited by T.A. Sebeok and J. Umiker-Sebeok, 65–78. Berlin: Mouton de Gruyter.
Skotko, B., E. Andrews, L. Tupler, D. Rubin, G. Einstein, and S. Corkin. Forthcoming. 'H.M.'s Language Skills: Clues about Language and the Medial Temporal Lobe.'
Šnejder, V.E., A.I. Sluckij, A.S. Šumov. 1978. *Kratkij kurs visšej matematiki (v 2–ch tomach).* Moscow: Vyšaja Škola.
Sokolov, B. 1997. *Enciklopedija Bulgakovskaja.* Moscow: Lokid-Mif.
Soloman, P.R., G.R. Goethals, C.M. Kelley, and B.R. Stephens, editors. 1989. *Memory: Interdisciplinary Approaches.* New York: Springer-Verlag.
Squire, L.R. 1987. *Memory and the Brain.* New York: Oxford University Press.
Sreznevskij, I.I. [1902] 1955. *Materialy dlja slovarja drevne-russkogo jazyka,* 1–3. Graz: Akademische Druck-u. Verlagsanstalt.
SSLRJa. 1950–1963. Slovar' sovremennogo literaturnogo russkogo jazyka. Moscow, Leningrad: AN SSSR.
Strauss, C., and N. Quinn. 1997. *A Cognitive Theory of Cultural Meaning.* Cambridge: Cambridge University Press.

Švarc, A. 1988. *Žizn' i smert' Mixaila Bulgakova.* Tenafly, NJ: Ermitaž.
Tanenhaus, M.K., et al. 1995. 'Integration of Visual and Linguistic Information in Spoken Language Comprehension.' *Science* 286: 1632–34.
Tielhard de Chardin, P. 1968. *Le prêtre.* Paris: Éditions du Seuil.
Thom, R. 1975. *Structural Stability and Morphogenesis.* Reading, MA: Benjamin/Cummings.
– 1983. *Mathematical Models of Morphogenesis.* New York: John Wiley and Sons.
Tikos, L. 1981. 'Some Notes on the Significance of Gerbert Awirllac in Bulgakov's *The Master and Margarita*.' *Canadian-American Slavic Studies* 15 (2/3): 321–9.
Timenčik, R.D. 1987. 'K simvolike tramvaja v russkoj poezii.' *Simvol v sisteme kul'tury, Trudy po znakovym sistemam XXI.* Tartu.
Tootell, R.B.H., M.S. Silverman, E. Switkes, and R.L. De Valois. 1982. 'Deoxyglucose Analysis of Retinotopic Organization in Primate Striate Cortex.' *Science* 218: 902–4.
Tootell, R.B.H., E. Switkes, M.S. Silverman, and S.L. Hamilton. 1988. 'Functional Anatomy of Macaque Striate Cortex.' 2. Retinotopic Organization. *Journal of Neuroscience* 8: 1531–68.
Torop, P., M. Lotman, and K. Kull, eds. 1998. *Sign Systems Studies* 26. Tartu: University of Tartu.
Traugott, E.C. 1989. 'On the Rise of Epistemic Meanings in English: An Example of Subjectification in Semantic Change.' *Language* 65: 31–55.
– 1991. 'English Speech Act Verbs: A Historical Perspective.' *New Vistas in Grammar: Invariance and Variation,* edited by L.R. Waugh and S. Rudy, 387–406. Amsterdam: John Benjamins.
Tulving, E. 1972. 'Episodic and Semantic Memory.' *Organization of Memory,* edited by E. Tulving and W. Donaldson, 381–403. New York: Academic Press.
– 1983. *Elements of Episodic Memory.* New York: Oxford University Press.
– 1985. 'How Many Memory Systems Are There?' *American Psychologist* 40: 385–98.
Tulving, E., and D.M. Thompson. 1973. 'Encoding Specificity and Retrieval Processes in Episodic Memory.' *Psychological Review* 80: 352–73.
Uexküll, J. von. 1928. *Theoretische Biologie.* Berlin: Springer.
– 1982. 'The Theory of Meaning.' *Semiotica* 42 (1): 25–87.
Uexküll, T. von. 1982. 'Introduction: Meaning and Science in Jakob von Uexküll's Concept of Biology.' *Semiotica* 42 (1): 1–24.
– 1986. 'Medicine and Semiotics.' *Semiotica* 61 (3/4): 201–17.
– 1987. 'The Sign Theory of Jakob von Uexküll.' *Classics of Semiotics,* edited by M. Krampen, K. Oehler, R. Pozner, and T.A. Sebeok. New York: Plenum Press, 147–79.
– 1989. 'Jakob von Uexküll's Umwelt-Theory.' *The Semiotic Web 1988,* edited by T.A. Sebeok and J. Umiker-Sebeok. Berlin: Mouton de Gruyter, 129–58.

- 1992. 'Varieties of Semiosis.' *Biosemiotics*, 455–70. Berlin: Mouton de Gruyter.
Vasmer [Fasmer], M. 1986–7. *Etimologičeskij slovar' russkogo jazyka*, revised and expanded by O.N. Trubačev 1–4. Moscow: Progress.
Vernadskij, V.I. 1926. *Biosfera*. Leningrad.
- 1934. *Očerki geoximii*. 4th ed. Moscow, Leningrad: AN SSSR.
- 1967. *Biosfera: Izbrannye trudy po biogeochimii*. Moscow: AN SSSR.
- 1989. *Biosfera i noosfera*. Moscow: Nauka
- 1993. *Otkrytija i sud'by*. Moscow: Sovremennik.
Voronskij, A.K. 1983. 'Iz perepiski s sovetskimi pisateljami.' In *Literaturnoe nasledstvo: Iz istorii sovetskoj literatury 1920–1930-x godov*, Berdnikov, T.P., 531–648. Moscow: Nauka.
Weeks, L.D., ed. 1996a. *The Master and Margarita: A Critical Companion*. Evanston, IL: Northwestern University Press.
- 1996b. 'Houses, Homes, and the Rhetoric of Inner Space in Mikhail Bulgakov.' *The Master and Margarita: A Critical Companion*, edited by Laura D. Weeks, 143–63. Evanston, IL: Northwestern University Press.
Weiskrantz, L., and E.K. Warrington. 1979. 'Conditioning in Amnesic Patients.' *Neuropsychologia* 17: 187–94.
White, J.J. [1966] 1988. 'Mathematical Imagery in Musil's *Young Torless* and Zamiatin's *We*.' *Zamiatin's We: A Collection of Critical Essays*, edited G. Kern, 228–35. Ann Arbor, MI: Ardis.
Winner, T. 1979. 'Some Fundamental Concepts Leading to a Semiotics of Culture: An Historical Overview.' *Semiotics of Culture*, edited by I. Portis-Winner and J. Umiker-Sebeok, 75–82. The Hague: Mouton.
Wright, A.C. 1978. *Mikhail Bulgakov: Life and Interpretations*. Toronto: University of Toronto Press.
Xoružij, S.S. 1990. 'O filosofii svjaščennika Pavla Florenskogo.' *P.A. Florenskij, t.1, Stolp i utverždenie istiny*. Moscow: izdatel'stvo Pravda.
Zamyatin, E.I. [1913] 1989. *Na kuličkax. My. Izbrannye proizvedenija*, 136–96. Moscow: Sovetskij pisatel.
- [1919] 1988. 'Zavtra.' *Sočinenija*, 407–8. Moscow: Kniga.
- [1921] 1989. 'O moix ženax, o ledokolax i o Rossii.' *Evgenij Zamjatin: MY - Roman, povesti, rasskazy, pjesy, statji i vospominanija*, edited by E.B. Skorospelova, 548–53. Kišenev: Literature artistike.
- [1922] 1988. 'O sintetizme.' *Sočinenija*, 412–19. Moscow: Kniga.
- [1923a] 1988. 'Novaja russkaja proza.' *Sočinenija*, 420–32. Moscow: Kniga.
- [1923b] 1988. 'O literature, revoljucii, entropii i pročem. ...' *Sočinenija*, 446–51. Moscow: Kniga.
- [1924] 1988. 'O segodnjašnem i o govremennom.' *Sočinenija*, 433–45. Moscow: Kniga.
- [1929] 1988. 'Zakulisy.' *Sočinenija*, 461–72. Moscow: Kniga.

- 1966. *The Dragon*. Trans by Mirra Ginsburg. New York: Random House.
- 1967. *Litsa*. New York: Inter-Language Literary Associates.
- 1970. *A Soviet Heretic: Essays by Yevgeny Zamjatin*, edited and translated by Mirra Ginsburg. Chicago: University of Chicago Press.
- 1988a. *Sočinenija v 4-x tomax*. Munich: A. Neimanis Buchvertrieb und Verlag.
- 1988b. *Sočinenija*. Moscow: Kniga.
- 1989a. *My. Izbrannye proizvedenija*. Moscow: Sovetskij pisatel'.
- 1989b. *Izbrannye sočinenija* . Moscow: Sovetskij pisatel'.

Zasorina, L.N., ed. 1977. *Častotnij slovar' russkogo jazyka*. Moscow: Russkij jazyk.

Zurek, W.H., ed. 1990. *Complexity, Entropy and The Physics of Information*. Cambridge: Cambridge University Press.

Index

'About My Wives, Ice Breakers, and Russia' (Zamyatin), 119
'About the Semiotic Mechanism of Culture' (Lotman and Uspenskij), 3–4
'About Synthesism' (Zamyatin), 126
'About Today and the Contemporary' (Zamyatin), 102
actual infinity, 86
Adams, V., 7
aesthetic function of a text, 77–8
Alexander Nevsky (ship), 119
alphanumeric names in Zamyatin's *We*, 113, 115–17
amnesia, 149, 153
Andrews, E., 176–7n4; markedness theory, 22; numerical texts, 115–17; Peircian semiosis, 23–4, 166n5; vision and language learning, 135–7; on Zamyatin, 96, 104, 174n6
anthroposemiotics, xiii
anti-entropic aspect of culture, 14
antiworld image, 104
aquarium image, 104, 173n9
artistic spaces, 80–92; author's role, 109–10, 112; boundaries, 80–1; continuity, 101, 173n11; creation of, 112; directionality, 80; fragmented non-space, 106, 173n11; imaginary, 84–6, 85f, infinity, 82, 83f, 86; in *Master* (Bulgakov), 86–92, 87f, 90–1f; 'road' images, 75–6, 80–1, 87–92, 97, 105–6
artistic texts, 77–80, 128–9, 170–1n5
associative memory, 159, 177n11
asymmetry of the semiosphere, 23, 33, 43–5; catastrophe theory, 54; centre and periphery, 44–5; temporal asymmetry, 39, 40–1; tension, 45
atemporality, 108–9
auditory signs in language learning, 133–46; phoneme perception, 142–4, 176n13
authorial intention, 109–10
autocommunication, 28–31, 29, 63
autonomy, 4, 11
Azadovskij, M., 6

'Backstage' (Zamyatin), 126
Baddeley, A., 150
Bailey, K.D., 27, 58
Bakhtin, M.M., 31, 109, 161–2n2

barrier images, 104
Beatie, B.A., 172n3
behaviour modification, 149
Belozerskaja, Ljudimila, 84
Berlioz (character), 87–9, 97–8, 102–5, 172–3n7–8
Besedy o russkoj kul'ture (Lotman, 1994), 163n3
Bethea, D.M., 161–2n2, 172n3
Bezdomnyj (character), 76, 87–8, 92, 97–8, 104
bilingual translation filter, 43, 46, 128
'Binary Models in the Dynamics of Russian Culture' (Lotman and Uspenskij, 1977), 108–9, 162–3n3
binary signs, xiv–xv, 4, 33, 43–6, 163–4n2; in Bulgakov's text, 76, 77f; versus triads, 21–5, 168n1
biological basis for the semiosphere, 35–6, 43–4, 168n4, 169n6
biological constructs of communication, 60–5, 61f
biological evolution, 55–6
biosphere, 43–4, 51–2, 55–7, 64–5, 168n5
blindness and language learning, 140–2, 176n11, 176n12
Bogatyrev, P., 8
Boni, A., 118
Boni, C., 118
boundaries, 10, 13–15, 33, 46–8, 166–7n3; artistic spaces, 80–1; centre/periphery, 44–7; continuity/discontinuity, 36–7, 47–8; cultural constructs, 46–7; in *Dead Souls* (Gogol'), 81; during explosions, 52, 62–3; external, 46–7; infinity, 82, 83f; integrals, 121; intertextuality, 94; language, 175n4; literary texts, 108–11;

translation, 43, 46–8, 62–3, 128; in *We* (Zamyatin), 128
'Brain and Language' (Jakobson), 145
brain function, 36, 44, 45f, 53
Brown, G.S., 14
Buchler, J., ed., 152
Buck, C.D., 135–6
Bulgakov, M.A., 73–92; binary versus triadic signs, 76, 77f; censorship, 93, 96–7; 'Diaboliad,' 94; fantastic realism, 81; letter to Stalin, 96; published works, 93, 96–7; relationhip with Zamyatin, 94–6, 169–70n3, 172n3. *See also The Master and Margarita*
Bulgakova, E.S., 94

Calvin, W.H., 53, 137
catastrophe theory, 53–4
categories, 14, 16, 50–1
censorship, 9, 93–7, 100, 110–11
centre/periphery, 44–7
cerebral cortex, 137
Černov, I.A., 5, 6, 9
channels, 29
chaotic spaces, 16, 33
Chekhov, A., 96
chreods, 54–5
Classicism and Modernism, 9–10
code, 17, 30–1, 165n2; versus addresser, 34–5, 34f; metalingual function, 66–7; in Uexküll's *Umwelt* theory, 64; used by Zamyatin, 125–6
code doubling, 50
cognition, 36, 53
cognitive science, xv, 163n4, 168n2
collective consciousness, 48, 168n2
collective memory, 13–14, 18, 39–41,

73, 146; in language, 40–1, 68–9, 153–60; metatexts, 68; oral versus written culture, 41, 156–7
colour imagery, 113, 174n6
communication acts, 30–2*f*; biological constructs, 60–5; cultural texts, 17–18; dialogue, 48; dynamic interpretants, 166n3; entropy, 26–8, 58–60; tension, 48–9. *See also* information exchange; translation
communication models, 17–21, 66–7; code versus addresser, 34–5, 34*f*; Jakobson's, 18–20, 20*f*, 29, 30–1*f*, 48; Lotman's, 17–18, 19*f*, 23, 29–31, 30–1*f*, 48, 166n1; Sebeok's, 20–1, 21*f*, 29–30, 33*f*, 48, 58–9; Thom's, 27–8, 59, 59*f*
Connolly, J.W., 174n6
consciousness, 168n2
continuity/discontinuity, 14, 16, 23, 35–40, 110, 163–4n2, 173n11; binary opposition, 45–6; encoding process, 53–5; explosions, 39, 49–50, 167n5
Conway, M.A., ed., 177n6
Cooke, L.B., 113, 115
Corkin, S., 176–7n4
Corti, M., 110
Craver-Lemley, C., 139, 176n10
creation of artistic spaces, 112
Čudakova, M., 94, 96–7, 100, 107, 171n1, 171n8
cueing, 153–4
cultural evolution, 46, 55–6
cultural organization, 3–4
culture, xiv, 3, 10, 13–16; discreteness of information, 36–7; versus natural phenomena, 43–4
Culture and Explosion (Lotman, 1992), 42–7, 55–9, 63, 67–9; asymmetry, 44–5; binary opposition, 4, 46, 163–4n2; on Bulgakov's *Master*, 87–8, 169–70nn3–5; collective memory, 41; continuity/discontinuity, 36–9; cultural texts, 51; describing the semiosphere, 32–6; dynamic aspects of culture, 15–16; explosions, 49–50; language and collective memory, 157; literary texts, 128–9; metalinguistic function, 50–1; naming function, 65–6; perspective, 52; road and path images, 105–6; tension, 48–9; triadic signs, 24–5
culture order-text axis, 111
culture texts, 3–4, 11, 18–21, 165n8; artistic, 77–80, 79*f*; boundaries, 62–3, 108–11; codification, 146; collective memory, 41, 69, 159; communication acts, 17–18; continuity/discontinuity, 110; exchange across boundaries, 47–8; language learning, 145–6; literary, 79–80, 79*f*, 108–11; tension and explosions, 50–2; verbal and nonverbal, 73

Dead Souls (Gogol'), 75–6, 80–1, 92
deafness and language learning, 141–2
declarative memory, 148, 150–1, 159–60
decoding of messages, 27
deconstructionism, 108–9
De Leonardis, D.M., 153
Derrida, J., 109
diagrams, 11, 175n1; in language learning, 135–7, 145–6; visual cortex, 138
dialogue, 168n1

directionality, 80–1, 112; in *Dead Souls* (Gogol'), 81; in *Master* (Bulgakov), 88
discontinuity. *See* continuity/discontinuity
distinctive features, phonological, 134, 138
doubling of codes, 50
'Drakon' (Zamyatin), 172n4, 172n6; historical context, 98–100; textual links with Bulgakov's *Master*, 93–111
Dudai, Y., 138–9, 153, 177n6
Dunlea, A., 140–1
dynamic change, 57
dynamic interpretants, 158, 166n3, 166n5
dynamic sign-complexes, 5

Eco, U., 165n1
Einstein, G., 176–7n4
Eisele, C., 175n1
Eixenbaum, Boris, 6
encoding/decoding process, 53, 147–52, 157–60, 177nn5–6
entropy, 21, 26–8, 58–60; metainterpretation, 68; in *We* (Zamyatin), 126–8
episodic memory, 148, 150–2, 153, 160, 177n6
escort symbols, 103–4
Essays (Zamyatin), 100
eternal home, 89
evolution, 46, 55–6
explicit references, 14
explosions, 39, 48–50, 52, 167n5; in *Master* (Bulgakov), 89, 92; in *We* (Zamyatin), 113–14
external boundaries, 46–7
external memory, 39–41

extracultural space, 10, 16
extralinguistic signs, 145–6

Fabbro, F., 177n6
facial recognition, 138–9, 177n7
false dialogue, 28
false home, 75–6, 169–70n3
false signs, 147
fantastic realism, 81, 171n7
final interpretants, 158
First Congress of Slavicists, 7
Fiske, J., 27, 58
Florensky, P.A., 84–6, 85*f*, 88, 171n8, 171n10
folklore, 74–5, 172n4
forgetting, 149
'For the Collection about My Book' (Zamyatin), 114
Frawley, W., 28, 163n4, 165n2, 168n2, 175n4, 177n10
Fundamental Theorem of Arithmetic, 116
Fusella, V., 176n10

Gardner, H., 163n4
Gasparov, B., xiv, 5, 97, 163–4n2, 164n6
geometric figures in Zamyatin's *We*, 117–25, 174n4
Ginsburg, L., 98–100
Gleitman, L., 141
Goethals, G.R., 148
Gogol', N., xvi, 92, 96, 171n7; artistic space, 80; fantastic realism, 81; fragmented non-space, 106, 173n11; images of home and road, 75–6, 106; impact on Bulgakov and Zamyatin, 172n3; infinity, 82
Greene, R.L., 175n8
Greer, P., 176n11

ground, 166n2
Gukovskij, G., 6
Gumilev, N.S., 101, 172–3n7

Hartley, J., 27, 58
Hasher, L., 148, 155
Hashtroudi, S., 154–5
'Hearing Lips and Seeing Voices' (McGurk and MacDonald), 142–4
Hebb, D.O., 150
Heller, L., 115, 174n4
hereticism, 95–6, 113–14
heterogeneity of the semiosphere, 33–4, 43
hierarchy of sign systems, 11, 51
historical approach, 8, 30–1, 165n2; artifacts of history, 46; role of language, 17, 35. *See also* cultural evolution
Hofstadter, D., 53
Hoisington, S., 174n6
home/anti-home/homelessness, 86–9, 87*f*, 105–6, 169–70n3, 170n4; concept of rest, 88, 92, 171n9; in *Dead Souls* (Gogol'), 81; point spaces, 80; in *Master* (Bulgakov), 74–6, 77*f*

iconicity, Peircian, 11, 135, 145
icons, 24
image, 137
imagery, visual: language learning, 142, 175–6, nn8–11; perception, 138–9
Imaginaries in Geometry (Florensky), 84–6, 85*f*
imaginary spaces, 84–6, 85*f*
Imbery, L., 174n6
immediate interpretants, 158

implicit references, 14
indexical signs, 24, 29
infinity, 82, 83*f*, 86; in *Master* (Bulgakov), 89; in *We* (Zamyatin), 122
information exchange: across boundaries, 47–8; cultural memory, 18; entropy, 58; new versus redundant, 14–16, 28; predictability, 27; role of entropy, 28; role of tension, 48–9
information versus meaning, 152
inner code, 165n2
integrals in Zamyatin's *We*, 119–23, 122*f*
intentionality, 109–10
internal boundaries, 47
internal memory, 39–41
interpretants, 147–8, 157–8
intertextuality of *Master* and 'Drakon,' 93–111; artistic space, 106; direct references, 107–8; lexical links, 98–104, 99, 102, 103; structural links, 104–6, 105
Ivanov, V.V., 7, 10, 161–2n2, 164n5
Izbrannye statji v trex tomax (Lotman, 1992–3): antiworld in *Master*, 104; artistic spaces, 80–1, 101, 112; artistic texts, 77–80; basic element of semiotic systems, 23; bilingual translation filters, 128; boundaries, 43, 46–8, 62–3; collective memory, 41, 69; construction of artistic space, 173n11; definition of culture, 3–5, 13; definition of semiosphere, 24; describing the semiosphere, 32–5; fragmented non-space, 106, 173n11; Gogol''s impact on Bulgakov and Zamyatin, 172n3; influ-

ence of Bakhtin, 61–2n2; language and collective memory, 157; metatexts, 67–8, 112; oppositions of home, 74–6, 77*f*

Jakobson, R.O., xiv, 8; 1960 visit to Moscow, 164n4; communication model, 4, 17–20, 20*f*, 29, 30–1*f*; contact, 29; diadic signs, 22–3; language learning, 145; markedness theory, 22; metonymy and metaphor, 24; travel to Tartu, 164n5; visual and auditory signs, 133–4, 140
James, W., 150
Jegorov, B.F., 5–10, 161–2n2, 164n4
Jeshua (character), 76, 87–9
Jessell, T.M., 138
Johnson, B., 143, 148, 153–5

Kajsarov, A., 7
Kandel, E.R., 138
Karamzin (Lotman, 1997), 162–3n3
Kelley, C.M., 148
Kidwell, A., 176n11
Klement, F., 9
'knowing' and 'seeing' lexemes, 135–6, 175nn2–3
Kosslyn, S.M.: associative memory, 177n11; imagery, 138–9, 142, 175–6nn8–10, 176n11; perception, 35, 53; viewer-oriented encoding, 153, 158–9, 176n1, 177n6
Kristeva, J., 93, 108–9
Kuljus, S., 97

Lahusen, T., 96, 104, 115–17, 174n6
Lakšin, B. Ya., 94, 96
Lamarck, J.B., 51
Landau, B., 141

language learning: collective memory, 40–1, 155–60; context, 156; extralinguistic signs, 145–6; phoneme perception, 142–4, 176n13; visual and auditory signs, 133–46, 176n13; visual perception, 137–9
language(s), 14, 30–1, 35, 40; abduction, 169n7; boundaries, 175n4; versus code, 17; consciousness, 168n2; doubling, in autocommunication, 29; information exchange, 16–18; Jakobson's model, 24; memory, 68–9, 153–60, 177n11; metatexts, 67; universal, 16, 165n1
lattice image, 104
laws of thermodynamics, 26
learning, 149
Le Roy, E., 51
Levin, J., 8
Levy Matvej (character), 87
Liberman, A.M., 176n13
linden tree symbol, 101–2
Lindsay, D.S., 154–5
linguistic model of memory, 159–60, 177n11
linguistic sign systems, 134
literary signs, 110–11
literary texts, 79–80, 79*f*, 108–11, 128–9
Literaturnaja Rossija, 112
Literaturnoe nasledstvo (Voronskij), 100
Lixachev, D., 31
Ljandres, S.A., 94
long-term memory, 148, 150–1, 160, 176–7n4
Lotman, Ju. M.: censorship and persecution, 9, 164–5n7; personal information, 5–7; published works,

xiii, 9, 74, 162–3n3, 169n1; travel, 9–10. *See also* names of specific publications
Lotman, Lidija Mixailovna, xiii–xiv, 5, 161–2n2
Lotman, Viktorija Mixailovna, 5
Lucid, D.P., 5
Luria, A.R., 149

MacDonald, J., 142–4, 176n13
MacLaurin series in Zamyatin's *We*, 119, 124
Majakovkij, V., 101
Maksimova, E., 96, 104, 115–17, 172n4, 174n6
Mandelker, A., 169n6
Mandler, G., 149, 152
Manuel, S.Y., 176n13
Margarita (character), 87, 89
markedness theory, 22, 23
marks, 13
Massaro, D.W., 143–4
The Master and Margarita (Bulgakov), 73–92; comparison with Zamyatin's 'Drakon,' 93–111; infinity, 82, 83*f*, 86, 92; oppositions of home, 74–6, 77*f*; replicas of texts, 87–8; textual links with 'Drakon,' 97–106; time and space, 86–92, 87*f*, 90–1*f*
Master (character), 87–8, 92
mathematical texts, 113, 118–25
Maturana, H.R., 35
McGurk, H., 142–4, 176n13
McNamara, T.P., 153
meaning: among cultural spaces, 14–15; boundaries, 46–8, 128; codification of culture texts, 146; versus information, 152; language learning, 144–6; memory, 155–60, 176–7n4; sign categories, 21–2;

Uexküll's *Umwelt* theory, 63–4; Vigotsky's three types, 168n2
Medvedev, P.M., 109
memory, 39–41, 146, 151*f*; associative, 159, 177n11; declarative, 148, 150–1, 159–60; definitions, 148–9; encoding/decoding process, 53, 148–52, 177nn5–6; episodic, 148, 150–3, 160, 177n6; interpretants, 157–8; language, 153–60, 177n11; linguistic model, 159–60; long-term, 148, 150–1, 160, 176–7n4; meaning, 155–60, 176–7n4; perception, 151, 157–60; perceptions, 53; personal, 69; priming, 147–8, 153–4, 177n9; procedural, 148, 151, 159–60; semantic, 148, 151–4, 160, 176n3, 177n6; short-term, 148, 150–1, 160; source, 148, 154–5. *See also* collective memory
memory disorders, 149–54, 177n9
metaconsciousness, 168n2
metainterpretation, 67–8
metalanguage of the semiosphere, 33–4, 50–1, 55, 66–7
metaphor, 137
metatexts, 66–8, 109–12, 128–9
metonymy and metaphor, 24
Mills, A.E., 141, 143–4
Milne, L., 96
The Mind's New Science (Gardner), 163n4
Mints, Z.G., 7, 164–5n7
modelling systems, 11, 14–18, 166n1. *See also* communication models
Montgomery, M., 27, 58
Mordovchenko, N., 6
morphogenesis, 36, 54
Morris, C., 23
Moscow Linguistics Circle, 8

Moscow Symposium of 1962, 7–8, 164n4
Mulford, R., 141, 176n12

Nakhimovski, A.D., 162–3n3
Nakhimovski, A.S., 162–3n3
Na kuličkax (Zamyatin), 104
naming function, 65–6, 169n8
'The New Russian Prose' (Novaja russkaja proza) (Zamyatin), 95–6, 126
Nikitin, N., 171–2n2
Nolde, S.F., 153
non-verbal texts, 113
noosphere, 51–2, 57, 168n5
numerical texts in Zamyatin's *We*, 113, 115–18, 174n4, 174nn7–8
nu-suffixed semelfactive perfective verbs, 104–5, 105t

Ob iskusstve (Lotman, 1998), 161–3nn2–3
October Revolution, 98–100, 105
Ojemann, G.A., 53, 137
O'Neill, J.J., 143
'On Literature, Revolution, and Entropy' (Zamyatin), 121
'On the Relation between Visual and Auditory Signs' (Jakobson), 133–4
O poetax i poezii (Lotman, 1996), 162–3n3
oral culture, 41, 156–7
O russkoj literature (Lotman, 1997), 161–3nn2–3
O'Sullivan, T., 27, 58

Pasternak, B., 101
Peirce, C.S., xiv, 53; compared to Thom's catastrophe theory, 55; continuity/discontinuity, 35–6; diagram, 175n1; dynamic texts, 50; ground, 166n2; iconicity, 11; interpretants, 147–8, 157–8, 166n3, 166n5; sign systems, 23–4, 64, 166n5; translation, 166–7n3; triadic model, xv, 21–2, 24, 45
perception, 53; continuity, 35–6; imaginary spaces, 84–6, 85f; memory, 151, 157–60; mental imagery, 138–9, 142; phonemes, 142–4, 176n13; Uexküll's *Umwelt* theory, 63–4
perspective, 52, 139, 173n11
Petelin, V.V., 95
phoneme perception, 142–4, 176n13
phonology, 134, 138
Pilate (character), 87, 88, 89, 92
Pillar and Confirmation of Eternal Truth (Florensky), 86
The Pillar of Fire (Gumilev), 172–3n7
Pis'ma (Lotman, 1997), 161–2n2
Pjatigorskij, A.M., 8, 10
Pomorska, K., 164n5
Portis-Winner, I., 11, 50
postformalism, xiv
poststructuralism, xiv
potential infinity, 86
Powell, P.W., 172n3
Prague School, 22–4
primary modelling systems, 11
primary texts, 50
primary visual cortex, 137–8
prime numbers, 116
priming memory, 147–8, 153–4, 177n9
principles of semiotics theory, xiv, 13–16
procedural memory, 148, 151, 159–60

Proffer, C.R., 113, 115, 174n6
Proffer, E., 169n2
Propp, V. Ya., 6, 172n4
Pushkin, E., 75
Puškin (Lotman), 5, 162–3n3

Radishchev, A., 8
reader-text axis, 111
recall/retrieval of memory, 149, 159, 176n1. *See also* encoding/decoding process
redundancy, 27–8
Reeves, A., 139, 176n10
references, 14
remembering. *See* encoding/decoding process
Repp, B.H., 176n13
representational signs, 133
revolution theme, 93–7, 100–3, 105, 121, 126, 172–3n7
Rezvin, I., 8
Rhopalocera, 114, 174n5
road images, 75–6, 80–1, 97; in *Masters* (Bulgakov), 87–92; versus path, 81, 105–6
Rose, S., 148–50, 152, 155–6, 176–7n4, 176n1
Rubin, D., 176–7n4
Rudy, S., 5
Russian/Soviet literary texts, 73, 169n1; anti-utopian literature, 112; bourgeois writing, 95; disruption of normal literary processes, 100; epic tales, 80; intertextuality, 110–11

Saltykov-Shchedrin, M., 96
Saunders, D., 27, 58
Saussure, F. de, 22–4
Savan, D., 21–2, 147, 158, 169n7

Schacter, D.L., 148–9, 152–3, 157, 159, 177n9
Scholarly Notes of Tartu State University, 7–8
Schwartz, J.H., 138
Sebeok, T.A., xiv, 11, 53, 164n6, 169n6; channels, 29; communication model, 17, 20–1, 21f, 29–30, 33f; entropy, 26–8, 58–9; information exchange, 27; memory, 69; naming function, 66, 169n8; principles of semiotic systems, 23–4; on Uexküll's *Umwelt* theory, 63–4
secondary modelling systems, 11, 16
secondary texts, 50
'seeing' and 'knowing' lexemes, 135–6, 175nn2–3
Segal, S.J., 176n10
Selected Works (Zamyatin), 100
self-description, 37–8, 50–1, 59–60, 127–8, 167n6
self-naming, 37–8, 167n6
semantic density, 54
semantic language learning, 141–6. *See also* language learning; meaning
semantic memory, 148, 151–4, 160, 176n3, 177n6
semantic structures, 135–7
Semiosfera (Lotman, 2000), 161–3nn2–3, 163–4n2
semiosis: information exchange, 27–8; in Peircean theory, 23–4, 166n5; recall and retrieval of memory, 159
semiosphere, xiv, 24, 32–5, 42–69; asymmetry, 23, 33, 39–41, 43–5, 54; biological basis, 43–4, 168n4, 169n6; centre and periphery, 44–6;

definition, 3, 42–3; discreteness of information, 36–7; entropy, 26–8; ground, 166n2; heterogeneity, 33–4, 43; intersection of language and memory, 156–60; mathematical basis, 168n4; metatexts, 66–8; origins, 51–2, 55–8; proper names, 65–6; section cuts, 44, 45f; sign types, 24; structural stability, 36
semiotics, definition, 53
Semiotics and History, 7
The Semiotics of Russian Cultural History (Nakhimovsky and Nakhimovsky, eds.), 162–3n3
semiotic space. *See* semiosphere
Shapiro, M., 137
Shcheglov, J., 8
Short, T.L., 147
short-term memory, 148, 150–1, 160
Shukman, A., 5, 161–2n2
sign systems, 21–5, 165n2; autocommunication, 29; Jakobson's theory, 22–3; memory, 147–8; Pierce's theory, 21–2, 166n3, 166n5; in Uexküll's *Umwelt* theory, 61–2, 64. *See also* binary signs; triadic signs
Sign Systems Studies series, 7, 9
Single State in Zamyatin's *We*, 119, 121–5
Skotko, B., 176–7n4
Sluckij, A.S., 122
Šnejder, V.E., 122
social entropy theory, 58
Sokolov, B., 84
Soloman, P.R., 148
source memory, 148, 154–5
Soviet Semiotics (Lucid, ed.), 162–3n3
spaces, 80–92, 168n1, 170n4. *See also* artistic spaces
sparrow symbol, 101–2

Spaulding, A., 143
speech acts. *See* communication acts
speech development. *See* language learning
Squire, L.R., 150–2, 176–7n4
Stephens, B.R., 148
Stockholm University, 9
St'opa Lixodeev (character), 87
'The Story about the Most Important Thing' (Zamyatin), 114
structuralism, xiii, 161n1
structural stability, 54–5
The Structure of the Artistic Text (Lotman, 1971), 4, 50, 162–3n3
Studdert-Kennedy, M., 176n13
Studia Russica Helsingiensia et Tartuensia, 9
Suess, E., 51
Šumov, A.S., 122
symbols, 24
synthesism, 95–6, 174n3, 174–5n11; in Zamyatin's works, 113, 114–29

Tanenhaus, M.K., et al., 144
Tartu-Moscow School of Semiotics, xiii, 5–12
Tartu Summer School, 8–9, 164n6
Tartu Teachers Institute, 6–7
Tartu University, 7
taxonomy of textual types, 11
Taylor, B., 124, 174n9
Taylor, F., 124, 174n9
Taylor, H.M., 174n9
Taylor series in Zamyatin's *We*, 119, 121, 123–5, 174n9
Teilhard de Chardin, 51, 55
tension, 15–16, 35, 42, 45, 48–9
texts. *See* culture texts
textual links between 'Drakon' and *Master*, 171–2n2; artistic space,

106; direct references, 107–8; lexical links, 98–104, 99*t*, 102*t*, 103*t*, 172n5; structural links, 104–6, 105*t*
thermodynamics, 26
Theses on the Semiotic Study of Culture, 10–11, 50
Thiem, R., 141, 144
Thom, R., xiv, 27–8; catastrophe theory, 53–4; continuity/discontinuity, 35–6; morphogenesis theory, 36
Thompson, D.M., 177n5
Timenčik, R.D., 101
time structures, 63–4
Tomashevskij, B., 6
Toporov, V.N., 7, 10, 164n4
touch, 140
tram symbol, 98, 100, 102–3, 105–6, 172–3n7, 173n10
translation, 35, 42–4, 166–7n3; across boundaries, 43, 47–8; artistic texts, 77–8; bilingual filters, 43, 46, 128
Traugott, E.C., 135
triadic signs, xv, 21–5, 168n1; in Bulgakov's text, 76, 77*f*; Peirce's views, 21–2, 45
Trubetzkoy, N.S., 164n4
Tulving, E., 149, 151–3, 177n5
Tupler, L., 176–7n4
Tynjanov, J., 6, 31

Uchenyje zapiski Tartuskogo gosudarstvennogo universiteta (Scholarly Notes of Tartu State University), 7–8
Uexküll, J. von, xiv, 24, 27, 44, 60–5, 61*f*, 159, 169n8; memory, 69; metainterpretation, 67–8
Uexküll, T. von, 60, 64–5, 169n8

Umiker-Sebeok, J., 164n6
Umwelt theory (Uexküll), xiv, 24, 27, 44, 60–5, 61*f*, 159, 169n8; memory, 69; metainterpretation, 67–8
unbounded texts, 108–9
unity, 10–11
universal language, 16, 165n1
Universe of the Mind: A Semiotic Theory of Culture (Lotman, 1990): autocommunication, 28–9, 63; binary opposition, 4; boundaries, 46–7; codification of texts, 146; collective memory, 40–1, 68–9; communication models, 18; continuity/discontinuity, 39; cultural memory, 146; entropy, 127–8; language learning, 156; metatexts, 67; self-description, 59–60; semiosphere, 32–5, 43–6, 55–6; sign types, 24; text as code, 165n2
University of Helsinki, 9
untranslatable texts, 77–8
Uspenskij, B.A., 3–4, 7, 8, 10

value of an information event, 15–16
Varela, F.J., 35
verb usage, 104–5, 105*t*
Vereški cycle (Zamyatin), 100
Vernadsky, V.I., 32, 168n4; biosphere, 43–4, 51–2, 55–7; noosphere, 168n5
visual cortex, 137–9
visual imagery, 138–9, 142, 175–6nn8–11
visual memory, 176n1
visual signs in language learning, 133–46, 175nn8–9; imagery, 142, 175–6nn8–11; oppositional features, 134; phoneme perception,

142–4, 176n13; Russian lexemes, 135–7; visual categories, 135–7
Voloshinov, V., 31
Voronskij, A.K., 100, 171–2n2, 172n6
'Vospominanija' (Lotman, 1999), 6–9
Vygotsky, L., 168n2, 175n4, 177n10
Vygotsky and Cognitive Science (Frawley), 168n2

Warrington, E.K., 153
Waugh, L.R., 133
Weiskrantz, L., 153
We (Zamyatin), 104, 112–29, 172n4; boundaries, 128; energy versus entropy, 126–8; heresy, 113–14; mathematical texts, 118–25; numerical texts, 115–18; synthetism of texts, 114–25
White, J.J., 113, 115
Woland (character), 87, 97–8, 101, 104–5
word frequency, 172n5
word recognition, 138–9, 177n7
working memory, 150
Works on Russian and Slavic Philology, 7
writing, 41, 156–7

Zacks, R.T., 155
Zaliznjak, A., 7

Zamjatin, E.I. *See* Zamyatin, E.I.
Zamyatin, E.I., 171n1; 'About My Wives, Ice Breakers, and Russia,' 119; 'About Synthesism,' 126; 'About Today and the Contemporary,' 102; 'Backstage,' 126; censorship, 93, 100; critical works, 95–6; 'Drakon,' 93–111, 172n4, 172n6; *Essays*, 100; fantastic realism, 81; 'For the Collection about my Book,' 114; hereticism, 95–6, 171–2n2; imprisonment, 118; letter to Stalin, 96; *Na kuličkax*, 104; 'Novaja russkaja proza,' 95–6, 126; 'On Literature, Revolution, and Entropy,' 121; place in Russian scholarship, 112–13; published works, 93, 95–6; relationship with Bulgakov, 94–6; reuse of images, 173n9; *Selected Works*, 100; similarities with Bulgakov, 169–70n3, 172n3; 'The Story about the Most Important Thing,' 114; synthesism, 113–29; textual construction, 118, 125–9; *We*, 104, 112–29, 174n4
Zapiski na man etax (Bulgakov), 96
Zasorina, L.N., 98, 172n5
Zhirmunskij, V., 6
Zholkovskij, A., 8

OHIO UNIVERSITY LIBRARY

Please return this book as soon as you have finished with it. In order to avoid a fine it must be returned by the latest date stamped below. All books are subject to recall after two weeks or immediately if needed for reserve.

APR 0 2 2010
RECEIVED
JUL 22 2011

CF